TRADING SYSTEMS

Secrets of the Masters

Joe Krutsinger

McGraw-Hill

New York San Francisco Washington, D.C. Auckland Bogotá
Caracas Lisbon London Madrid Mexico City Milan
Montreal New Delhi San Juan Singapore
Sydney Tokyo Toronto

Library of Congress Cataloging-in-Publication Data

Author: Krutsinger, Joe.
Title: Trading systems : secrets of the masters / Joe Krutsinger.
Published: New York : McGraw-Hill, 1997.
Description: p. cm.
LC Call No.:   HG4515.95 .K78 1997
ISBN: 1557389128
Subjects: Electronic trading of securities.
               System analysis.
               System design.
Control No.:   97009644

McGraw-Hill

A Division of The McGraw·Hill Companies

3 4 5 6 7 8 9 0   DOC/DOC   9 0 2 1 0 9 8

ISBN 1-55738-912-8

The sponsoring editor for this book was Stephen Isaacs, the editing supervisor was Donna Namorato, and the production supervisor was Pamela Pelton. It was set in Times Roman by Jana Fisher through the services of Barry E. Brown (Broker—Editing, Design and Production).

Printed and bound by R. R. Donnelley and Sons.

McGraw-Hill books are available at special quantity discounts to use as premiums and sales promotions, or for use in corporate training programs. For more information, please write to the Director of Special Sales, McGraw-Hill, 11 West 19th Street, New York, NY 10011. Or contact your local bookstore.

This book was printed on recycled, acid-free paper containing a minimum of 50% recycled, de-inked fiber.

There are many people who would love to be Larry Williams.

Larry is a world reknowned futures trader, educator, system designer, and entrepreneur. As the old saying goes, "He's handsome, rich and he sings well, too!"

Larry taught me how to write trading systems, along with thousands of other people.

This book is dedicated to the man I believe to be the greatest system developer of all time, my friend—Larry Williams.

C O N T E N T S

Acknowledgments vii

Preface ix

PART 1

THE MASTERS

Michael Connor 3

Joseph DiNapoli 20

Stan Ehrlich 33

David W. Fox 47

Nelson F. Freeburg 51

Lee Gettess 61

Cynthia A. Kase 78

Joe Krutsinger 96

Glenn Neely 106

Jeffrey Roy 120

Richard Saidenberg 134

Randy Stuckey 147

Gary Wagner 162

Bill Williams 185

Larry Williams 194

PART 2

THE SYSTEMS

Michael Connor 207

Joseph DiNapoli 209

Stan Ehrlich   211

David W. Fox   213

Nelson F. Freeburg   215

Lee Gettess   217

Cynthia A. Kase   219

Joe Krutsinger   221

Glenn Neely   227

Jeffrey Roy   230

Richard Saidenberg   232

Randy Stuckey   234

Gary Wagner   236

Bill Williams   238

Larry Williams   240

INDEX   242

ACKNOWLEDGMENTS

Jeff Roy has helped me tremendously in organizing and by writing a couple of the systems and indicators in this book. In the years to come you will be hearing great things from and about Jeff.

Joel Robbins and Larry Herst, my close friends who encourage me in everything I do.

My wife Caren, my mother Helen, and my kids—Susan, Tracy, Angela, Stacey, and Chris—my family and the source of my inspiration.

As traders, you depend on systems to provide you with an edge, and in my experience, most traders are unwilling to part with their secrets. This book was assembled, not written in the traditional manner. I sent 31 questions and a blank tape to 15 system developers. The publisher edited their responses. I read their answers and wrote a trading system or indicator in Omega Research's easy language. These trading systems make up Part Two.

The traders defined the concept of "training system" in many different ways, demonstrating once again that trading systems depend as much on traders' individual style as on their knowledge of the markets. They also revealed how they keep even their highly successful systems from going stale. It was a challenge to construct a trading system from their answers, but it can be done by asking some basic questions. It was an enjoyable experience. I hope it will be for you as well, and I also hope that you will be able to translate some of their thoughts and ideas into a system and indicator of your own.

Contact me anytime with brickbats or roses at 888-455-4612 or joekrut@aol.com, or P.O. Box 822 Centerville, IA 52544.

PART 1

THE MASTERS

Michael Connor

INTRODUCTION

Mike Connor has an excellent fax service called Market Watch (Phone: 630-858-6107). You should all take a complimentary look at it; tell him you read about it in the book. He will be glad to fax you a couple of copies. He is also available on the Internet at MarketWatch@Internetmci.com. Mike's system is another variation of that channel breakout system he discusses in his answer to question number 19. If you notice that many of the system developers have used some variation of channel breakout as either their first system or the base of their current system, that's not coincidental.

1. *Tell me about yourself. If someone were to say, "Tell me about Mike Connor," what would you want them to know? Give me a brief biography of you before you got into commodities, and a brief biography of what you have done since you got into commodities.*

I graduated from Indiana State University in 1971. Before entering the brokerage industry, I had a career as a journalist, working on a financial desk and as a general assignment reporter for major metropolitan newspapers.

I have been involved as a trader in the futures markets since 1974. From 1979 through 1989, I was a registered floor broker and member of the Chicago Mercantile Exchange, trading my own accounts, customer accounts and proprietary accounts of several clearing firms. From March 1984 through February 1986, I was also a registered associate of Glasgow & Gorman Futures Corporation. I was a registered securities representative with Winthrop Securities Inc. from November 1984 through December 1986, and I was with Rodman & Renshaw, Inc. from January through August 1986. Prior to that I have been an inactive registered representative with Republic Securities, Inc.

In March 1988, I became registered as a sole proprietor commodity trading advisor and incorporated the business as Market Watch, Inc. in September 1989. A year later, the firm was additionally registered as a commodity pool operator. At first, Market Watch produced market letters and market price information primarily oriented towards professional traders. In addition to editing and producing Market Watch, Inc. publications, I also managed trading in proprietary accounts for clearing firms on the floor of the Chicago Mercantile Exchange until shortly before June 1989, when I sold my CME membership to devote myself exclusively to customer advisory activities through Market Watch, Inc.

2. *Tell me about your technique. What makes it exclusively yours? How did you develop it?*

It's just a commonsense technique. It's not exclusively mine. I am sure thousands of other people have thought about it, and have used it. I do two types of trading. One, I look to buy higher highs or sell lower lows. The second thing I look to do is trade at retracements of standard links, 33 percent, 50 percent, and then finally at a 61.8 percent retracement with a stop placed either on a dollar value or at some technical point underneath or above the last current high or low. So again, I would say this is common sense. In trending markets, I try to buy higher highs or sell lower lows. In sideways markets, I try to do just the opposite: I try to buy retracements and hope that the market will move back higher or lower before it hits my stop point.

A successful long-term trading campaign should be built on a technical foundation of buying higher highs or selling lower lows along with the use of a better than average money management routine. Following this approach should not only let the market tell you when it is going to move higher or lower, but also avoids the amateur trading approach of trying to guess the direction the market should be heading.

As far as stop-loss routines go, you do not have to be a rocket scientist to realize that protective stops are usually located in very vulnerable locations. The lyrics from an old rock n' roll classic, "I was at the right place, but at the wrong time," could be the theme song of futures trading. Generally there are stops waiting at the weekly and monthly highs and lows, and the market will generally penetrate these critical areas, and then as often as not, move from the stop location before regrouping for another unannounced charge at this same stop location. As any mark see-saws between price point, the poor quality of stop-loss executions can cause amateur traders to feel they were unjustly ripped-off. Most futures markets function with hours of boredom and minutes of terror. It is during these few moments of terror when a market wanders into a pocket of vulnerable protective stops, that price slippage and poor market execution become just another normal indirect expense of your trading business. Until the mentality to cheerfully accept stop-loss adversity is in place, all other efforts to run a successful trading business will be placed on hold.

Another obvious point: for day trades we often use the familiar pivot formula to generate our market location. I think everybody is pretty familiar with this routine. Familiarity breeds contempt, and this is why this particular technique may often produce less than favorable short term market location. By the way, there have been a couple of books written about the pivot method. Listed below is one routine that will work with TradeStation. System vendors sell this same program for $4,900, and if you are not happy paying $4,900, I know where you can pay as high as $10,000 for the same concept, along with a book of written rules that Solomon would have trouble following.

```
TradeStation Code:
Var:NewDay(0),PrCB2(0),Avg(0),Hi1(0),Hi2(0);
If NewDay = 1 then Begin ;
          Avg = ( High of Data2 + Low of Data2 + Close of Data2 ) / 3;
          Hi1 = (2*Avg) - Low of Data2 ;
          Hi2 = Avg + Hi1 - ( (2*Avg) - High of Data2) ;
End ;
If NewDay = 1 then NewDay = 0 ;
If CurrentBar of Data2 < > PrCB2 then Begin
          NewDay = 1 ;
          PrCB2 = CurrentBar of Data2 ;
End ;
If CurrentBar of Data2 >= 1 then Begin
          Plot1(Avg, "AVG") ;
          Plot2(Hi1, "HI1") ;
          Plot3(Hi2, "HI2") ;
End ;
```

```
Var:NewDay(0),PrCB2(0),Avg(0),Lo1(0),Lo2(0);
If NewDay = 1 then Begin ;
          Avg = ( High of Data2 + Low of Data2 + Close of Data2 ) / 3 ;
          Lo1 = (2*Avg) - High of Data2 ;
          Lo2 = Avg + Lo1 - ( (2*Avg) - Low of Data2) ;
End ;
If NewDay = 1 then NewDay = 0 ;
If CurrentBar of Data2 < > PrCB2 then Begin
          NewDay = 1 ;
          PrCB2 = CurrentBar of Data2 ;
End ;
If CurrentBar of Data2 >= 1 then Begin
          Plot1(Lo1, "LO1") ;
          Plot2(Lo2, "LO2") ;
End ;
```

3. *Tell me about your best current trading system. What makes it tick? What are the features that make it the best trading system? Why do you trade this system?*

The best concept I have is the simple method of buying markets when they make new highs or selling markets when they make new lows. These highs or low points could come from several different technical patterns and not from new high or new low water marks. Nobody ever boarded a plane in Chicago and arrived in Los Angeles on a flight sched-uled for New York City, but unfortunately several trading plans are de-signed with this flawed flight plan.

4. *How long ago did you write your first trading system?*

I hate to tell you how long ago that was because then you would real-ize that instead of being a "state-of-the-art Eddy," I am just another "moldy oldie." Oh well, back in the early '70s, I was a member of the MidAmerica Commodity Exchange, and we used to fool around with oscillators on soy-beans spreads. Old-timers might remember Miller-Lane, a MidAm clearing firm. George Lane, the developer of the stochastic trading method, was the owner of this firm, and we tried to leverage our thinking off this popular os-cillator. In addition, I fumbled around with moving averages and Donchian's ideas about channel break-outs. Most Chicago traders realize that the Donchian work on channel break-outs is the backbone of the fa-mous "Turtle Trading Method." I have included some of Donchian's fa-vorite rules compiled in 1934.[1] Simple is always better, and this list of commonsense rules can be the foundation for any trading system.

---

1 *Technical Tools Journal,* December 1991

1. Beware of acting immediately on widespread public opinion. Even if correct, it will usually delay the move.
2. From a period of dullness and inactivity, watch for and prepare to follow a move in the direction in which volume increases.
3. Limit losses, ride profits—irrespective of all other rules.
4. Light commitments are advisable when a market position is not certain. Clearly defined moves are signaled frequently enough to make life interesting, and concentration on these moves to the virtual exclusion of others will prevent unprofitable "whipsawing."
5. Seldom take a position in the direction of an immediately preceding three-day move. Wait for a one-day reversal.
6. A move followed by a sideways range often precedes another move of almost equal extent in the same direction of the original move. Generally, when the second move from the sideways range has run its course, a counter-move approaching the sideways range may be expected.
7. Watch for "crawling along" or repeated bumping of minor or major trend lines and prepare to see such trend lines broken.
8. Breaking of minor trend lines counter to the major trend gives most other important position-taking signals. Positions can be taken or reversed on stops at such places.
9. During a move, take or increase positions in the direction of the move at the market the morning following any one day reversal, however slight the reversal may be, especially if volume declines on the reversal.

5. *Remember back to your first trading system. Can you tell us the rules?*

While I was trading at the MidAmerica Commodity Exchange, I used to go with the market out of the opening range and add to the position if the market took out the previous high or low. Intraday, I would use either the opposite low or high from the previous session as a stop loss, or if I would add to the position at either the new high or new low, I would use either the top or bottom of that day's opening range as the stop loss point. Final rule: *Go home flat!!!*

6. *What caused you to abandon or modify that trading system the very first time?*

I think what happened is that I did not really abandon the trading plan, but as personal computers became more and more popular, it became a no-brainer to expand your trading concepts. My thinking evolved as technology became more advanced and user friendly. Now with TradeStation, I think you could teach a six-year-old kid how to run the computer, but I still use the same simple concepts I was using years ago. I think you will find the simpler the trading program, the better chance it has of working. If your trading model has 19 entry variables and 20 stop-loss routines, and so many different rules that the concept is so optimized and so set up to pick only one specific pattern, the trading system is doomed. You want to use simple rules that do not clog the machine with any excess baggage. Use tight stops; use money management stops; use retracement bars, but keep it simple. With any system, if you are in a position where you can sit and watch the markets, you almost always want to use indicators side by side with the trading system. In any trading system, no matter what, you still employ some human judgment. The trading system is only as good as the person following it, and to carte blanche charge in and do what a system says can be just as bad as not taking all the trades. So I think you have to have some judgment as a trader to know when to enter the market, when not to enter the market, how to balance your trading capital so you do not overexpose and let leverage become your tragic flaw. One of the biggest tricks to commodity trading is money management. A minor league system with major league money management rules would work much better than a system that had major league trading parameters and minor league money management rules. Money management and strong discipline are what makes for great traders, not great trading systems.

7. *When you look at another person's trading system, what is the very first thing you look for to tell if it's a good or a bad system?*

The first thing I look at is how much it lost. I do not care how profitable the system is. What is the worst drawdown? How much pain did you have to endure? The next important issue is the average winning trade size. Is it $10 or $100? Is it $250? The other thing I would look for would be the number of rights and wrongs. Most people want the thing to be right 70-85 percent of the time. They cannot stand to be wrong, but the system could actually only be right less than 50 percent of the time and still produce great results. If the money management rules are right and if the average trade is right and the drawdown is not too aggressive, then there is a chance of being successful. Just to satisfy your ego and be right, right, right has nothing to do with good trading. You know, if you talk to people long enough, you will find they all say they want to make money trading, but very, very few people say they want to make good trades. It is the good trades that lead to successful trading, and not the other way around.

8. *What is the least important aspect of a trading system as far as you are concerned?*

The number of wins versus the number of losses is not that important. My personality can handle controlled losses. You can ask any of the order desks that I work with, and I am sure they would tell you I immediately place a stop-loss order when a fill is reported. The number one fatality of most novice traders is the lack of stop-loss protection.

9. *In your current work, are you using a mechanical approach or is there judgment involved in your trading?*

I always use judgment. I use a lot of indicators; I use a lot of trend line concepts. I use a lot of parallel lines, and I run systems in the background. What I do is watch the system to trip the market; then I look at the trend lines and the other indicators to help make some type of value judgment. For systems that I run on a day trading basis, I always use a money management stop routine. Generally, if it's in the S&P, it might be a $650 risk; if it's in the currencies, it might be a $350-$400 risk. If I am using longer-term systems where I plan to take the position overnight, then it's some type of a low or high. These market locations can either be written into the system, or marked off with a horizontal line as an alert on the chart. That's one advantage to the TradeStation programs, all the systems and indicators' alerts will take you directly to the page where the market action is occurring.

10. *Are you currently using TradeStation or System Writer? If not, what software do you use to run your trading system?*

I am probably going to say something that will offend somebody, but I will say it anyway. I use TradeStation, and I would say that people who really know how to trade are much stronger with indicators than people that have to rely totally on systems. I have never seen one single trading system that you could consistently produce a living from year in and year out. Now someone can probably stick one in my face and show me that I am wrong. Systems go through drawdowns, and they need not only to be managed but also to be massaged. People are looking for the Holy Grail to trading, and there is no Holy Grail; there is only hard work. Unfortunately, most traders do not have the luxury that I do of being able to sit and watch the screen all day, so they have to rely on systems. If they are prepared correctly, systems can help, but you also have to make a value judgment for each signal about whether your account is in the position where it can accept this trade. If you have a $25,000 account that will be overmargined with this additional new position, then you might want to think about canceling the new position. In addition, you have to look at your total portfolio of where you are in the market instead of just blindly adding a new position. This opens up a whole new can of worms: portfolio management. It's the control, again; it's the control of your trading capital that makes for a good trader, and not the system development.

11. *Is your current trading system for sale? For lease? On a fax line? How do you provide this information to clients?*

A small part of my business is selling systems and indicators. I give prospective clients a 45-day trial, and then if they like what I have, they can purchase the program. I also do seminars where I outline several of my methods along with some options trading concepts. Finally, I publish an overnight fax line that has become very popular. I have been publishing the overnight newsletters for six or seven years now. The fax line newsletters are easy to use and have reasonable money management controls. The other thing is that I do not try to make any predictions about how far the market is going to run. If the person on the fax line is in the trade, and the trade goes his way, it's up to either him or his broker to decide where to pull the trigger. The fax lines can be used in conjunction with some of the support and resistance software that I have or market estimates that other analysts produce.

12. *Can you share the concept behind your trading system? For example, your main entry technique, your exit if you are wrong, and your exit if you are right?*

The big money in the commodity market is made on the overnight moves, not from day trading. I look to buy higher highs and sell lower lows. Constantly trying to buy the bottom and pick the bottom is stupid. Picking tops and bottoms is like trying to catch a safe falling from a window in a cartoon. Let the market bottom come up above the top of the low bar and then think about being a buyer or vice versa on the sell side. Top and bottom picking is digging your own grave.

13. *If you could advise system developers to do one thing when they are starting out, what would that be?*

I would tell them that the best thing to do before they try to program a system is to use indicators and see how their thinking looks on the drawing board. See how your idea tests out by taking it out on the track and running it. Then, if you have some idea of how to set the computer, you may not even have to program in a trading system, but you can use alerts and different types of market action toggles. You do not necessarily need a system. The problem with the systems in the TradeStation, unless you use market orders, is that the program does not enter the market until the end of the bar. The problem with market orders is you cannot always see the entry signal coming, so you need additional indicators to alert you to what is on the horizon.

14. *Other than yourself, who do you think is the best system developer, or who do you think is the best teacher of system development?*

I think probably the best system developer is each individual. You have to find something that makes you comfortable. There are plenty of tools out there, but you have to find what works with your personality. Early on you have to realize that there is no Holy Grail. There is nothing that is going to make you a lot of money without blood, sweat, and tears. Only a fool pays $4,000 or $5,000 for a system without some warm-up ride. Think about this, you would not pay $50 for a pair of shoes without trying them on, but traders are standing in line to pay $5,000 for a dream. You are going to have to work at this. There is going to have to be some adversity involved with your research, and you are going to have to be able to accept the adversity.

Most people cannot accept the adversity. They become disappointed because they buy something and they think it's going to go their way, and when it does not, or when there is a stumbling block, they stop. It's very, very hard to find people who have the ability to persevere against strange circumstances. The market, when you stop to think about it, can only do three things: go up, go down, or go nowhere. It frustrates most people. It's like playing golf; I mean, how can a person with a massive amount of education not figure out something so simple? If you went to the Merc or to the Board of Trade, you would find the professionals who have done really well trading are not the guys with the fancy educational backgrounds or keen business backgrounds. Generally, they are fellows who are very competitive; a lot of them were fairly decent athletes, probably in high school or college. My own observation is that at the Merc, a disproportionate number of locals appear to be left-handed. Left-handers generally process numbers very well. (Unfortunately, the press and several market commentators portray most of the floor traders as being underhanded.) The average guy off the street cannot deal with adversity. He wants to be immediately successful, and he wants to make a lot of money fast. John Q.

RetailAccount never thinks about making good trades that revolve around cutting your losses.

Over the years, my children have been heavily involved in soccer, and every summer they tour the Midwest playing in several soccer tournaments. At these soccer tournaments there are always vendors selling T-shirts that say, "Offense wins games; defense wins championships." Most traders need to accept this simple concept. When most people trade, they fail to think about the defense (stop-loss protection). You wouldn't jump out of plane without a parachute; don't jump into the market with out a stop-loss routine. Anybody can get into a trade, but the pros know how to get out. Even with successful trades, there will always be problems and setbacks, but the proper defense lets you confidently ride out these storms.

To get back to who the good traders are, I also enjoyed reading most of the books that Joe Ross wrote. Ross probably is one of the best futures writers that I have ever read. Some of his option concepts are a little bit confused, as well as his ideas about being able to move stop-loss and profit targets, but his entry concepts are excellent. Unfortunately, Ross' biggest drawdown is that he is very, very hard on the exchanges, the regulators and the integrity of the exchange members as well as the clearing firms. I think some of Jake Berstein's stuff about people and their heads is pretty good. I also like seasonal research.

I would have to say that I have learned something from every book I have ever bought. I would say that I am a little bit suspect of authors who are always promising pie-in-the-sky profits. There are plenty of good books around, but you have to know how to weed through them. The problem with all the books written on futures trading is that if the Exchanges are correct about 95 percent of the accounts losing, then all the trading books written to date have been flawed. Then to date, there has been no one complete book that successfully tells you how to trade commodities. I like books that make me think, and I will feel successful if this book can do that for other traders. So, I would take marketing efforts that present great trading results with caution. I do believe that traders can take a number of different ideas and come up with some great trading concepts that will fit their personality.

15. *When you devise a trading system, what time frames do you use most? For example, do you use daily bars, weekly bars, 1-minute bars, 10-minute bars, or 60-minute bars?*

The measure of market volatility is how fast the market might move, but the direction is still an unknown variable. If you have any doubt about volatility, options traders know the primary driving force of the Black-Scholes Model, the options pricing model, is based heavily on the volatility of the futures markets. It depends on how fast the market is moving. I think that people are kidding themselves if they try to day trade under a five-minute chart. If you consider that by the time the last trade gets to you, the computer processes the trade, the trading system marks your bar, you make up your mind, you pick up the phone, you try to call the floor, the boat has sailed, and you are left with a sloppy fill. You cannot be in California and trade like a local on the floor of a Chicago Exchange. This is my favorite marketing bug-a-boo. Computer generated programs can give the off-floor trader a big edge, but you have to be standing in the middle of the pit to capture the "bid and offer." Just watch!! The trading fatalities from market access on the Information SuperHighway will make driving on New Year's Eve look like amateur night. Expand your time horizons! Try to think long-term! Look at any chart; the big success stories are from overnight gap openings.

16. *If for some reason they closed every commodity in the world except one, and you were the guy in charge of deciding which one would stay open, which commodity would you choose? Why? What hours would it be open?*

British Pound has a tendency to move nicely. It trends nicely. The overnight gaps are good. It trends very, very, smoothly. It's orderly, and it has a reasonable tick value. The market that could be great for trending markets would be feeder cattle. The feeder cattle contract is based on the cattle fax index, and the market settles to cash, so you do not have to worry about being squeezed or the delivery process as you do in the live cattle market. Unfortunately, the volume has just never materialized in the feeder cattle market. So I am going to say the British Pound. That probably will surprise people.

17. *If you were to choose one commodity you could never trade again and you could never include in a trading system, which commodity would this be? Why?*

Coffee. I know that once coffee gets going that it trends very, very well, and that it has had some monstrous moves. In the coffee market, there are so many games played to confuse and irritate traders. The coffee market will open up the limit, then close for a few minutes only to re-open down the limit. So the games they play in coffee are not good, but if you can survive and catch trending market, it's usually a big move.

The same thing is true in orange juice. I think orange juice is an absolute horrible market, but it does not do enough volume to warrant any attention. I would never even waste my time trying to figure out a system for orange juice. If I had to close one market, it would be coffee.

18. *Where do you get your ideas for your system? A chart? A pattern? Observations? Trades that you have done before? What is your favorite technique for coming up with a trading system?*

I get a lot of my ideas from observations, and I also get a lot of new ideas from talking with other traders. I talk to a lot of people, and when people call me asking for help, they tell me things that give me ideas. Most of the things people tell me do not work. But parts of what someone tells me might work, and parts of what someone else tells me might work, and then I come up with a new idea. I have to tell you though, I do not change a lot of stuff, and I have left a hundred dark alleys empty handed. If you met people who were really successful in this industry, you would find that most of their systems are very simple and that they are very pleasant and simple people to be with. Successful ideas are not flashy. If you went to a futures industry convention and tried to market these simple successful concepts, they would probably lose out to the flashy complicated ideas from individuals who knew a great deal less about the market, but much more about marketing. Just like buying dog food. "Man's best friend" will eat almost anything; so for the pet owner, it's not what's in the can, but how the can's promoted that sells the pet owner on the product. Do not fall into the dog food trap when you are thinking about purchasing computer trading software. Just about any dog food program will run with today's high-tech personal computers. Buy the steak and not the sizzle!!

19. *I want you to write a trading system for me. I want you to give me all the rules. I want you to tell me what commodity, what time frame, whether it is daily bars, whatever. What your entry rule is, your exit rule with a profit, your exit rule with a loss. It does not have to be a great system. Just give me an idea of something you would look at, something you would test to see if there was any validity.*

This is going to be kind of hard, but I will try something. We are looking for an overnight situation. The market is going to make four consecutive lows. We are going to look to be a buyer. Four consecutive lows. Boom. Boom. Boom. Boom. Four consecutive lows. When it takes up the high of the lowest low, we go long and put our stop at the low of the low bar. Let's take the first low when it made its first consecutive low, which would be four days back. Let's take the low of that day and make that our profit target. If that would appear too tight, then let's take the middle range of that day or the high of that day. Remember four days back. Stop-loss is two ticks under the fourth low. You just put your stop there, GTC, and try to forget it for a while (a very difficult thing to do). If the market takes off you go with it. It gets up to that low of four days ago, profitably close the position. If market location is too tight, use the middle value, that bar or the high of that session.

20. *What is the typical day in the life of a system developer? What time do you start? What time do you end? What is it you do all day long? How are your orders placed? How is your system run?*

I am a lucky guy. I work in my house, so I just wander or stumble down to my basement about seven o'clock in the morning. I stop in the afternoon. (I used to be in an afternoon car pool with my grade school daughter, but fortunately we moved into junior high. Most males do not understand the strict discipline of school car pool rules. For those who do not know, grade school car pools are dominated by suburban females, who are no less unforgiving than futures markets.) I write my newsletters at night, so I usually do not stop until around 10:00 P.M., but my day is not anywhere close to 18 hours long. I think I found the perfect work at home business. I place all my orders with an off-floor trading desk. I always try to avoid going directly to the trading floor. All these guys who think they get better service by going right to the floor are wrong. I call an order desk, place the orders, talk to somebody who has some idea of what they are doing, and have them place the orders. With this procedure, I have a buffer between some screaming phone clerk and myself on the trading floor. The phone clerk on the floor is the lowest guy in the food chain. People risk thousands of dollars listening to industry level novices telling them the locals are pushing the market, and that is enough said about that.

My systems run only on OmegaResearch products. Again, I use systems, and I also use a lot of indicators. I would place more stock in the indicators than I would in the systems. That is not to say that the systems are not valid. The systems just do not get there as fast as the indicators.

21. *If you could have your system run in any manner, what would be the preferable method? Would you have the person whose money is at risk run the system, or would you have a third party run the system and just arbitrarily take the trades as they are generated, regardless of consequence?*

While I was a member of the CME, I always operated with a clerk. On markets, other than the pit I was trading in, I would always tell him what I wanted to do, what I expected to do, and when to call me. It is always better to have somebody place orders for you than to try to do it yourself because you will wind up second-guessing yourself, especially on the stop-loss routines. If you give the guy specific instructions, I want to do this at this price, or when the market trades here. You are better off using a third party, but not somebody on the floor of the exchange, or getting flash fills is not for me.

22. *Let's pretend I do not have a single book on commodities, and I am interested in writing systems. Other than your own work, what book would you recommend? Along these same lines, is there anything you would avoid—whether it's software, books, lectures, whatever?*

What I would tell people to do is to call the Chicago Mercantile Exchange and get a list of the books they sell to the public. I would try to read some of Joe Ross' books; I would take advantage of some of the videos and pamphlets the two Chicago Exchanges offer. I would read *Market Wizard* for hints on how to accept adversity. I would page through *Futures* magazine to acquaint yourself with the standard list of market gurus and charlatans. There are lots of things you can do, but if you are really serious about trading, do two things: (A) Come to Chicago but instead of going to the exchange floors, visit the exchanges' libraries and learn what a wonderful trading resource they can become for you.

(B) I am not plugging OmegaResearch, but if you are going to be involved in the 1990s in futures markets, I think you at least need to have SuperCharts or another compatible computer program. I think you have to have some type of charting capability. I would also encourage people to get *The New York Times*, and *The London Times*. I think that I would use a book by Perry Kaufman. I think his books are good. *Computer Analysis of the Futures Market* by LaBeau and Lucas is also a good starting point.

23. *Do you think it is necessary for a software developer/real-time trader to have tick-by-tick real-time quotes? Why or why not?*

If you are going to do some of the things I do, you will probably need real-time quotes or a good broker. A deep-discount broker may not be able to help, because what happens if you are going to buy a higher high or sell a lower low and you have the order placed, but you cannot place your protective stop-loss until after the stop-entry price has been triggered. Otherwise, you might first be hit on the downside protective stop-loss before the market goes high enough to elect your original stop-entry price. Since this type of trading always enters the market on stops, you probably need a better-than-average broker that will service your account—a broker you can count on to call you when the market trips your stop-entry price.

What kind of quotation vendor you need depends on the length of your trading time-frame. If you are day trading, tick-by-tick quotes would probably be important. If you are trading overnight, it would not be nearly as important. Overnight traders could probably go down to 10-minute delay or end of day quotes. Actually, sometimes the less you know, the better off you are. Also on certain trades, placing stop-loss and OCO (one cancels the other), profit target, contingency order makes good sense. Your broker can tell you at which Exchanges this type of order is acceptable.

24. *What kind of quotes do you have? What kind of software would you recommend? Are there any systems or software that you would definitely not recommend?*

I do not know about quotes. I mean, I have used Signal; I have used CQG. Recently, there has been lots of noise on several internet e-mail lists about which quote vendor is faster. Since 99.9 percent of my stuff is done on day bars, I guess smoke signals would be fine for me.

I would not recommend any trading system that said you were going to make a lot of money with it. With any trading system, you first have to test the system to see if it works not only in the market but also with your personality. If the system vendor will not let you test the system in real-time, do not buy it. Anybody who knows much about writing trading systems knows the tricks of the scammers who can make any trading system appear to be successful. If the results are too good to be believed, they usually are!!!

I use TradeStation; I use Excel; I use Dial Data; sometimes I use Signal. I get tick-by-tick stuff off an internet bulletin board. I buy old data. I would say I would never go more than 48 months back in testing a system. The world changes, the market changes, and that type of information, anything older than 48 months, is probably going only to confuse your expectations.

25. *How much data do you think is necessary to be tested as far as assessing a day trade session on five-minute bars? A daily bar system? A 60-minute system?*

I do not trade five-minute bars. With a daily system, you could test one year, that should give you a clue about what to expect. A 60-minute system you probably test 99 to 120 days. Remember, I always use some discretionary judgment about my entries and profit targets. You have to be careful when you are dealing with shorter time frames. The successful patterns you think you have found may not be valid with every time fame. You just have to be extra careful when you are doing day trades. Instead of using just one trading system, what you could do is you look for strong support numbers and strong resistance numbers, and then buy the bottom of channels and sell the top of channels with a dollar stop-loss routine. Think twice about short-term trading. I think day traders really risk about $2 to make $1. Remember the real success stories come from the big overnight moves.

26. *Why do some systems consistently perform year after year, and other systems fail or need to be continually optimized?*

This is the story of life. Simple things perform. The simpler the system, the more likely it is going to be successful year after year. The simpler the trading system, the better. The market entry point is important; the stop-loss point is critical. All these fancy input rules just do not make a lot of sense in the long run.

27. *How important are drawdowns in your research? How important is average trade size?*

Drawdowns are the most important thing. How much money are you going to lose before you are right? How much pain can you stand? How far can I twist your arm before you give up? It is the most important thing. Most people look at how much money the trading system made and forget what the drawdown pain threshold is.

How important is the average trade size? That is also very, very important. I would say that is the second most important thing. Like anyone else running a business, you want your average trade size (ticket size) to be reasonable. Just like in any other business, if your average ticket size is not reasonable, your business is going to be spinning out of control, and you are going to have to do a lot more trading volume just to try to stay in the black. So the ticket size, or the average trade size, is very, very important. The average trade size of your futures business has to overcome these variable expenses: trading losses; execution slippage; missed profitable trading opportunities due to capital or portfolio adjustments (very subjective item); commissions and other administrative costs.

28. *Do you do portfolio management—linking several commodities of different systems together? Do you do pyramiding? Why or why not?*

I have no academic background in portfolio management. I do watch what my position is and my equity or margin commitment. I do not pyramid. Actually, I de-pyramid. I look to get out when I am right along the way. Why? I think pyramiding is an amateur move. You have moved your average price up, and when the market finally turns, it's going to get you a lot quicker. You are always better off getting out of the market on your terms, and that means scheduled profit targets. You are never going to capture the whole move. If you let the market run and run and run, it's going to come back and take you out anyway. Since you are getting out on your terms instead of letting the market take you out on its terms, if you have profit targets along the way, psychologically you are much better. Finally, as we begin to close this century, the old sage trading advice about "cutting your losses, and letting your profits run" might need to be reworked. Maybe today this would be better advice: "cut your losses, and manage your profits." Sounds yuppie enough to me.

29. *Let's get a little morbid. You have died. You have left a sealed letter to your heirs. It contains the secret of your fortune. It's the secret to allow them to continue the lifestyle to which they have been accustomed. What one sentence is in the letter?*

The key word would be *perseverance.* You have to be able to persevere. The other thing I would tell my heirs would be to plan for the worst and hope for the best.

30. *Without giving the secret of life, how would you write an imitation of your system in two lines or less in TradeStation language? For example, I have an S&P system called Buy Monday. "Monday you buy it, put in a $1,400 stop, get out on the close." That's how you write that.*

I would revert back to what I said earlier, we will try this, buy the high of the four bar, from four consecutive lows and risk to the bottom of the two ticks under the last low bar. Vice versa on the sell side.

31. *Give us an example of some of your work and put it in English-type language for a system.*

Take the 21 bar mean moving average, buy the second breakout of the 21 bar mean moving average. Use an envelope of a price channel as a stop on the downside and two and one-half times the price channel as a profit target.

Joseph DiNapoli

INTRODUCTION

Joe DiNapoli is president of Coast Investment Software in Sarasota, FL, and a trader for more than 25 years. He has taught his trading techniques and spoken at numerous conferences and seminars around the world and is the author of the "Fibonacci Money Management and Trend Analysis" home training course.

1. *Tell me about yourself. If someone were to say, "Tell me about Joe DiNapoli," what would you want them to know? Give me a brief biography of you before you got into commodities, and a brief biography of what you have done since you got into commodities.*

It seems that in one way or another, I've been involved with trading all my life. In 1967 I finished engineering college and began seriously trading. Back in those days, I was dealing with low capitalized, small, over-the-counter issues, where you'd lose 15-25 percent just in the bid/asked spread. We used to margin those "equities," that's using the term loosely, at the company's credit union where I was working. It was definitely spooky. I was also involved in trading options on stocks. That's before they were listed on exchanges like they are today. You talk about volatility. When you wanted to sell, the broker would say, "to whom?" It was strictly a bid by appointment situation. We'd generally end up paying for an exercise to exit a position.

So, to answer your question about how long I've been trading, it seems like I've been trading as far back as I can remember; before that I watched my father trade, quite actively. That's something I really haven't mentioned much because when he was alive, I didn't want anyone bothering him. Now that he's gone, I have no reticence to say he was a good trader, primarily in stocks and certain other cash markets.

My educational background is electrical engineering. Of course, I really didn't like engineering, but that background has been an unbelievable help to me as a trader. Good engineers think in structured patterns. That's the way I think, disciplined and structured. It's not in the same sense that a computer programmer's thinking is structured. They tend to be too rigid for the game. Programmers tend to shy away from unpredictability, regardless of how small a portion of unpredictability there is in the overall plan.

I got involved in trading commodities in about 1980. I like the commodity markets. If you can develop strategies to effectively deal with the risk, the advantages far outweigh those of other markets. Since I've learned how to do that, I have substantially decreased the amount of stock and options trading that I do, but I'm still involved.

About 1986 I began speaking, initially with Jake Bernstein, at the Futures Symposium International. That's when I started letting myself out to the public. It really mushroomed from there. I've spoken all over the world, in major centers in Asia, Europe, and the Middle East. In 1996, I spoke in about 22 different countries. That was a bit much, but I couldn't give up the opportunity to speak in places like Tallin, Estonia, St. Petersburg, Russia, and Bombay. I've met fantastic people all over the globe, and the industry has been nothing but good to me.

Commodity traders tend to be risk-takers, self-made people, and I enjoy them immensely. The public always wonders why someone, if he is profitable and making plenty of money trading commodities, would talk about what he does or expose his methodologies. The public doesn't realize some of the advantages you receive by doing so. Obviously, there's the money that one can make from selling a system or teaching. But the contacts you make, literally around the world, couldn't be bought at any price. If you have something worthwhile to say, exposure also gives you access to other professional traders, and that access can be intellectually stimulating as well as financially beneficial. You can fine tune your trading methods by brainstorming with others.

At this point, I trade my own account; I don't manage money and don't want to. I teach and have a software company, Coast Investment Software Inc. That company produces trading courses, as well as certain proprietary software, which enables my clients and myself to trade much more effectively.

I've been a registered CTA since 1986 or 1987.

2. *Tell me about your technique. What makes it exclusively yours? How did you develop it?*

The trading techniques I use are substantially different than those used by other people. I mix leading and lagging indicators and interact with prices based on that approach. I use certain lagging indicators like displaced moving averages and the MACD/Stochastic combination to determine the trend. Once I'm in a trend, I use Fibonacci analysis as a leading indicator to position myself within that trend. The last step is to take logical profit objectives. Those profit objectives are calculated by certain Fibonacci techniques.

What makes the system mine is that I've spent an awful lot of time developing it. I use displaced moving averages, for example, in very specific and unique ways. I think I've really done my homework on that one, about 3 years worth of research in the early '80s. During the mid-'80s, I spent another three years or so determining the most effective method to utilize **Fibonacci** techniques. I think I've done a good job of separating the best from the good or the average. Sometimes it's not a matter of developing a brand new indicator. It's a matter of utilizing an existing indicator in a more effective manner. For example, instead of using standard moving averages, I use displaced moving averages. In fact, back in the mid-'80s, when I started speaking about this, there weren't any computer programs out there available, except our own, that would displace a moving average. Prior to that, some people used the opens instead of the close to determine the moving average before the end of the day. When you displace a moving average say five days, you know what the moving average is going to be up to five days out. There is no longer any reason to use the open. Unfortunately, many of the graphics software programs that displace moving averages don't show them past the last day's price action. It's an example of programmers rather than traders creating trading software.

3. *Tell me about your best current trading system. What makes it tick? What are the features that make it the best trading system? Why do you trade this system?*

My best and my current trading system is an approach that I've used continuously for years. I buy dips in an uptrend and sell rallies in a downtrend. The lagging indicators allow me to determine trend. The leading indicators, primarily **Fibonacci** analysis, allow me to "safely" place myself within that trend. I use logical profit objectives continually, and I have oscillators, that are used as filters, to keep me from entering in the direction of a trend which is too dangerous.

I also have about eight trading patterns or conditions which act to give me the direction of a market. If they are in conflict with the trend analysis, I always go with what the patterns are telling me.

4. *How long ago did you write your first trading system?*

About 1981, 1982, when I began applying my engineering background to the formulation of a commodity trading strategy. I could get away with a more sloppy approach trading equities; commodities are more demanding.

5. *Remember back to your first trading system. Can you tell us the rules?*

The first trading system I had that I thought was at least reasonably good had to do with price crossing over certain Displaced Moving Averages on a closing basis. What I used then, and continue to use today, was a three-day simple moving average of the close, displaced forward three days, a seven-day moving average of the close, displaced forward five days, and a 25-day moving average of the close, displaced forward five days. Those numbers were not easily determined. It took literally years of research, but I didn't do the research from an optimization point of view. I did it from the point of view of an experienced trader. Remember, I <u>was</u> an experienced trader by that time. So I had a software package developed that would displace moving averages and one that would allow me to view these moving averages and price action on a screen. I bought some data and literally viewed thousands upon thousands of different data sets with different moving averages until I came up with something that a trader could live with, that a trader could actually trade! That's a lot different than doing some sort of optimization routine where you're immune to the psychological consequences and emotions created by your system parameters.

6. *What caused you to abandon or modify that trading system the very first time?*

I certainly didn't abandon the initial system. I added to it and made it better. There were two specific additions that I made. I added an overbought oversold oscillator, a detrended oscillator, to the displaced moving

average system. This acted to filter out-of-range moves, those that were expired or at least expired for a period of time. The detrend filtered the trades
and kept me out of dangerous situations. The next thing I did, which I think
was really my first big development, a sort of inspirational development,
was to create an indicator that I call the Oscillator Predictor. This indicator
would tell me, a day ahead of time, where overbought and oversold was in
the marketplace. It was truly a leading indicator. Using it, I could capture
profit. With the old system, I would watch a commodity fly through a displaced moving average, go strongly my way, and then I would sit there. I
would have to wait and wait and wait and wait and watch price deterioration. Under the old system, I was not able to exit until price passed through
the moving average again on close. I was giving back an awful lot. With
the Oscillator Predictor, I was able to capture profits for the first time at a
logical place. I think that's key, the ability to capture profits. When you use
logical profit objectives, you begin to experience a very high percentage of
winning trades. As long as your techniques are good enough to get you
back in, you don't have to worry about missing a move. Besides, one thing
my Dad taught me was that a businessman's profit should be booked. He
never got piggish about his trades, and I don't either.

7. *When you look at another person's trading system, what is the very
first thing you look for to tell if it's a good or a bad system?*

I actually don't look at another person's trading system; first, I look
at the person. I look at where he is coming from, how much experience he
has in the marketplace. Most people that develop trading systems don't
have an awful lot of experience in the marketplace. They are cerebral
types or programmers, and they don't understand order flow. If you don't
understand order flow, it will kill you. So that's the first thing I look at.

8. *What is the least important aspect of a trading system as far as you are
concerned?*

That's a tough question to answer. What's the least important thing?
I think the amount that it trades. To be more specific, I'd rather trade less
and have safer trades than just be trading all the time, which is what most
people want to do. They trade just for the sake of trading. They love action. So, the frequency with which a system trades is the least important
thing to me. Obviously, I don't want one trade a year, but I don't need to
be trading all the time. That was a big lesson for me to learn, but a critical
one.

9. *In your current work, are you using a mechanical approach or is there judgment involved in your trading?*

I use a mechanical approach, and judgment is involved. A key point in any judgmental trading system is to make as much of it as nonjudgmental as possible. I think I've achieved that.

10. *Are you currently using TradeStation or System Writer? If not, what software do you use to run your trading system?*

I currently use Aspen Graphics for the development of bar charts and indicators, and I use my own company's **Fibnode** software for determining precise buy and sell entry points. Then I use **Fibnodes** to determine profit objectives.

11. *Is your current trading system for sale? For lease? On a fax line? How do you provide this information to clients?*

My trading approach is available by means of an in-home trading course and private seminars. I will have a book out shortly, which should also provide a lot of high quality information for traders. That's my objective anyway. We'll see if it's achieved. I don't provide fax updates or any sort of advisory services. I provide after-purchase support, of course, at no charge. One of the reasons I trade commodities is that I want an ample amount of time to myself, and if I were running a fax service or advisory, I don't think my life would be my own anymore. The way it is now is tremendously advantageous. I can take as much time off as I want. If I want a break, I turn off the monitors. I don't schedule seminars, and I leave other people in control of filling orders for the products Coast offers. Why achieve success in a field and drive yourself mad with overwork?

The in-home trading course is available at $475. There is a less expensive version available, but it really doesn't sell as well as the bigger course, which is sold strictly by word-of-mouth. Right now the private seminars are $1,000. They are two-day events, a maximum of three attendees. That price and the structure of the private seminars may change down the line. I have a larger facility now. Perhaps I could offer ten or twelve people a more thorough experience involving other experts over a longer period of time. What I have in mind is to conduct most of the seminar myself, including the analysis of real-time trading situations. Perhaps I would bring in people that I know have something to offer and whose approach would dove-tail with mine. I think it would be a great learning experience and a lot of fun. I really enjoy teaching.

12. *Can you share the concept behind your trading system, for example, your main entry technique, your exit if you are wrong, and your exit if you are right?*

I think I've already covered the main concepts of the trading systems. First, I determine trend or direction. As I alluded to earlier, direction is generally derived from certain patterns. This initial analysis tells me whether the market is likely to go up or down. But that's not enough. You need to position yourself on a retracement as safely as possible. Let's say we're going up. You need to position yourself on a retracement level, a safe level for entry. Then, you need to immediately calculate a profit objective. It's most beneficial for intraday trading to have that profit objective in place before the market gets there. By definition, whether you are using a **Fib** expansion or the Oscillator Predictor, these price points are unstable. You simply may not have time to get on the telephone and exit the market at the most favorable place unless you have a resting order. If the position were established on the long side, I would choose a more distant **Fibonacci** support point as my "get out" on the loss side. If I go down to the vicinity of the stop, it doesn't need to be a physical stop; I reevaluate the trade. Basically, I determine if I am wrong in my position. If so, I take the first rally back to get out. Therefore, I minimize or eliminate my loss. Using the approach that I've developed, there is not a lot of question about whether you're right or wrong. If the trends or the direction is in your favor, then you are right in the trade. If they are not, you are wrong. If you are wrong, you either get out, or you look for a way out. Looking for a way out usually saves a lot of money, rather than just exiting. It can however, on occasion, create a larger than expected loss. I prefer looking for a way out because most of the time I can mitigate any damage or trouble that I get into.

13. *If you could advise system developers to do one thing when they are starting out, what would that be?*

Get a dose of reality. Most people who develop trading systems have absolutely no idea of what's happening on the floor. It's a huge area of misunderstanding, and unless you have ample experience, trying to develop a trading system in your office using TradeStation without adequate knowledge of order flow is a recipe for disaster or at least disappointment. This is where a good broker can be invaluable. Someone who has been around for a long time and understands order flow is going to be able to help you evaluate your system, your entry and exit points. It's difficult to find brokers that have experience in the markets and the time to help you. They are available however, and the <u>least</u> significant issue in all this, is an extra few dollars for commission. I know people will disagree with me on that point, but it's an absolute fact as far as I'm concerned. Someone who can save you money in the way your position is executed, someone who can give you sound advice and understands market order flow, can save you a lot.

14. *Other than yourself, who do you think is the best system developer, or who do you think is the best teacher of system development?*

I don't think I'm really qualified to make judgments about system developers because I think the question is really meant to pertain to developers of nonjudgmental systems, and that is not where my expertise lies. I have, however, recently become involved with an individual overseas, who is using some, let's say, incredible assets from which he is developing a neural net. Although I really don't believe in neural nets, I've consented to consult with this individual because of the talent that's behind this project. Maybe I could recommend him some day, but for now, the jury is out.

15. *When you devise a trading system, what time frame do you use most? For example, do you use daily bars, weekly bars, 1-minute bars, 10-minute bars, or 60-minute bars?*

The approach I take to the market is exactly the same, whether I use monthly charts or five minute charts. In 1980, I was trading primarily daily charts, and in 1983, I went down to the 5-minute world. I could learn more and develop my approach more quickly in the 5-minute world than on dailies, particularly relative to **Fibonacci** analysis. So, in the development phase of it, I gained more experience in less time by trading 5 minutes charts. I went through this development process by actually trading, not by theorizing.

I think most good systems should be applicable across time frames. If they are not, it's a red flag.

16. *If for some reason they closed every commodity in the world except one, and you were the guy in charge of deciding which one would stay open, which commodity would you choose? Why? What hours would it be open?*

Well, that's got to be the S&P. I mean, it's the most incredible futures contract out there. I was trading it in 1982, and I was trading the value line before it. If you can understand its action, it can be a money machine. I actually thought it was going to die after the 1987 crash. It was more than sad, but it's still alive and reasonably well today. If I had control, I'd trade the S&P from about 3 P.M. until 9 P.M. I love those civilized European hours.

17. *If you were to choose one commodity you could never trade again and you could never include in a trading system, which commodity would this be? Why?*

That's really a funny question. I don't have any hesitation on that one. It's wheat. If I never saw another wheat contract, I wouldn't be sad. In the early days, more money went from the Merc to the Board of Trade while I was trying to trade wheat. I mean, it was incredible! I finally followed the advice of a friend of mine. We were sitting in a bar and I was complaining about the wheat market. "Look," he said, "I'm going to tell you how to handle wheat so you're never going to lose any money on it again, but it's going to cost you $500 to find out what the secret is." He guaranteed the results. He said, "If this doesn't work, I'll give you back the $500 and $500 more to boot." So I gave him $500 on the spot. He looked at me with kind of a silly grin and said, "Don't trade wheat." I never got my money back, and I never traded wheat again!

18. *Where do you get your ideas for your system? A chart? A pattern? Observations? Trades that you have done before? What is your favorite technique for coming up with a trading system?*

Observation of markets. Observation and experience. My very best directional signals come from the disasters that I've had. I mean, I can still remember them, clearly. If I didn't understand why the market did what it did, I studied it, and I said, well, let's see if that happens again. Over the years I've found some very consistent situations, which have fully mitigated those disastrous moments. In other words, if you are going to lose money, just be sure you learn something in the process. If you are going to lose money, you've got to be sure you learn something, because from what you have learned, you can get that money back tenfold on down the line.

19. *I want you to write a trading system for me. I want you to give me all the rules. I want you to tell me what commodity, what time frame, whether it is daily bars, whatever. What your entry rule is, your exit rule with a profit, your exit rule with a loss. It doesn't have to be a great system. Just give me an idea of something you would look at, something you would test to see if there was any validity.*

We don't have enough paper for me to go through all the details of an entire trading system here. As far as market or time frame, it doesn't matter. I pretty much approach the markets and time frames in the same way, with the exception of wheat of course, but let me give you a brief recap and a little more about my approach. Look at the MACD/Stochastic combination. Let's say those two trend indicators are both indicating an up market. Let's also assume that we have made the Stochastic a deliberately weak indicator, so that it will show us when the weak longs are bailing out, and when the weak shorts are coming in. But, by using the correct inputs, we keep the MACD strong. That way, we can observe whether or not the trend remains intact. The MACD is telling us where the strong money is. When the pull-back comes in the direction of the weak stochastic, we will be able to position ourselves on a <u>properly constructed</u> **Fibonacci** retracement series as long as the MACD remains intact in an up trend. Once we have positioned ourselves within that series, we then calculate a **Fibonacci** objective for our profit or look at the Oscillator Predictor. We look at the properly developed retracement series again to determine more distant support. That's where our stops should be. If we lose the trend on the MACD, we look for a way out of the trade on any retracement back up to our entry. That's about as specific I can get without really taking up some space.

20. *What's the typical day in the life of a system developer? What time do you start? What time do you end? What is it you do all day long? How are your orders placed? How is your system run?*

My system is and has been an ongoing effort over a period of 16 years, so it's not what I do in a single day. I will take this opportunity to tell you one thing I try to do that affects my performance as a trader every single day. I think, at least for a few hours a week, every commodity trader should do something that he really enjoys. Something that does not involve the markets or his computer. I like working with my hands. I restore classic cars, things like that. You need to be able to settle the mind and avoid all that frenetic activity. The graveyard of past traders is littered with those who couldn't get the needle out of their arm. I mean that in a literal as well as a figurative sense. Markets can destroy you emotionally, physically, and financially. You must keep perspective.

21. *If you could have your system run in any manner, what would be the preferable method? Would you have the person whose money is at risk run the system, or would you have a third party run the system and just*

*arbitrarily take the trades as they are generated, regardless of conse-
quence?*

If I had a nonjudgmental system, I would turn it over to someone
else that was competent, but I'd always keep an eye on things. Since I use
a judgmental system, I won't turn over its implementation to anyone.

22. *Let's pretend I don't have a single book on commodities, and I'm interested in writing systems. Other than your own work, what book would
you recommend? Along these same lines, is there anything you would
avoid—whether it's software, books, lectures, whatever?*

The Commodity Futures Game by Teweles, Harlow & Stone. It's a
soft-covered, inexpensive book. It's a great book. There is an immense
amount that I would avoid, like the plague, but I would not feel free to list
them.

23. *Do you think it is necessary for a software developer/real-time trader
to have tick-by-tick real-time quotes? Why or why not?*

No, I don't think it's necessary. It might be desirable at some point,
but certainly there's an awful lot of data that can be had for low dollars
that you can use for development work. There's even programs now that
will spit this data out just like it was live data, except it's data from, say,
1982 or 1993. You can develop your system cheaply. Why spend money if
you don't need to? Develop it, test it historically and tweak it, then test it
real-time to see if you are on the right track. Spend money for real-time
quotes <u>after</u> all the development is in.

24. *What kind of quotes do you have? What kind of software would you
recommend? Are there any systems or software that you would definitely
not recommend?*

I used to have three different types of quotes coming in to my office.
Now I only use Signal. Again, I use Aspen Graphics, and I use my own
Fibnode software. I also use my end-of-day graphics package, the CIS
Trading Package, for some proprietary studies like the Oscillator
Predictor that are in there.

25. *How much data do you think is necessary to be tested as far as assessing a day-trade session on five-minute bars? A daily bar system? A
60-minute system?*

I would look at snap shots from 1988 to the present time for any of the time frames that you are suggesting in your question.

26. *Why do some systems consistently perform year after year, and other systems fail or need to be continually optimized?*

Over-optimization leads to inconsistency. Unhappily, many of the so-called consistent performers have very poor win-to-loss ratios and involve substantial drawdowns. You need to look at how a system makes its money, not just at a summary sheet or equity run.

27. *How important are drawdowns in your research? How important is average trade size?*

Drawdowns for me are critical. I don't like drawdowns. I like very good risk-to-reward situations. I'm far more interested in avoiding risk than I am in capturing every opportunity. My philosophy says that loss of opportunity is preferable to loss of capital.

28. *Do you do portfolio management—linking several commodities of different systems together? Do you do pyramiding? Why or why not?*

I do portfolio management, but I don't do it in a typical "optimal F" way. I definitely will pyramid when the situation calls for it, for example, when my directional indicators come into play.

29. *Let's get a little morbid. You've died. You've left a sealed letter to your heirs. It contains the secret of your fortune. It's the secret to allow them to continue the lifestyle to which they have been accustomed. What one sentence is in the letter?*

Assuming I had someone that was interested and capable, the one sentence would be to study the work that I have done, particularly the work that is in the trading course, my upcoming book, as well as the output of the **Fibnodes** software.

30. *Without giving the secret of life, how would you write an imitation of your system in two lines or less in Trade Station language? For example, I have an S&P system called Buy Monday. "Monday you buy it, put in a $1,400 stop, get out on the close." That's how you write that.*

I have no idea.

31._Give an example of some of your work and put it in English-type language for a system._

I believe I already have. I find methods of buying dips in an uptrend or selling rallies in a downtrend. I take precalculated profits whenever I can. I manage risk as well as my psychology.

Stan Ehrlich

INTRODUCTION

Stan Ehrlich graduated from Southern Illinois University in 1971 and joined Conti Commodities Services in the fall of that year. It was in 1976, when I first joined Conti, that I met Stan. After trading for a few years, Stan invented the Ehrlich Cycle Finder, a physical, accordian-like device used to find cycle activity in any chart. The oldest mechanical, technical analysis tool in the futures industry, traders can use the Ehrlich Cycle Finder on all kinds of markets worldwide.

Often quoted in publications such as *Bond Week*, *Successful Farming Magazine*, *Crane Chicago Business Weekly*, *Futures Magazine*, and *Technical Analysis of Stocks and Commodities Magazine*, Stan has appeared numerous times on television and radio. Several Technical Analysis texts mention or detail the Ehrlich Cycle Finder.

Stan has taught at dozens of investment seminars around the world, including some real-time trading seminars. In the past Stan has worked with such well-known investment personalities as Jake Bernstein, Robert Prechter and Robert Saperstein. Stan currently faxes a timely technical analysis market letter to his clients every few days.

1. *Tell me about yourself. If someone were to say, "Tell me about Stan Ehrlich," what would you want them to know? Give me a brief biography of you before you got into commodities, and a brief biography of what you have done since you got into commodities.*

My interest in the futures market began when I was in college at Southern Illinois University. I didn't know what the futures market was. Jeff, my new stepbrother, told me a little bit about it. He was an egg market expert. As a sophomore in college he said, "Hey, Stan, I'm going to make a trade for you. If the trade succeeds, I'll send you a check for whatever the profit is. If it fails, I'll eat it, no big deal." A couple of weeks later, I got a check in the mail for $200. In those days, around 1970, that was good beer money. And it impressed me a little bit. I looked into the futures industry a little bit more. Jeff was able to provide me with a start in the industry with Conti Commodity Services as a runner on the old Franklin Street Mercantile Exchange. I was a runner back when they were trading eggs and milo and there were, of course, the standard meat markets—milo and eggs aren't traded anymore as you know—but there were also bellies and hogs and cattle and feeder cattle and lumber. And that was pretty much it on the Merc in those days.

After being a runner on the Mercantile Exchange for a few months, I was a runner on the Board of Trade, the traditional floor, of course, back when the old cement parking garage was in the back, and of course the windows overlooked LaSalle Street; now they are boarded up because of night trading. That was a fantastic experience. I got to meet Gene Cashman and several other pretty famous pit brokers in those days. Actually, I used to deliver his paychecks because he was a trader for Conti, one of the brokers who filled orders for Conti. Then I worked as a research assistant in the back offices of Conti in the Board of Trade Building in 1971, learning to draw vertical bar charts. And I worked with Ivan Auer in the fundamental research department, tallying up numbers, crop statistics, import/export statistics, etcetera. For a short while, I was also a phone man on the floor of the Board of Trade, and for a short while I was also an out trade clerk. So I knew pretty much what was going on, including all of the mistakes and how to correct them and so on and so forth. By the end of my first year, I had a pretty good experience in the futures industry. They referred to me as the original broker trainee because that's what my training program was, being a runner or an out trade clerk phone man, etcetera, on the exchange floors.

In 1972, I believe in October, which is my birthday month, I got my broker's license. At the time, I also went through a couple of the Board of

Trade classes on hedging and fundamental analysis, and a little bit of technical analysis. It wasn't all that popular in the very early 1970s. And I was trading grains in eighths before they switched to quarters. I was trading soybean in the three dollar price range, very low prices in those days. And then all of the sudden, along came OPEC and cranked the price of petroleum sky high and the "Russian Grain Deal." So in the next one to two years, from the fall of 1972 through 1973 and 1974, especially 1973, I got to learn the futures industry as things went through the roof. I mean, this was for a while the average day. Most markets were limit up. I thought that was the way it was. There was, in fact, approximately a three-week time frame when most markets were limit up bid on the opening bell and sometimes stayed there all day or dropped off a bit and closed limit up again. So that was an incredible situation. They actually took an order like this: "Buy 5 soybeans on an open order at the market." Please notice I didn't say anything about a contract month and it was an open order at the market. So I didn't care what damn month it was; the specification was buy a quantity of course, at the market on an open order any month, and sometimes it wouldn't be filled for days. Absolutely incredible.

As time passed in the 1970s, I got an opportunity to be on TV, Channel 26 on the top of the Board of Trade, approximately 20 times. A couple of the times were invitations, as opposed to Conti having bought the half hour time frame called "Ask the Expert." And the other time frames were, I think, "The Market Basket," where Terry Lee Savage interviewed me a couple of times. The studio was very small, a little antiquated on the very top of the Board of the Trade, just under the Goddess of Harvest, Ceres, which is the statue on the top of the Board, as you probably know.

During the next several years into the later 1970s, as a result of one of my appearances on Channel 26, Jake Bernstein responded to an appearance, and we got to know each other. And we hit it off. It was great. And we got to be friends. I turned out to be his broker. He raised the money, opened the accounts and traded through me, managed the accounts, and ended up being a friend of mine for many, many years, although we don't talk very often now. He was a very ambitious, very workaholic, very brilliant person.

I was supposed to be a substitute speaker for Jake in Kuala Lumpur, Malaysia around 1980 or so, but he still went. This was the Global Technical Tours seminar provided by Art Lavally who used to run and be a part owner of Commodity Perspective Chart Service. Art was a very tall, black-bearded, imposing figure who recognized when he first heard about

the Ehrlich Cycle Finder—that it was something he would be able to promote and do something with financially, so he approached me and said,
let's put a flyer in the Commodity Perspective Chart book, a blow-in, and
for five weeks in a row—I believe it was November of 1978—he did so,
and we sold hundreds of the tool very, very quickly, of course, and it was
a godsend. It was fantastic. Art Lavally gave me my first initial exposure
to the public with the Ehrlich Cycle Finder, and I owe him for that. Of
course, several years later he passed away from a heart attack.

It was a very fun trip when I got to go to Kuala Lumpur, Malaysia. It
was five days around the world, first class. Cindy, my wife, accompanied
me. If I remember correctly, the airfare alone was over $8,000. I ended up
only speaking for 15 minutes, while Jake took an hour and 45 minutes of
his original two hours. What it boiled down to was that I was the most expensive gopher you ever saw. I was asking all the time what I could do,
how I could help, and so on.

One particular situation I remember very vividly. When I arrived at
the hotel in Kuala Lumpur on Friday evening, the seminar was already underway. Everybody knew I was coming in on a certain flight at a certain
time; I couldn't make it earlier. I went up to my room, changed into a nice
suit, and came down toward the ballroom. As I approached the series of
double doors entering the ballroom, I heard Art Lavally's voice in the
background saying something to the effect of and now ladies and gentlemen, I would like to announce that we have a guest surprise speaker. His
name is Stan Ehrlich and blah, blah, blah. As he was saying blah, blah,
blah, I opened the double doors because I was a little late and I was wanting to get up on stage and sit down with the rest of the speakers, but the
audience thought that this was some sort of a grand entrance situation that
was possibly preplanned.

It was a total coincidence. Half the audience of Malaysians got up
out of their seats, and we're talking, 200, 300, 400 people, something like
that, and came over and surrounded me. I felt very, very special for a few
minutes, and it was an absolute total coincidence that I walked in at that
particular moment. That was a very memorable situation.

I've done many different seminars since approximately the late
1970s when I invented the Ehrlich Cycle Finder tool. I like to do seminars,
and I get good reviews, and they keep asking me to come back.

Okay, a quick little story about the cycle finder. How I invented the
cycle finder is a common question. Before Computrac, there wasn't any
real software you could buy that would run on anything. There wasn't
anything to draw charts. Along came the Apple Computer and Computrac,

and boy oh boy, you could download it 300 baud on your floppy disks on a 64K machine and end up printing charts on a Epson FX80 dot matrix printer. In a few minutes, you had yourself a nice looking chart. Absolutely amazing. Well, I ran out and got one, and a little while later I got a second one. For years I had a couple of Computrac memberships. Tim Slater apparently liked the idea of having a speaker that was an inventor of a tool. He asked me to speak, and as a result I ended up being a speaker at the first seven or so of the Computrac seminars. I've been the broker for Robert Prechter, the Elliott wave theorist. During that time frame, Bob Prechter and I, mostly due to Bob's expertise, but I was hopefully a bit of help, made 666 percent on his money in about six weeks. It was a great educational experience learning "Elliott Wave Theory" from the master. Bob was trying to break his previous contest winning record of 444 percent in four months. But his profitable streak slipped and the results were not high enough to win. He is the only client I've ever had that bought the low and sold the high in a market in one day. He took 100 percent of the range out of a day, not an easy task.

I've also been the broker for Beatrice Foods Corporation. At one point they were hedging a shipload of sugar from Australia mixed with cocoa powder and sold short sugar approximately in the 40-cent area while it was on its way up to 66, on a weekly basis with about 16 contracts short, they margined up approximately $100,000 a week to the tune of over half a mil. Sugar topped out at 66 in a radical manner with what I nicknamed a pagoda top because it gapped up, gapped up, gapped up, gapped up, in those days a 400 tick limit, and then ended up having a gigantic opening limit up, closing limit down, key reversal and gapping down, gapping down, gapping down, so if you draw little horizontal lines through all the gaps you ended up having something on the chart looking like a pagoda. No other market to my knowledge, except maybe the Hunt Brothers Top in silver and gold, had that kind of formation at such an incredibly radical rise and collapse.

I was also the broker for a banking institution out of Denver, Colorado. On one particular day they bought and sold 200 bond futures contracts at a time day trading, five times that day, for a total of 1,000 contracts in and out in one day.

Another little story. Because the cycle finder turned out to be such a success, the president of Conti Commodity Services, Walter Goldsmidt, came to my desk one day. He approached smiling very broadly, and said, I understand you have a tool that you invented. Tell me something about it. So I gave him the usual quick spiel. He ended up, before leaving my desk, buying 200 cycle finders. I found out months later that they were still in the boxes in a storage closet. He never did anything with them. He obviously bought them from me as a present, you know, as a congratulations of sorts.

2. *Tell me about your technique. What makes it exclusively yours? How did you develop it?*

My technique is cyclical analysis. Static equal time span cycles and price action. What makes it exclusively mine? The Ehrlich Cycle Finder is the only tool of its kind in the futures industry. It has nine points across one end and five across the other, allowing you to empirically—the definition of empirical in the dictionary is a nonscientific visual investigative process—find rhythms in price and action that hopefully will repeat themselves. With the tool, you forecast into the future the next potential cyclic high and low and watch to see, watching your other technical tools, indicators, techniques, methods, approach, whatever, to see if they generate buy and sell signals at about the point in time that you expected the cyclic turning point to occur, because of the prior rhythm that you had found. Now I like the little phrase Jake Bernstein thought up, "a window on time." I think it's very applicable, so I refer to a cyclic high occurring within a small space of time, maybe a few days early or late, but a "window of time." I am unique in the industry in terms of inventing a physical device that is used worldwide, approximately 8,000 sales since it became public in late 1978.

How did I develop it? Back in 1976-77 everybody used chart paper, either 8 grid or 10 grid, which allows you to plot a full year's worth of price action on one large sheet, eighths for grains and tenths for any other market. These sheets of paper were 18 x 12 or 18 x 16 inches, fairly sizable pieces of paper for a year. If you had a runaway bull market, which we had plenty of in those days, you could have two to five pages tall sometimes, depending on the price scale you used. But after two years, you had two pages left to right; after five years, five pages left to right. My charts began to be six, seven, eight pages long in the late 1970s because I started all of them around 1971 or 1972. As it turns out, they became a bit of a show themselves, these big charts, because I brought them in a large cardboard tube to the seminars that I was asked to participate in. On a few occasions, I had the whole wall of the ballroom, the length of it, with a series of tables covered with white tablecloths covered with these charts. One evening at home, I had this series of charts on the dining room table back in Evanston, Illinois. The kids were toddlers, and we had a child gate in the doorway between the living room and the kitchen to keep them from falling down the kitchen stairwell. The child gate was the old wooden criss-cross mechanism. The story goes that I'm working on my charts with an old compass, going back and forth trying to average rhythms that I found in the price action, chewing up my paper, I looked over at the child gate and realized that it had a series of points across the top. They were all an equal distance apart because of the geometry of the gate, no matter how wide your doorway might be. And if you took it out of the doorway and laid this child gate on these large charts and expanded and contracted the gate, you would still have a series of equally spaced points on the top. A little crude, but nevertheless, that's it. That's how I thought of the idea of the Ehrlich Cycle Finder. I miniaturized it. Got a lawyer to do a patent search, added the middle points between the larger ones and added a few refinements. So that's how I developed the "Ehrlich Cycle Finder." After one year at the very most, I ended up having a mold made that would make the parts within one thousandths of an inch tolerance.

Another little story. At one point, we had a Computrac seminar in New Orleans; this was when the tool was new and a hot item. My wife, Cindy, was with me; we had a booth, and we were selling the tool. There were like three layers of people around my table trying to watch me demonstrate how it was used on charts, and Cindy mentioned to me, "Gee, Stan, we only have two tools left." All of a sudden, credit cards, cash, wallets, purses, you name it, any form of payment came flying over shoulders onto the table in an effort to grab what was the last two tools. Well, obviously it was a real psychological rush to have such a response. We sold out the two tools instantly and took orders for many more tools, which we delivered after we got back home.

3. *Tell me about your best current trading system. What makes it tick? What are the features that make it the best trading system? Why do you trade this system?*

Well, I probably answered that already. Equal time span cycles and price action. One of the more impressive examples of this is a four-year cycle, starting about October-November 1994 and then going backward in time from October approximately in four-year increments, the lowest low was November in this last case, which was 1994. If you go back every four years in the Dow Jones or in the stock market index basically, you will come right back to major, long-term buying points. One whopping cycle, the four-years cycle in the Dow Jones. This is the chart that I use in my lectures.

What makes it tick? Cycles and price patterns of course. What are the features that make it the best trading system? I think it is an extremely valuable tool to set up a psychological expectation, that the market may be heading into a "point in time" when the classic situations develop for turning points which most people realize in retrospect, 20/20 hindsight, it happens when contrary opinion is often at extremes. Calling, i.e., predicting turns, basically makes you look like a wizard to the average trader. You said it was coming, "the turn," here it comes, here it is. Listeners lived through it, and they are still going around with their mouths wide open not realizing that they just made a mistake by not taking action. That's what happens frequently with neophyte traders who don't see the light of day as the market is turning. They're just a little too slow to pull the trigger. They always want some sort of time to pass and some sort of price action to develop to be convinced that the market topped. Well, great, now everything is gone. But cycles come to pass so often, so frequently, that if you know how to work with them they are great.

I use the system because it tends to work fabulously well. And by the way, there is a major edge that you have here. When the pieces of the puzzle fall into place properly, you have a great psychological edge. You are able to pull the trigger usually much more quickly, much more accurately, closer to tops and bottoms. When it turns out that you are wrong, you have a small loss because your stop goes just beyond the recent high or low you thought was the major turning point. When you are correct, you end up with a much better profit than you would have had otherwise. So your profits are larger and your losses are small! And even if it was only a 50-50 proposition, this would still end up providing you with an excellent edge as far as trading systems are concerned. I see this as a very valuable tool in almost any type of trading system, i.e., cycles.

4. *How long ago did you write your first trading system?*

Well, that's when I invented the tool: 1978.

5. *Remember back to your first trading system. Can you tell us the rules?*

Using the Ehrlich Cycle Finder, you empirically find rhythms in price action, and then after averaging the cycle, you forecast the next possible turning point. You also use other type of trading "studies" that you are versed in using. When they end up providing you with the pieces of the puzzle that fit into place, then you have a trade you should be trying, that you should put on and see what happens. I always use trailing stops to be able to quickly limit my losses and allow the profits to run.

6. *What caused you to abandon or modify that trading system the very first time?*

Well, I really didn't. It's just the process of learning how cycles work and don't work. What they can help you with and can't help you with. How to manage the market movements when they occur at cyclical turning points. So I never really abandoned it at all; it's just a refinement of the basics over the years.

7. *When you look at another person's trading system, what is the very first thing you look for to tell if it's a good or a bad system?*

I really don't look at other people's trading systems very much. They've got their own systems. More power to them. They've got a technique that works for them. I think that's one of the marvelous things about this industry: You can come up with your own system that does what it does for you the way you want it to, and you can live with that. Fundamentalists take good-sized chunks out of the middle of the market after the fundamentals have been solidly in place and the market has turned for awhile. Technicians, on the other hand, although they may be more actively trading generally, get closer to major turning points than fundamentalists, on the average. So I really don't look at other trading systems and see what's good or bad about them per se.

8. *What is the least important aspect of a trading system as far as you are concerned?*

Trying to find out why cycles work. Don't ask why, just do it. Find the rhythms. Maybe experience a few of the revolutions without doing anything about it per se. The process of following rhythms, living through them for better or worse, and finding out how they develop is the teaching process. The least important thing, I think, is trying to figure it out. Why do cycles exist? It's a natural phenomenon. There are cycles all around us, everything from your heartbeat, obviously very short, to the Kondratiev wave: 50-, 54-, 55-, 60-year economic cycles in capitalistic societies. That's one of the longest ones I can think of. Double sun spot cycles. Drought cycles. Lunar cycles. You name it.

9. *In your current work, are you using a mechanical approach or is there judgment involved in your trading?*

Well, the mechanical approach, of course, is calculating the cycles and the judgment part of it is seeing the other parts of the puzzle fall into place. It's a judgment call to an extent as to whether you are getting the key reversals to develop, the island reversal to develop, the head and shoulder tops to come into play, the double or triple tops to occur, breakouts of pennant formations, trend perpetuating techniques, percentage retracements that might come back and fill gaps or test trend lines or test tops or bottoms of channels. So you are looking at a variety of other aspects in correlation with rhythms to justify that the time is right and the price is right using various vis-a-vis charting techniques. The percentage retracements, gap closures, trend-line tests, channel tests, breakout of formations and the like are personal calls to an extent.

10. *Are you currently using TradeStation or System Writer? If not, what software do you use to run your trading system?*

I do use TradeStation and Super Charts, but it's to keep track of my cycles and to see the chart formations and to experience real-time charting. I'm trying to develop the "Ehrlich cycle forecaster," which will be the new software version of the Ehrlich Cycle Finder. The vertical cycle lines will not look the same on the screen, and it will act totally differently than any other cyclical tool or study ever developed in the futures industry because of what it does and how it does it and how it shows things to you. It is still a judgment call on the trader's part, like these other programs, as to whether you got what you want and are going to do something about it.

11. *Is your current trading system for sale? For lease? On a fax line? How do you provide this information to clients?*

I have a verbal *hot line* which uses these principles to generate buy and sell recommendations.

12. *If you could advise system developers to do one thing when they are starting out, what would that be?*

Be consistent about what you do. Only change your underlying methodology when you are convinced that you are doing something that will improve your results.

13. *When you devise a trading system, what time frame do you use most? For example, do you use daily bars, weekly bars, 1-minute bars, 10-minute bars, or 60-minute bars?*

I use any time frame. Last fall, around Thanksgiving, if I remember correctly, we had a three and one-third year cycle low in pork. That's the hog market in particular, not bellies. Plus we were at 15-year lows. The combination seemed to me an ideal situation for the beginning of bull market in hogs. Of course, that's 20/20 hindsight now.

14. *If for some reason they closed every commodity in the world except one, and you were the guy in charge of deciding which one would stay open, which commodity would you choose? Why? What hours would it be open?*

I suppose it would be the stock market indexes because of their wide appeal and wide scope.

15. *If you were to choose one commodity you could never trade again and you could never include in a trading system, which commodity would this be? Why?*

Let me see. All of them are cyclical. Very highly so at times and less highly so at times, but I can't answer that question. It's not applicable to my particular approach.

16. *Where do you get your ideas for your system? A chart? A pattern? Observations? Trades that you have done before? What is your favorite technique for coming up with a trading system?*

Patterns in charts! For breakouts and for turning points of cycles, I use observations. Of course, this is an *empirical approach.*

Trades that I've done before? What is your favorite technique for coming up with a trading system? I've got two stories that I tell at my seminars all the time. Years ago, when I was writing my market letter, I said there was going to be a buying opportunity in bonds on a certain date. The day before the supposed low day, the money supply numbers came out very bearish! Friday afternoon, dollar supply was up a hell of a lot more than expected. The cash market collapsed a limit and a half. Next Monday morning, that's the date I expected a cyclic turning point for bonds. The market opened limit down. But it ended up rallying to limit up and went straight up for the rest of the week. It was one incredible turning point in the bond market and came exactly when I had forecasted it would weeks before because of a long-term cycle in bonds that I had put in black and white in my market letter. That's the short version of the story.

Here's the second story. A client is short 30 contracts—10 Swiss, 10 Deutsche, 10 Yen—expecting a cycle low to develop that day. The market gaps down about 80 ticks on the opening bell on the average. He's already in the black for $30,000. Prices drop another 35 ticks during the first two hours on the average, going into a sideways trading range that the client and I realize is a small head-and-shoulder bottom in that two-hour time frame that morning. We reverse. We get out of 10, 10, 10; we went long 10, 10, Swiss, Deutsche, Yen; the currency markets end rallied so damn much they close approximately 90 ticks higher on the day for a net gain of $101,000 for that client that single day. Because we were expecting a turn and we saw a pattern that was telling us what it was trying to turn, we did something about it. It worked phenomenally well.

17. *I want you to write a trading system for me. I want you to give me all the rules. I want you to tell me what commodity, what time frame, whether it is daily bars, whatever. What your entry rule is, your exit rule with a profit, your exit rule with a loss. It doesn't have to be a great system. Just give me an idea of something you would look at, something you would test to see if there was any validity.*

I would take a look at any market. Don't even tell me the name of the market; I don't care. Don't tell me what price range it is, just a chart. In normal market circumstances, any market, using daily vertical bar chart usually, investigate for cycles, find reliable dominant ones that have occurred over a significant number of years. I'd forecast them forward in time, then watch the market as it comes into those time frames, and put on trades when my indicators agree with my cyclical expectations. I'd use stops immediately, a few ticks probably beyond the highest high or the lowest low for the turning point. Usually, you will have a very low risk, usually a few hundred dollars and as quickly as you can, within a day or three, raising or lowering or just plain moving the stops so that it's a break even situation, or at least covering costs. Be patient and try to milk the most you can out of the trade as time passes. Some trades will end up developing into fantastic moves for months; some trades will end up being only a few days or several days old. It might be very small losses or small profits.

18. *What's the typical day in the life of a system developer? What time do you start? What time do you end? What is it you do all day long? How are your orders placed? How is your system run?*

I really don't necessarily consider myself a system developer. I'm a broker basically, and I start at 5:00 A.M. California time. My day ends when I'm pretty much exhausted or when I have other things to do after all the markets have closed.

What is it you do all day long? Well I watch the market, handle clients, orders, and the daily business. I place my orders through normal phone calls.

How is your system run? It's not computerized so you really don't "run" it.

19. *If you could have your system run in any manner, what would be the preferable method? Would you have the person whose money is at risk run the system, or would you have a third party run the system and just arbitrarily take the trades as they are generated, regardless of consequence?*

First of all, I would not have the person whose money was involved run any system! Too much subjectivity. As for the rest, I'd have the trades taken when the pieces of the puzzle fit into place properly, and I would have somebody who really doesn't know anything about the market learn this technique and follow it. It's the old monkey with the banana routine, right? I want to hire someone who would learn to put A B C D E F together, and every time ABCDEF fell into place, he would do what he was supposed to do. So, yes, you do want to have somebody do it in a relatively mechanical way.

20. *Let's pretend I don't have a single book on commodities, and I'm interested in writing systems. Other than your own work, what book would you recommend? Along these same lines, is there anything you would avoid—whether it's software, books, lectures, whatever?*

I don't think this question applies to me very well. I'm mostly self-taught because of my 25 years as a broker.

21. *Do you think it is necessary for a software developer/real-time trader to have tick-by-tick real-time quotes? Why or why not?*

In this particular case, for a cyclical analysis, it would be of some help if you knew how to use a quote machine in terms of watching the market and not jumping the gun constantly and being a little on the patient side. Delayed quotes are of no use to me, might as well use newspaper prices.

22. *What kind of quotes do you have? What kind of software would you recommend? Are there any systems or software that you would definitely not recommend?*

I like Super Charts and TradeStation. I have a dish that splits the feed to two computers, real-time feed, so I am feeding quotes to signal software on one quotation system simultaneously with another FM receiver box to TradeStation. Each system has its advantages.

23. *Why do some systems consistently perform year after year, and other systems fail or need to be continually optimized?*

Because Futures market characteristics change. For several years, the precious metal markets were involved in a major bull market into the top of the Hunt Brothers, and then for 13 years they were basically in a bear market after the Hunt Brothers topped. So it was a totally different characteristic for many, many, many years.

24. *How important are drawdowns in your research? How important is average trade size?*

Well, drawdowns are obviously important because if you have too many of them, you won't survive. The average trade size is totally dependent upon the account size. It's not a question that is particularly applicable to my technique.

25. *Do you do portfolio management—linking several commodities of different systems together? Do you do pyramiding? Why or why not?*

I don't pyramid too much. Generally speaking, I try to get into my trade at the turning points and that's it. I stick with it until I get out. If it's a large position or a small position, that's that.

26. *Let's get a little morbid. You've died. You've left a sealed letter to your heirs. It contains the secret of your fortune. It's the secret to allow them to continue the lifestyle to which they have been accustomed. What one sentence is in the letter?*

Do your own thinking. Don't follow the crowd when the crowd becomes too loud. Become a contrary thinker. You're buying bottoms because the bottom contains everybody being bearish at the same time. You are selling into highs and the tops because everybody is bullish at the same.

David Fox

INTRODUCTION

Dave Fox is a very, very interesting person and trader. I've known Dave now for about three or four years, and he's always one of the friendliest, most helpful people with clients that there is in the industry. Dave is a very modest sort. He's written one system, and he's kept that one system number-one many years in *Futures Truth* ranking. I think you'll enjoy his commentary. One thing I will mention about Dave's answers to questions; he's very succinct. He answers yes or no, or it doesn't apply. Don't be put off by that. Dave is a very long-term trader, dollar trader. For instance, he only trades eight or nine times a year. The system I wrote at the end called Fox 31 is really not any code from Dave, but it's an idea or a technique that once you read the commentary, you can see how it was derived. Looking at the code for Fox 31, it is a Quick Editor system so that means it can be done in Super Charts or TradeStation. Basically, it says if the close is above the 220 day, the highest high of the last 220 days, you buy, and if it's below the lowest low of the last 220 days, you sell. In other words, it's the channel breakout system in a reversing mode put on a currency, and you can see that when we put it on the yen, the drawdown is very small. The length of trade is very long, and it hasn't lost yet over a 10-year period. It may not be something you want to trade, but it's something you sure want to respect, and you want to look at channel breakouts because they are the base of many, many, good trading systems. Dave's system, Dollar Trader, is not a simple channel breakout, it's much more complex than this, but it's

a very good value. I think it sells for less than $500, and you should take
a hard look at it.

1. *Tell me about yourself. If someone were to say, "Tell me about David
Fox," what would you want them to know? Give me a brief biography of
you before you got into commodities, and a brief biography of what you
have done since you got into commodities.*

I served as a trustee of a mutual savings bank in the state of Maine,
getting a good education in the financial markets. I assisted another person in the development of an S&P trading system and was registered as a
commodity trading advisor in 1984. I placed Dollar Trader with Futures
Truth in early 1991 and, when it was immediately ranked number one, I
proceeded to market it.

2. *Tell me about your technique. What makes it exclusively yours? How
did you develop it?*

I believe my strength to be in the proper application of an indicator
and finding ways to corroborate signals.

3. *Tell me about your best current trading system. What makes it tick?
What are the features that make it the best trading system? Why do you
trade this system?*

Indicators built into Dollar Trader must confirm the direction of a trade.
So, while we may be late to enter in a new direction, it is usually productive.

4. *How long ago did you write your first trading system?*

Dollar Trader, in 1990.

5. *Remember back to your first trading system. Can you tell us the rules?*

Dollar Trader has the rules I use. The system calculates *pivot points*
in price above or below the market that, when hit, indicate that the *high* or
low for this cycle should occur on this day or the succeeding two days.
The point to *buy* or *sell* will then be one tick above or below the 3-day
high or *low* of this period. Initial protective stop is at the 20-day *high/low*.
A filter is employed, an Average Modified Moving Average (AMMA). If
this points in the opposite direction from the indicated trade, then an in-
struction to *go flat* will result.

6. *When you look at another person's trading system, what is the very
first thing you look for to tell if it's a good or a bad system?*

I have had little experience with other systems; however, in an inter-
mediate-term system, I would not want three losses in a row.

7. *In your current work, are you using a mechanical approach, or is there judgment involved in your trading?*

Mechanical; however, I provide a fax advisory to deal with close calls.

8. *Are you currently using a TradeStation or System Writer? If not, what software do you use to run your trading system?*

The program is customized to read all leading data formats.

9. *Is your current trading system for sale? For lease? On a fax line? How do you provide this information to clients?*

Dollar Trader sells for $475, which includes a fax advisory for one year. For those wishing to continue the advisory, it is $75 per year for the USDX alone or $100 for the USDX and currencies.

10. *If you can advise system developers to do one thing when they are starting out, what would that advice be?*

Use walk-forward testing with individual contracts.

11. *Other than yourself, who do you think is the best system developer, or who do you think is the best teacher of system development?*

Gerald Appel is my choice for the S&P.

12. *When you devise a trading system, what time frame do you use most? For example, do you use daily bars, weekly bars, 1-minute bars, 10-minute bars, or 60-minute bars?*

Daily bars.

13. *If for some reason they closed every commodity in the world except one, and you were the guy in charge of deciding which one would stay open, which commodity would you choose? Why? What hours would it be open?*

USDX, around the clock, with close at 3:00 P.M. EST.

14. *Where do you get your ideas for your system? A chart? A pattern? Observations? Trades that you have done before? What is your favorite technique for coming up with a trading system?*

I get ideas from Futures, S & C, and my customers.

15. *What's the typical day in the life of a system developer? What time to you start? What time do you end? What is it you do all day long? How are your orders placed? How is your system run?*

I am available at my listed phone number at all times for customers. My system runs on any PC, and orders are placed with *full service* brokers.

16. *If you could have your system run in any manner, what would be the preferable method? Would you have the person whose money is at risk run the system, or would you have a third party run the system and just arbitrarily take the trades as they are generated, regardless of consequence?*

I prefer that users make their own trades.

17. *Let's pretend I don't have a single book on commodities, and I'm interested in writing systems. Other than your own work, what book would you recommend? Along these same lines, is there anything you would avoid—whether it's software, books, lectures, whatever?*

New Commodity Trading Systems & Methods by Kaufman.

18. *Do you think it is necessary for a software developer/real-time trader to have tick-by-tick real-time quotes? Why or why not?*

I find 10-minute snapshots from FutureLink to be adequate.

19. *What kind of quotes do you have? What kind of software would you recommend? Are there any systems or software that you would definitely not recommend?*

I find 10-minute snapshots from FutureLink to be adequate.

20. *How much data do you think is necessary to be tested as far as assessing a day-trade session on five-minute bars? A daily bar system? A 60-minute system?*

For a daily bar system, five years.

21. *Why do some systems consistently perform year after year, and other systems fail or need to be continually optimized?*

If we only knew!

22. *How important are drawdowns in your research? How important is average trade size?*

Drawdowns exceeding two times the margin are excessive.

23. *Do you do portfolio management—linking several commodities of different systems together? Do you do pyramiding? Why or why not?*

I believe that one can enter or add positions on retracements where the risk is 30 ticks or less, in the currencies.

Nelson Freeberg

INTRODUCTION

Nelson Freeberg is one of the most thorough researchers that I know. A couple of years ago he reviewed my One Night Stand. He did over 60,000 tests on it trying to break it. Couldn't break it, wrote me a glowing letter about how much he liked it. But Nelson is very, very thorough in his own work, too. I think you'll enjoy his chapter, and you'll enjoy his system Path Finder.

1. *Tell me about yourself. If someone were to say, "Tell me about Nelson F. Freeberg," what would you want them to know? Give me a brief biography of you before you got into commodities, and a brief biography of what you have done since you got into commodities.*

I was working on a Ph.D. in world politics at Columbia University when I got drawn to trading. I put aside my dissertation so I could absorb everything possible about technical analysis. Despite reading widely, my trading results were inconsistent. In time, I shifted the focus to mechanical trading systems. I found that some of the same quantitative tools I had used to pattern the strategic arms race could help me develop effective timing models.

A curiosity from the past: I went to a small high school in Memphis, Tennessee with just 175 students. One of them was Paul Tudor Jones. Later I went to a small liberal arts college in Wisconsin. Tom DeMark was a graduating senior the year I arrived. Twenty years later, Tom wound up in New York working with Paul.

2. *Tell me about your technique. What makes it exclusively yours? How did you develop it?*

My approach to system development stresses three principles. First, the system must be robust across time. I test all of my systems on an out-of-sample basis. This means using one segment of data to develop the timing logic and then applying the trading rules to a different time span. Reasonably consistent performance across time reinforces confidence in the signal logic.

 Second, the system must be robust across parameter sets. If profits depend on a narrow range of signals, results in actual trading will suffer. I try to make sure my systems hold up regardless of the precise signal mix.

Third, trading systems should be sensitive to price, but I often add a fundamental component. Many of my timing models reach beyond price to capture some of the governing forces that shape and determine price behavior. A good example is the stock market. Most of my index systems explicitly factor in interest rates.

3. *Tell me about your best current trading system. What makes it tick? What are the features that make it the best trading system? Why do you trade this system?*

The *Pathfinder Currency System* is a case study in fusing technical and fundamental elements. *Pathfinder* works off of a pair of trend indicators that are purely price-based. But the prospective trade must be confirmed by a governing filter.

Foreign currencies tend to swing up and down with T-bond futures. For instance, since 1977, the correlation of T-bonds with the Japanese yen has been 0.86. With Pathfinder, no trade is possible without support from this key association. The upshot is higher signal accuracy, higher gains per trade, and lower drawdown. By the way, one reason the Pathfinder system has remained profitable since I published it is because the buy and sell signals were derived from out-of-sample testing.

4. *How long ago did you write your first trading system?*

I distinctly remember building my first trading system in early 1979. It was a simple moving-average crossover system. I got tired of doing the calculations by hand, so later that year I bought my first computer, a Tandy TRS-80. The machine cost $600 and had 4K of RAM.

FORMULA RESEARCH PATHFINDER CURRENCY SYSTEM

MARKETS TESTED: B-POUND, D-MARK, J-YEN, S-FRANC

Trading Rules:

Enter long on tomorrow's open if:

1) 6-day moving average of currency > yesterday's 6-day MA
2) 9-day moving average of currency > 18-day MA
3) 3-day moving average of US T-bond futures > 25-day MA

Exit long on tomorrow's open if:

1) 9-day moving average of currency < 18-day MA

Protective Stop: $2,000
Short-side rules are the mirror image of buy-side rules.

Pathfinder Currency System: Single-Contract Profits					
Time Frame	B-Pound	D-Mark	J-Yen	S-Franc	Total
Nov-77–Dec-93[1]	$104,844	$80,650	$104,138	$93,525	$383,157
Jan-94–Sep-95	$(5,787)	$(500)	$41,363	$6,363	$41,439
					$424,596

[1] Date First Published in Formula Research   *Transaction costs: $100/trade*

5. *Remember back to your first trading system. Can you tell us the rules?*

You simply go long when the close climbs above the moving average, and exit or go short when the close drops below the smoothing.

6. *What caused you to abandon or modify that trading system the very first time?*

My expectations for the moving-average system were so high. Unfortunately, I found out soon that no single moving average worked all the time, a point some of the technical trading texts neglected to mention.

7. *When you look at another person's trading system, what is the very first thing you look for to tell if it's a good or a bad system?*

For me, a key indicator of system performance is the ratio of profit to drawdown, a point Joe Krutsinger stressed, this risk/reward measure, in *Trading Systems Toolkit* (Chicago: Irwin, 1993).

8. *What is the least important aspect of a trading system as far as you are concerned?*

After four years of publishing a new trading system each month, I find value in most of the conventional performance statistics. If I ever judged one insignificant, you can be sure a subscriber would claim it was the best measure of all.

9. *In your current work, are you using a mechanical approach, or is there judgment involved in your trading?*

In the last four years *Formula Research* has published about 100 trading systems. Sometimes the models give conflicting signals. The ideal solution is to develop a composite system that balances the weight of the evidence. Unfortunately, I'm so busy building new trading systems that I haven't had a chance to properly integrate all of our prior findings. In the absence of such a composite model, I am not afraid to rely on judgment.

Also, I have never done any systematic studies of money management, a field ripe for quantitative analysis. Pending such studies, I use discretion in sizing positions and other aspects of money management.

10. *Are you currently using TradeStation or System Writer? If not, what software do you use to run your trading system?*

I use both System Writer and TradeStation. TradeStation offers superior graphics, but there are features of the older System Writer I still find appealing. Either way, my work would not be possible but for the programming flexibility that each platform offers.

By the way, I use the versatile command language not just for system testing but for a variety of helpful tasks. You can customize the code to generate compound annual returns and peak-to-valley equity dip, performance measures vital to any CTA. As a matter of fact, I use System Writer to automatically build all of my spread-adjusted continuous futures contracts. It's much easier than with a spreadsheet. For simple applications like moving-average crossovers, no testing software is faster than MetaStock, which I also use daily.

11. *Is your current trading system for sale? For lease? On a fax line? How do you provide this information to clients?*

My newsletter *Formula Research* is devoted to building high performance teaching systems. All of my past timing models are for sale at prices ranging from $25 to $40. I deliberately keep our systems economically priced. Formula Research is to a degree a collaborative effort. I learn from my subscribers. By expanding the reach of the newsletter, we collectively profit from the contributions of a broad and knowledgeable subscriber base.

12. *Can you share the concept behind your trading system, for example, your main entry technique, your exit if you are wrong, and your exit if you are right?*

The Pathfinder Currency System is very easy to implement. All of the trading rules are featured on page xx.

13. *If you could advise system developers to do one thing when they are starting out, what would that be?*

Three fine books on system design are recommended to anyone who would build a trading system, whether novice or veteran: Bruce Babcock's *Business One/Irwin Guide to Commodity Trading Systems*, Chuck LeBeau and Dave Lucas' *Technical Traders Guide to Computerized Analysis of the Futures Markets*, and Perry Kaufman's *Smarter Trading*.

14. *Other than yourself, who do you think is the best system developer, or who do you think is the best teacher of system development?*

I cannot pick out any single towering figure in the field of system building. The authors cited above qualify as experts in model design and testing. When it comes to finding profitable price patterns, Tom DeMark and Larry Williams have no peers. Finally, let's not forget some great system designers better known in the cash markets: Gerald Appel, Marty Zweig, and Ned Davis.

15. *When you devise a trading system, what time frame do you use most? For example, do you use daily bars, weekly bars, 1-minute bars, 10-minute bars, or 60-minute bars?*

Most of my futures systems work off daily bars. We are expanding our research into intraday price behavior. Half of my subscribers are equity portfolio managers. For them, weekly price history is appropriate. By the way, many of my favorite futures systems are filtered with weekly data from the cash markets.

16. *If for some reason they closed every commodity in the world except one, and you were the guy in charge of deciding which one would stay open, which commodity would you choose? Why? What hours would it be open?*

Without a doubt, stock indexes are my preferred market. They are a challenge to trade, but the risks are matched by the potential gains. Whether trending sharply or in a violent trading range, stocks offer plenty of action. There is also good liquidity. If that liquidity holds up, I would favor 24-hour index trading.

17. *If you were to choose one commodity you could never trade again and you could never include in a trading system, which commodity would this be? Why?*

I stay away from all weather-sensitive commodities. Yes, my models often work off fundamentals, but I draw the line at acts of the Almighty.

18. *Where do you get your ideas for your system? A chart? A pattern? Observations? Trades that you have done before? What is your favorite technique for coming up with a trading system?*

My favorite systems factor in both technical price action and some external determinant of price. For the technical component, I look at either a trend-following or a countertrend indicator. For the external indicator, I try to find strong correlations with other markets or indicators.

To illustrate, I just published a gold/silver trading system that gained $400,000 a contract since 1975. To go long, the close must be above a simple moving average. This trend-following signal helps assure prices are moving in the right direction.

But the entry is not valid unless two fundamental conditions are met. Foreign currencies must be trending higher, and real interest rates must be trending lower. Analysis shows these two external conditions are highly correlated with action in the precious metals.

19. *I want you to write a trading system for me. I want you to give me all the rules. I want you to tell me what commodity, what time frame, whether it is daily bars, whatever. What your entry rule is, your exit rule with a profit, your exit rule with a loss. It doesn't have to be a great system. Just give me an idea of something you would look at, something you would test to see if there was any validity.*

Take as illustration the S&P 500. Research shows you can use this week's close of the Dow Jones 20 Bond Average to help forecast the S&P

500 next week. In fact, since index futures began trading in 1982, the Dow Jones Bond average has shown a strong .92 correlation with next week's S&P 500 close.

You could use this powerful relationship to build a variety of daily and intraday S&P trading systems. For instance, you might use a volatility breakout to signal to get stopped into a position. As always with the S&P 500, you have to give the trade ample opportunity to progress. A wide stop of $2,000 or more is recommended. If you use a profit target, it should be fairly generous, on the order of $4,000 to $5,000.

20. *What's the typical day in the life of a system developer? What time do you start? What time do you end? What is it you do all day long? How are your orders placed? How is your system run?*

I'm a night owl and get my best work done after the office is closed. Weekends are highly productive for me also. Unless I have to monitor the open of a critical market, I often arrive at my desk at 8:30 or 9:00 in the morning, central time.

I could be happy doing nothing but trading and developing timing models all day long. For several years I did just that. But today I have a small staff to manage and a newsletter to publish. This means dealing with clients, vendors, and colleagues.

21. *If you could have your system run in any manner, what would be the preferable method? Would you have the person whose money is at risk run the system, or would you have a third party run the system and just arbitrarily take the trades as they are generated, regardless of consequence?*

Personally, I enjoy the excitement of trading and always place my own orders. But with a system as straightforward and effective as the Pathfinder Currency System, a user could easily have an independent third party manage the trading.

22. *Let's pretend I don't have a single book on commodities, and I'm interested in writing systems. Other than your own work, what book would you recommend? Along these same lines, is there anything you would avoid—whether it's software, books, lectures, whatever?*

In addition to the three texts I already cited, consider John Murphy's *Intermarket Technical Analysis*, Martin Pring's *All-Season Investor*, and Martin Zweig's *Winning On Wall Street*. All of Jack Schwager's books are also highly recommended.

As for the overhyped commodity trading systems we are all familiar with, early on I was naive enough to sample more than one. My unfortunate experience convinced me I was better off building my own trading systems. That's why I started a newsletter devoted to trading systems.

23. *Do you think it is necessary for a software developer/real-time trader to have tick-by-tick real-time quotes? Why or why not?*

It is not necessary to rely on an intraday quote stream, whether you are a trader or a system developer. Many systems work better by capturing longer-term price trends that tick data can obscure.

Unlike some analysts I respect, I believe it is possible to develop good intraday timing models. But for a longer-term system, real-time quotes are unnecessary and potentially counterproductive.

24. *What kind of quotes do you have? What kind of software would you recommend? Are there any systems or software that you would definitely not recommend?*

I download my quotes on an end-of-day basis. As for software I would avoid, stay away from, black box trading systems with undisclosed rules.

25. *How much data do you think is necessary to be tested as far as assessing a day-trade session on five-minute bars? A daily bar system? A 60-minute system?*

Our research effort is not geared to day trading. In time, we will focus more attention on this risky but promising area.

I tend to be risk averse, so I like to examine as much data as possible. The last time I tested an S&P day trading system, I took it all the way back to 1982, when index futures first started. Since the system works off five-minute bars, this is the equivalent of testing a daily system back to the turn of the century.

I try to test in historical depth because price behavior evolves over time. If profitability holds up despite the shifting patterns, the system has probably captured a fundamental element of price behavior. All of the future systems I have published—whether for the S&P, T-Bonds, precious metals, or currencies—have been profitable since the inception of trading in that market.

26. *Why do some systems consistently perform year after year, and other systems fail or need to be continually optimized?*

I don't know of any systems that actually produce uniform compound annual gains. Even the most profitable trading systems show periodic uneven performance.

Still, there are systems that manage to show a profit pretty much year in and year out. My favorite short-term S&P index system is called Quadram. It has been profitable in 12 of 14 years since index futures started trading, with the largest annual loss held to $1,300. In the six months since we published Quadram, it is up $12,500 a contract.

Why does Quadram seem to work? Well, its timing logic grew out of the three principles of system design stressed earlier. The buy and sell signals were derived from strict out-of-sample testing. Second, the gains do not depend on an arbitrary parameter set. (If we substituted other signals, performance might actually improve.) Third, Quadram incorporates a monetary filter that helps insure the trade does not run counter to larger trends in the financial markets.

27. *How important are drawdowns in your research? How important is average trade size?*

For me, equity drawdown is the single most important dimension of risk. The Sharpe ratio is the traditional measure of risk-adjusted return, and for the benefit of clients who rely on it, I often report the Sharpe Ratio in my performance summaries. But a better specification of risk than the standard deviation of returns is the depth and duration of equity retracements, a point stressed by Jack Schwager 10 years ago in *A Complete Guide to the Futures Markets*.

28. *Do you do portfolio management—linking several commodities of different systems together? Do you do pyramiding? Why or why not?*

I am just starting to investigate systematic portfolio management. But the studies I have done suggest you can reduce risk without penalizing gains by trading multiple markets. Nor do the markets necessarily have to be uncorrelated, as is often said. Trading a basket of currencies in moderate size is apt to produce a more consistent equity curve with less punishing drawdowns than trading in a single market with much larger positions.

As for pyramiding, I haven't had a chance to formally analyze the many strategies available. I look forward to testing Ralph Vince's Optimal F and other promising money-management formulas.

29. *Let's get a little morbid. You've died. You've left a sealed letter to your heirs. It contains the secret of your fortune. It's the secret to allow them to continue the lifestyle to which they have been accustomed. What one sentence is in the letter?*

"Trade with the trend"? "Follow your system"? "Blow not thy wad"? There are many paths to success. In the end, perhaps the best advice is *to work hard.*

30. *Without giving the secret of life, how would you write an imitation of your system in two lines or less in Trade Station language? For example, I have an S&P system called Buy Monday. "Monday you buy it, put in a $1,400 stop, get out on the close." That's how you write that.*

If average (c,6)>average (c,6)[1] and average (c,9)> average (c,18) and average (c of data2,3)> average (c of data2, 25) then buy at market. If average (c,9)< average (c,18) then exit long at market.

31. *Give us an example of some of your work put in English-type language for a system.*

See page 53 for a summary of the logic of this simple but effective trading method.

Lee Gettess

INTRODUCTION

Lee Gettess is a very, very smart system developer and very proficient. I think you'll get a real kick out of both his commentary and his system. The system developed from Lee's commentary is called Gettess 30. It's a buy only strategy in the S&P, and it reads basically: If the most recent occurrence where the close is greater than or equal to the close of one bar ago, and the open is tomorrow is less than the close, then once that happens, you are going to buy at the market. And then once the open of tomorrow is above the entry price, you are going to exit. Other than that use a $4,000 stop. You can see from the track record it's got a very high percent accuracy, 79 percent, 17 winners in a row. A very good addition to anyone's trading system library.

1. *Tell me about yourself. If someone were to say, "Tell me about Lee Gettess," what would you want them to know? Give me a brief biography of you before you got into commodities, and a brief biography of what you have done since you got into commodities.*

I'm just basically a street kid from Detroit, and I mean that sincerely. I was the only white boy on my high school football team. I went to college basically to play football and between semesters of football took a job at General Motors as a janitor because my parents, who were both retired in their late sixties by then, were not in great financial shape. I wound up staying on full-time as a janitor and eventually worked my way into the computer department at Fisher Body. I worked there for seven years. I eventually got transferred over to Electronic Data System, which I think is a very important part of the story. General Motors purchased EDS from Ross Perot and took all of their General Motors computer employees and said that they weren't General Motors employees anymore, that they were now EDS employees. That meant we no longer had our GM benefits and the stock plan and 401K and what have you. That was a colossal shock to me. I thought General Motors was about as secure as you could possibly be, that they would definitely take care of you in the future, and I woke up one day and didn't work for them anymore, and didn't have all my future plans laid out. EDS was a wonderful company to work for, and I very sincerely admire and like Ross Perot as a person. I've had lunch with him several times and I enjoyed working for him, but it was just a big wake-up call to me about security. I started reading about how you can work to make money or you can have your money work for you, and the money working for you is open-ended. Since your money can just continue to compound and work for you indefinitely, letting it work instead of me seemed like the wisest thing to do. I took the normal route I think most people do. I did mutual funds and stocks and things like that. That's kind of like walking. If you want to run—and I wanted to run—you've got to trade commodities. I've been doing it since the mid-1980s, trading for a living since 1987.

2. *Tell me about your technique. What makes it exclusively yours? How did you develop it?*

There are multiple techniques. I probably have 150 to 200 different things that I've developed over the years, and I don't know that any of them really would be considered exclusively mine. I don't know that I know anything that isn't public domain, that other people don't know. The way I put them together may be a little different, but the way I developed them is both through trial and error, beating up computers viciously to find out what works and doesn't work, as well as observation. I've been sitting and looking at markets better than a decade. I'd like to believe that anyone who would do that would pick up a few things along the way. So basically, the unfortunate truth is the way you develop these things is probably by getting your brains beat in for a while.

3. *Tell me about your best current trading system. What makes it tick? What are the features that make it the best trading system? Why do you trade this system?*

Again, I have numerous trading systems. I guess my best trading system has to be the one I'm working on currently. Hope springs eternal; I'm an optimist, and I'd like to believe that whatever I'm working on currently is going to be the best. What I'm doing is sort of a momentum-based thing where I am going with the market when it shows strong enough momentum, but I may fade the market if the momentum appears to be lessening. That is to say that the market may be dropping, but it seems to be doing so with very little momentum, so I may fade it; I may buy a dropping market and then go with it on the upside when it's strong enough. I'm trying to do both in one system, which down the road may not work out, but that's what I'm trying to do.

Incidentally, I trade the system to find out if it works. I hope to make a lot of money with it. At this point, it appears to make more money than anything I've ever seen, but what I usually do with any system I develop is at least open a small account to trade one lots with it. Things can look great on paper or on a computer printout, but there is still the question of whether you can really logistically and physically do this in the market. Consequently, I have small accounts at numerous brokers so I can trade this system, this system, and this system and at least get a feel for whether it really works to any degree.

4. *How long ago did you write your first trading system?*

I wrote my first trading system in the mid-1980s. I had a big computer background, but I didn't know squat about PCs, so I had to kind of teach myself to trade basic from a Microsoft manual. Boy, that's an experience.

5. *Remember back to your first trading system. Can you tell us the rules?*

I used volatility breakout. I used 60 percent of one day's range displaced from the open to buy or sell the S&P 500. I used a $1,000 stop and exited market on close, and I also traded the treasury bond market. I used, I can't remember if it was 38 percent or 45 percent of one day's range. It was a gun caliber one way or another, and that was a volatility reversal system. I bought or sold that far off of the open and simply held the position until I got a signal in the opposite direction and used it to reverse.

6. *What caused you to abandon or modify that trading system the very first time?*

What caused to me abandon or modify it originally was I noticed too many times that I had good profits in the trade that I wasn't really capturing.

I believe the margin to trade bonds at that time was only about $2,000, and numerous times I would have at least $1,000 in the trade, which was 50 percent on the margin, and yet I was unable to bank profits. I'd wind up getting reversed at a five- or six-tick loss, so I set out to try to beat up a computer and find out if there weren't ways I could capture the money that I was leaving on the table. Just a typical greedy human being response, I think.

7. *When you look at another person's trading system, what is the very first thing you look for to tell you if it's a good or a bad system?*

There are really two things I look for. One is sample size. If somebody shows me something that looks phenomenal for six months to a year and a half or whatever, that doesn't impress me a whole lot. Markets change so much over time, and if you show me something that is biased to the buy side in a bull market it ought to look great. But you need to see a bear market in a congestion to see how it works, so sample size is a large part of it.

The other aspect of it is the logic behind it. I like to feel there is at least some validity to the reason that you are buying or selling, and it probably has to be a relatively simple thing. If somebody showed me a system that only traded on days that began with T, provided the date was an odd number instead of an even number, gee, that might work; I mean, I'm not going to tell you that it won't work. But I'd have a tough time trading it because the logic doesn't make any sense to me. I don't see why it should work. I like to see something that makes logical sense to me as well as have a reasonable sample size.

8. *What is the least important aspect of a trading system as far as you are concerned?*

Again, I'm going to give you two answers. The least important probably is total profits. If too much of the profit is made up from a very small number of trades, it's not a system that I'd really like to trade, regardless of how much money it makes. I want to see some consistency, and total profit isn't that important for that.

The other thing that is very unimportant to me is maximum drawdown. I think max drawdown is about the most unreliable figure you ever see in a trading system. It's not a guarantee that things will ever get worse than whatever that number is, and it is certainly not an indication that things ever have to get that bad again. The example that I like to give people is if I show you a system that makes $150,000 with a $2,000 drawdown, you'd probably think it was a pretty good system. If you go trade it and the drawdown triples in size, I'd think you'd assume the system is failing. However, if you were to come across a system that makes $150,000 with a $6,000 drawdown, that still looks like a pretty good system. So it's all relative; it's all a matter of where you are looking in the distribution of trades, and I just don't think max drawdown is a very reliable figure at all. I don't have a really good replacement to tell you how much capital is necessary to trade a given system. There has been some Ralph Vince's optimal left type stuff, but max drawdown means nothing to me.

9. *In your current work, are you using a mechanical approach, or is there judgment involved in your trading?*

I use several mechanical approaches, and I also use a little bit of judgment. The judgment that I use is twofold. One is for day trading, probably for ego purposes as much as anything else. I want to believe I know something, and so going in to buy or sell during the course of the day helps soothe my ego because it lets me prove that I either do or don't know something. I definitely trade much less size in that fashion than I do on systems, which I guess ought to tell you how much I really do know.

The other thing I use a little bit of judgment with is lightening up positions. If I'm trading a system and I load up a position and things are going well and I think I see what might be, say, a resistance area and the system isn't based on support resistance at all, it's just going to hold the position, I may take 10 percent of the position off, or something like that, just so I can bank a little profit. Again, it's an ego thing. I just feel better that I have at least put a little money in my account. If the market continues going, that's fine; I feel really smart because I'm still positioned. And if the market stops there, I feel really smart because I was able to take some off. So it is an ego thing probably that tells me to use the judgment. I don't know that it makes me any more money than the mechanical things do; the majority of the trading I do is really totally mechanical.

10. *Are you currently using TradeStation or System Writer? If not, what software do you use to run your trading system?*

I have access to both System Writer and TradeStation. I've had System Writer a lot longer, and I'm a lot more comfortable with it. I'm sort of gravitating more and more towards TradeStation because I find it a little easier to do certain things with, once I figure out how to do them. They operate in different fashions, but they are both really powerful products that have allowed me to find things that I really couldn't figure out how to program when I was just doing things on my own. They have certainly made a difference in the things that I've discovered in my development work.

11. *Is your current trading system for sale? For lease? On a fax line? How do you provide this information to clients?*

A couple of my systems are out for sale through various avenues, but I think probably the best value I can offer anyone is a nightly fax service, which basically just details what I'm looking at doing personally the next day. It allows me to use a blend of systems, several of them that trade on what I'd call an intermediate time frame, holding trades on average from two days to two weeks. I also use several short-term systems for the bonds and S&P that normally hold trades for about a day or two. And I do a running commentary on the bond and S&P markets that's primarily, I guess, good for a day-trade basis or maybe slightly beyond. For the day-trade part, it's not specific buy here or sell here things because it's virtually impossible for me to do that the night before, but I try to identify areas where I think the market will be interesting and whether I expect the market to basically go up or down and what I think the overall picture is. I think that's probably a better value for most people than anything else that I've seen. I feel better about it because I'm actually giving them exactly what I think about the markets the next day. I certainly reserve the right to be every bit as wrong as anybody else, but I've been doing this for a living for better than eight years now, and I hope that means I know a thing or two. And I'm more than willing to share what I think with other people.

12. *Can you share the concept behind your trading system, for example, your main entry technique, your exit if you are wrong, and your exit if you are right?*

Well, again, I have so many. If I were to sort of summarize, the vast majority of the things that I do are going with the market, buying on stops, and doing so either at a calculation or at a chart point, something like that. And the exit, if I'm wrong, is the same thing. It's taking out a calculation in the wrong direction or taking out a chart point in the wrong direction. The exit, if I'm right, that changes based on the time frame of the system. With short term systems, I take profits rather quickly. After all, they are short term! With longer term systems I may take partial profits, but I will trail a stop behind the position to protect some of the open equity. I may trail it by a certain percentage of daily ranges, or a percentage of open equity. Something along those lines. But the real key, I think, is going with the market, going with the momentum. Here's an analogy: You're in Kansas City, and you want to go to San Francisco. If you jump a train that's heading toward North Carolina, it may go there, turn around, and go to San Francisco. But I like your odds a lot better if you just hop on a westbound train. That's what I try to do in my trading basically, get to where I want to go in the shortest time possible. So the market basically has to already be moving in my direction before I get aboard the vast majority of the time.

13. *If you could advise system developers to do one thing when they are starting out, what would that be?*

The best thing I think system developers can do is just keep things easy; don't try to be the smartest guy. Traders in general like to believe they are really smart, I think, and the more complicated something is, the better. I just don't think that's true. You know, the limited slope, least squares, linear regression oscillator, often-inverted, outer Mongolian-head-and-shoulders pattern with a cherry twist, that might be a good entry. So might buying over the highest high of the last 10 days. I think the simple stuff works better. So that's what I would recommend. Just see what you think you see in the market and charts particularly and try to quantify it as simply as possible.

14. *Other than yourself, who do you think is the best system developer, or who do you think is the best teacher of system development?*

There are a lot of guys who have put very good, interesting, unique systems out there, and it would be hard to mention any of them without mentioning a lot of them. There are also a bunch of guys probably sitting in their basements and dens beating up their little PCs with data and finding good stuff there, too, that we'll be seeing in the next few months or years. So it's tough to pick anybody. However, Larry Williams has been both a mentor and a very good friend to me. We swap ideas and swap systems. Larry has probably done more to promote systems to the trading public than anyone else in the industry. Not all Larry's ideas are wonderful; in fact I think some of them are just outright bad. But, hey, 98 percent of the things I think are great turn out to be useless once I test them thoroughly. If I had to pick one guy, it would be Larry, but there are a lot of people with quick, inventive minds out there developing systems. I know of at least a couple of people, including one who does some programming for me, that I think are excellent developers, but they aren't in the public eye.

15. *When you devise a trading system, what time frame do you use most? For example, do you use daily bars, weekly bars, 1-minute bars, 10-minute bars, or 60-minute bars?*

The time frame that you use for developing a system is certainly relative to your own personality and character. I think one of the most exciting things that I'm working on currently is finding ways to combine time frames, not using a single time frame to develop a system, but rather using multiple time frames to get the rules of a system together. I'm working on a system that I go down in time frame as far as 10-minute bars, and yet it probably trades only once or twice a week. I'm using daily, hourly, and 10-minute bars. You would think with 10-minute bars you'd be trading two or three times a day, but all I'm doing is using the 10-minute bars to fine-tune what I'm seeing on the hourly bars, which I only use to fine-tune what I see happening on the daily bars. I think the combining of time frames like that is probably the direction that a lot of my research is going to go in the future because I just think there are much better things to discover there than just being one-dimensional.

So I think the combination of time frames is important, and those time frames are, again, relative to your personal time horizon; I mean, monthly, weekly, daily is fine. You can use quarterly, monthly, and weekly if you are an incredibly long-term trader. Basically, what you are trying to do is identify the big picture, what's going on on a higher-up time frame, and then use a shorter time frame to fine-tune your entries and perhaps quantify the risk better. At least that's the basic idea.

16. *If for some reason they closed every commodity in the world except one, and you were the guy in charge of deciding which one would stay open, which commodity would you choose? Why? What hours would it be open?*

If they closed every commodity in the world, I hope they'd leave the bond market open. Treasury bonds are by far my favorite vehicle. The liquidity is so wonderful; they have good volatility, good volume; the executions are great. You can trade almost limitless size without running into a problem. The profit potential versus the margin is a very, very good ratio; you are not restricted to super large accounts to be able to trade them. I'd love for them to be open from 8:00 to 2:00 Chicago time like they were back in the mid-1980s because the stuff I had in bonds in the mid-1980s just worked phenomenally and hasn't worked as well since they changed the times. I realize that's wishful thinking; it's not just the timing of the market that has made a difference I'm sure. But boy, it's hard not to long for the good old days, which I've got to tell you, makes me feel like a real old man.

17. *If you were to choose one commodity you could never trade again and you could never include in a trading system, which commodity would this be? Why?*

You know, you can have everything that trades in New York and I couldn't care less. That's perhaps unfair, but the execution problems, the fill quality and everything is just, in my experience, so poor in New York. The market is almost irrelevant; anything over there is just ugly. Sugar and crude oil both have reasonable volume and reasonable liquidity but, you know, you can get raped there too. So the way I would answer that is I don't trade much that is in New York. I can analyze it, and I can publish things that say, gee, this market looks interesting and I have a signal in this market, but I personally don't do too many trades in New York. This is a shame; there are good markets, good opportunities there. But for me, personally, the fill quality and execution is so poor that I just don't think the aggravation that I deal with is worth the profit potential.

18. *Where do you get your ideas for your system? A chart? A pattern? Observations? Trades that you have done before? What is your favorite technique for coming up with a trading system?*

I have found price pattern to be the most reliable thing I can base things off of. There are numerous things you can base a system off of, but the systems that I've developed based on price pattern have tended to hold up better over time, to be a little more stable. There are a couple of ways you come up with those things. You can just beat up a computer and try a bunch of different patterns, but most of the things that I've come up with, at least originally, came from thinking I saw something in the market. I think when bonds take out the previous hour's low in the last hour that they continue the next day. I think any time we have a really, really big outside day and close right at the lows that we don't follow through very often the next day. Things that I think I see, I then attempt to quantify; I try to code up exactly what it is that I do see and, as I alluded to earlier, I've got to admit that 98 percent of what I think I see turns out to be of absolutely no use to me when I go to test it out. It doesn't work like I think it should, and it isn't bad enough that I can use it to buy when I thought it should sell. I can't use it at all. That's the nature of the beast.

But I think that's basically the way it comes: You start to notice something that you think you see in the market and try to quantify it, try to find a way to test it over a large enough sample size to prove to yourself that there really is something there.

19. *I want you to write a trading system for me. I want you to give me all the rules. I want you to tell me what commodity, what time frame, whether it is daily bars, whatever. What your entry rule is, your exit rule with a profit, your exit rule with a loss. It doesn't have to be a great system. Just give me an idea of something you would look at, something you would test to see if there was any validity.*

We'll use a simple volatility breakout concept. We'll take 60 percent of the previous day's range, that's pretty simple. Not true range, just actual range, high to low. Take 60 percent of that and displace it from the open, the 7:20 Chicago time open in the bond markets, and we'll be buyers if it goes up that far from the open or sellers if it goes down that far from the open. But we're not going to trade immediately; we'll wait until 8:00 Chicago time, 40 minutes after the open, and we'll look at what the high and low of the day is at that point, and we'll either buy 60 percent up from the open or at the high of the day plus four ticks, whichever is higher. That'll prevent us from getting whipsawed too badly when some of the "news nonsense" occurs. As anybody who has ever watched T-Bonds trade after one of those 7:30 Chicago time news reports come out knows, they create carnage. It sometimes looks like a Vietnam memorial search and destroy mission—they run the market all over the place. We don't use stops during that time period; we'll just stay out. We will make this a reversal system. If we get long, we'll use a stop that's four ticks below the low of the first 40 minutes of the day; and if we get short, we'll use a stop that's four ticks above the high, and we'll simply stay in the market reversing that way. I suspect that might make four or five grand a year on average, not a bad system. Couple a hundred percent on your margin.

I've tested things like that. I haven't tested that specifically, but that seems like a logical thing; that's something that I would go look for.

20. *What's the typical day in the life of a system developer? What time do you start? What time do you end? What is it you do all day long? How are your orders placed? How is your system run?*

Like there is anything typical for anybody who's in the market! For me, the day starts at about 4:30 in the morning. I hit the gym to hit the weights pretty hard. When I stopped playing football, I stopped hitting people on the weekend, but I didn't stop wanting to, so I have to take that aggression out somewhere, and working hard, intensely, in a physical fashion like that, I think, makes me sharper mentally. I feel much more alert, much more aware and capable of doing things during the course of the day.

During the day, I'm placing orders, following my systems, and I'm doing things intraday; I'm looking at 10-, 15-, 20-, 30-minute charts. I don't go down to fives and ones too often but sometimes down as low as a three-minute chart. Just trying to fine-tune things, see what's going on, take a few little day-trade positions that I trade relatively small. That's basically how the day goes by. I also have three computers in the office. I may having something else run various tests for me to see if some idea that I have has worked out, and then I try to see how the things are setting up for the next day after the markets have closed and write the fax for the next day for my subscribers, and for myself, too.

As an aside, I should tell you, writing a fax service has really helped my trading immensely because what I think and what I'm planning to do is right there in my words. It really helps my discipline to see my own words staring at me; my trading has actually gotten a lot better since I've started writing things down.

21. *If you could have your system run in any manner, what would be the preferable method? Would you have the person whose money is at risk run the system, or would you have a third party run the system and just arbitrarily take the trades as they are generated, regardless of consequence?*

I'm not exactly a control freak, but I'm not as comfortable with anybody else handling things as I am with myself. I think a lot of good traders have large egos, and I find it hard to believe that anybody is going to do a better job than I do. I recognize that different personalities react differently and that some people would do a lot better having someone else run a system for them, trade their money for them. That's a rather difficult thing for me to do. It's hard for me to have confidence in someone else, regardless of whether it's my system. I'd always be suspicious that they'd be doing something wrong. I certainly am aware of other people who have others execute their systems for them with good results. We all seem to come to the markets with our own psychological defects, and for people whose defects show up in their execution, they can work around that by having someone else execute the system for them. That is not an issue with me. I would much rather see to it that the execution is done to my satisfaction.

22. *Let's pretend I don't have a single book on commodities, and I'm interested in writing systems. Other than your own work, what book would you recommend? Along these same lines, is there anything you would avoid—whether it's software, books, lectures, whatever.*

My pet peeve relates to people wanting that one book or course that will teach them to trade or design systems. It is such an open ended field of study that it is impossible to have an ultimate book that suits everyone. It is a question that I get asked frequently. There are a lot of reasonably good books out there and a lot of books that address certain aspects of trading or system development, but none that really cover the entire process, and I don't think it's possible that there ever could be. There are so many things to look at. I think Alexander Elder's book, *Trading for a Living*, is a good book. I think Joe Ross has written some good books. Although the actual execution of trading plans as he lays them out may not be doable, they are good concepts to pay attention to. Larry Williams wrote a couple of books. There are good books to give you ideas, give you a little starting point. But there's really nothing that just lays it all out for you, and I don't think there ever will be, can be.

23. *Do you think it is necessary for a software developer/real-time trader to have tick-by-tick real-time quotes? Why or why not?*

Real-time quotes are absolutely not necessary. Again, we're getting into a personality issue. I like having real-time quotes; I like to see every tick the market does; I like being able to do something if I think it is prudent. You can tell a mechanical system that a particular structure is a buy every time you see it, but you can't tell it that it's a buy unless Saddam Hussein happens to be launching a scud at that moment. I like to be there on top of the market so that I can see how things are transpiring and maybe recognize trouble before my systems do. But when I first got real-time quotes, there was a good 18-month learning curve where it actually cost me money seeing the real-time charts in front of me. It's a reasonably expensive proposition; I mean, it's hard to get real-time quotes for less than $500 to $800 a month. So you have to make at least that much a month to justify the expense. I don't think for most people it's necessarily a good idea. For people who enjoy being right on top of the market and who want to use their five-minute chart as the long-term chart and trade a one-minute, it's doable; there are people who can do that. When I do that, at the end of the day, I feel like I've been in the ring with Larry Holmes and Mike Tyson at the same time. It's not preferable for me. But I do have real-time quotes, so I guess that shows what sort of character flaws I have.

24. *What kind of quotes do you have? What kind of software would you recommend? Are there any systems or software that you would definitely not recommend?*

I use a BMI data feed, and I have both Aspen Graphics and access to a TradeStation for the real-time charts and all. I find Aspen a little more pleasant to look at, easier on my eyes, and TradeStation is, of course, just an incredibly powerful analytical tool. If you can think of it, you can probably find a way to code it up and test it and at least show it on your charts. So both of those are good pieces of software as far as I'm concerned.

25. *How much data do you think is necessary to be tested as far as assessing a day-trade session on five-minute bars? A daily bar system? A 60-minute system?*

The amount of data necessary is an open-ended question. It's impossible to give a definitive answer on that for day trades or a daily system or anything. You want a sample size that is large enough so that you can see the various types of trading that a market can give you. I mean, you want an uptrend, a downtrend, a strong uptrend, a strong downtrend. You need sideways markets, and you need the wide, swinging-sideways congestions as well as a real tight sideways congestion.

How much data is required to encompass these various types of trends and congestions is an impossible question to answer. You want to have a reasonable sample size of each in your system. You'd like to see a minimum of 30 trades is what the statisticians tell me, but I'd like to see even more than that under each type of circumstance to make sure that I don't have just a good trend system that falls apart in other markets. You can probably develop very good daily-based systems on five years of data, provided you have a simple enough entry that you get enough sample size.

26. *Why do some systems consistently perform year after year, and other systems fail or need to be continually optimized?*

I guess if I knew exactly why some systems perform year after year and others need to be tinkered with, I'd design all of mine to perform year after year. First of all, the different types of markets can affect a system, and sometimes you simply have to accept the fact that in certain markets your system is going to underperform. There is a difference between underperforming and falling apart. Again, if you have a system that is designed to work really well in trends and you go an entire year without having a trend, you can't expect that system to do terribly well. That's just the design of the system. Continually reoptimizing is something that I'm just not a big fan of at all. I think you're always chasing after what was the perfect parameter and you'll never be on top of what it is currently, so I don't reoptimize things myself. I try to design things that are robust and basic enough that reoptimization is not necessary. As far as consistency year to year, though, you are definitely at the whim of market conditions. You can't force the markets to behave in any particular fashion; all you can do is try to design a system that is able to handle varying types of market conditions without falling flat on its face.

27. *How important are drawdowns in your research? How important is average trade size?*

I think drawdowns are just a terribly unreliable figure. I think how much you're risking on any given trade and what your return is versus your risk are more important things to look at. Average trade size is a very interesting thing. When you run a system and you get a large average trade, that would seem to indicate that you have a very good system. If you attempt to use some aggressive money-management strategy, such as Ralph Vince's Optimal F, you'll find that systems with smaller average trade sizes are actually much better systems, usually.

Let me explain it this way. Let's assume you have a system that is 50 percent accurate, and the average win is twice as big as the average loss. Well, if the average win is 2,000 and the average loss is 1,000, that's a good system; I mean, that's something worth trading, definitely. But if you take the exact same 50 percent accurate and the exact same ratio of average win to loss, but the average win is 500 and the average loss is 250, your average trade is going to be quite a bit smaller with that system, yet it's actually a system you can be far more aggressive with. And, again, if you are using an aggressive form of money management, you should make a lot more money with that system. So average trade is important, but it is a little bit misleading. A larger average trade is not necessarily a better system; in fact, a smaller average trade may be desirable, providing you have a reasonable amount of trade frequency and the average loss tends to be smaller with systems that trade more frequently. If your average trade is smaller, 90 percent of the time your average loss is going to be smaller. And I think that's more important really than the average trade itself.

28. *Do you do portfolio management—linking several commodities of different systems together? Do you do pyramiding? Why or why not?*

I find the diversification among 2 or 3 markets is preferable to 20. I think you just dilute your performance that way. I think Fred Gehm did some studies years back that showed that. Ralph Vince said so as well. I think you make more money if you concentrate on just a couple of markets than if you trade too big a basket. Although, looking across markets and picking and choosing where good opportunities are is not a bad way to go. If your system is such that it's not terribly active, that you are only looking for certain types of market activities, it's fine to go across a group of markets to find those because odds are you'll only be in two or three of them at a time anyway.

I don't do any pyramiding personally; it's a psychology question. I don't like increasing my risk. I mean, I'm in a trade, I'm making money, and I feel good about it. If I put any additional positions on, I feel like I am increasing the risk. I may not really be doing so monetarily, but often I am. Either way, it always feels like I am. I don't like the concept of addition to that position. Also, I'm not very long-term oriented. In fact, I'm much more inclined to take part of my position off than I am to add to it. Probabilitywise, the markets just don't run in a straight line; therefore, your probabilities of making money are better when you are peeling contracts off rather than adding to them, and that tends to be the way I approach things.

29. *Let's get a little morbid. You've died. You've left a sealed letter to your heirs. It contains the secret of your fortune. It's the secret to allow them to continue the lifestyle to which they have been accustomed. What one sentence is in the letter?*

This is a very good, deep, interesting question. I'm going to give you an answer that you probably don't really want because you want a trading secret, but I'm going to give you a very honest answer. What I would tell any of my heirs is that the secret to fortune is doing exactly what you want to do with your life. Make sure you know that this isn't a dress rehearsal and you're doing what you want to do. The amount of money that I've made trading cannot compare to the freedom that I have. I have a two-and-a-half-year-old daughter, and my choice of job has allowed me to see every little aspect of her growth. I've seen her first step, her first smile, her first word, the first time she sat up. I've been able to be right there for all of that because of my choice of job. The little things in life that you get, they're so much more important than the amount of money that you make, so I wouldn't say here's the secret to how to buy bonds or whatever. That's not important. Success in life is not about counting the money you make.

I have the ultimate job. I have no one to listen to, nobody to complain to, no one to tell me what to do. The only problem I have is when things go wrong, I don't have anybody to blame, but that's the ideal thing for me. So again, the secret is that you've got to do what you want to do with your life because nobody promised you another chance.

30. *Without giving the secret of life, how would you write an imitation of your system in two lines or less in TradeStation language? For example, I have an S&P system called Buy Monday. "Monday you buy it, put in a $1,400 stop, get out on the close." That's how you write that.*

Heck, I gave you the secret of life in my last answer! Let's assume the S&P has had two consecutive down closes and then opens lower the next day. Buy it, put in a $4,000 stop and exit on the first profitable open, meaning you have to hold it that day. That's not a system I'd recommend anybody trade necessarily, but it works about 85 percent of the time, and it may be a starting point for developing something else. For instance, you have the setup on the daily, you've had two down closes and you've opened lower—maybe that's a good starting point for researching some intraday charts now and seeing if there isn't a way you can get long-based on them with a lot less than $4,000 risk. Incidentally, that will work with different stops; it will work in the bond market as well.

31. *Give us an example of some of your work put in English-type language for a system.*

Let's say we've identified a market that is heading higher with a fair amount of volatility; then we get a pullback, the market going down for two to three days but with lower volatility. We'll buy the market as soon as it starts up again, and we'll trail a stop and try to protect 50 percent of whatever profits we get into the trade. That would be an example in English of some of the intermediate-type trading that I do, trying to take advantage of trends as I think they present themselves.

I'd like to provide a little summary here that isn't an answer to one of your questions. I kind of beat people over the head with this any time I give seminars or talk to them over the phone or anything. I really believe that the key to success at this is twofold. One is you have to find a methodology that is compatible with your personality and temperament. This psychology being a rather trite buzz word these days, you know, if you don't have a viable methodology, all the psychology in the world doesn't mean squat. You can't make money with psychology. The real key to psychology is trying to find out what time frame and what type of methodology you're most comfortable with and then designing a methodology around that. That's not always possible, I mean, obviously what we'd all like to do is be 95 percent accurate or 100 percent accurate and never take any risk, but that's not realistic. But basically whether you're long term, short term, whatever suits your personality, even if that methodology doesn't make as much money as another, it's probably a better methodology for you if it's something you are comfortable with and able to execute well.

The other thing I'd like to stress is that I really think the primary job of the trader is to control the risk. I mentioned not trading if Saddam Hussein is launching scuds. Controlling the risk is the only thing a trader really has control over. You get in the market and you want to make money, that's what you are trading for, but you can't make it happen. You can try to find as good entries as possible and research and what have you, but you simply can't make the market go your way. If you decide that you don't want to risk more than $1,000 per trade, given that there is some execution costs and slippage and things like that, you can come really close to making sure that you don't risk more than $1,000 per trade. But if you want to make $1,000 per trade, there is nothing you can do. You get in the market, you hope, wish, pray, whatever you have to do, but you can't make the market go your way. You are powerless. Consequently, focusing on the risk is I think what most people need to do in their trading in general, whether it's trading system development or if they are going to trade by the seat of their pants, they still better damn well control the risk because that's really the only thing they can do.

Cynthia Kase

INTRODUCTION

Cynthia Kase is president of Kase and Company, Inc., a registered commodity trading advisor, in Albuquerque, New Mexico. She is known for developing fresh approaches to technical trading, blending financial engineering techniques learned in derivatives trading with a classical technical understanding of the market. A master's level chemical engineer, she advises major institutional and corporate clients, primarily in the energy sector, where she has more than 23 years of experience. Her new book *Trading with the Odds* (Chicago: Irwin, 1996) has recently been published.

1. *Tell me about yourself. If someone were to say, "Tell me about Cynthia Kase," what would you want them to know? Give me a brief biography of you before you got into commodities, and a brief biography of what you have done since you got into commodities.*

I am a veteran energy trader and an expert on the application of quantitative and technical price risk management and price optimization strategies to achieve business objectives. As a registered Commodity Trading Advisor, and Certified Market Technician, I provide strategic business advice to energy-industry corporate and government clients.

As CMT, I am now acknowledged as a leading innovator in the field. I am well known for our acclaimed high-tech indicator library, including statistically based money management and trade filtering systems. In the energy market, I am known by many as the top technical and quantitative advisor, blending my technical expertise with a thorough familiarity of the needs and concerns of the energy business.

I have a B.S. in Chemical Engineering from the University of Massachusetts, and a Masters of Engineering degree, also in Chemical Engineering, from Northeastern University. I joined Polaroid in 1973, as a design engineer, and taught Reactor Design and Kinetics at University of Massachusetts at Lowell.

In 1977, I was commissioned as an engineering duty officer with the United States Naval Reserves and moved to California to work for Stauffer Chemical Company as a process and project engineer. In 1980, I was recruited by Standard Oil Company of California's (now Chevron) corporation engineering department as a project engineer until 1983, then moved to *Chevron International* as a Senior Trading Coordinator.

In 1985, I moved to New York as the Manager of Clean Products trading. This region included most of Canada, the U.S. East Coast, the Caribbean and much of Latin America. During the following five years, I managed trading and hedging, term business, asset utilization, processing, and joint ventures and became expert in futures trading, technical analysis and risk management.

In early 1990, I accepted a position at *Chemical Bank* as the Vice President of Commodity Risk Management. Chemical Bank allowed me to carry on private consulting, thus the practice which is now known as *Kase and Company*, was launched at that time. My first client was *Petronal* (BVI), the international arm of the Saudi downstream government company, Samarec.

After launching Kase and Company formally in 1992, I now provide comprehensive risk management consulting, advisory, and software services to over 30 major energy clients and have designed over 15 risk management programs.

One key element is that I made the transition from engineering to trading in 1983. This was an important year for trading energy for a couple of reasons. First of all, 1983 was the year that the crude oil contract was introduced. Also in 1983, I believe, or it could have been 1982, the first Lotus programs were making their way into the public domain. So as I joined trading there were, in fact, no PCs in the entire building. But my background in engineering was such that I was familiar with spreadsheet programs, and it was I who introduced the use of the PC into the trading operation and computerized Chevron's trading group. Also, again, crude oil futures were introduced in 1983, and the use of futures and the introduction of futures and commoditization of the energy market began almost simultaneously with my setting foot into the trading organization. So, in a sense, I belong to a transitional generation that saw both the old way of doing business, which was rife with both inefficiency and unethical behavior. That is, there was a lot of bribery and doing of favors in order to get business done. The transition into the futures market not only made the business a lot more honest, it made it a lot more competitive. People had to buy low and sell high. You couldn't succeed in the business just because you knew where to obtain the right height and hair color gal for the oil administer of a third-world country. In any case, the transparency in the futures market changed the whole face of the energy market, and of course we all know how much computerization changed the business as well. It was my early interest in PCs and computerization that supported my transition not only into being a trader but being a technical trader at the same time.

2. *Tell me about your technique. What makes it exclusively yours? How did you develop it?*

Of course, nothing is ever exclusively one's own. One always builds on the past. So in the sense that I use, for example, bars on my screen, there is commonality between my technique and other people's techniques. But what makes my technique exclusively my own is that I've developed all of my indicators from scratch, and I don't use any traditional indicators whatsoever. Again, we built on the past, but for example, my PeakOscillator study, the math is unique and my own. Same thing with the KaseCD. In a nutshell, our techniques are high-probability, low-risk techniques that are designed for corporate and institutional traders, who as a general rule do not trade portfolio or baskets of commodities but are employed to trade either a single or a very narrow group of futures or physical commodities on an intraday basis, and because of the corporate environment have to be highly accurate.

I've developed my techniques over time, but I would say that I was most highly influenced by my time on the derivatives desk, trading over-the-counter derivatives for Chemical Bank. The reason is that banks tend to employ very intelligent geeks that sit in the corner and play with numbers, including people who are financial engineers and highly educated in math and higher-level statistics. And sitting next to these people for two years I picked up a lot of statistics and probability theory, and that influenced my work in technical analysis. To a certain degree, the technical approach that

I use is a conflation of both quantitative, that is, statistical analysis and technical analysis.

3. *Tell me about your best current trading system. What makes it tick? What are the features that make it the best trading system? Why do you trade this system?*

My current trading system is complex and simple at the same time. It is a multiple time frame trading system where we use two time frames in three levels. Basically, we use a very short-term time frame screened by a medium-term time frame screened by a daily and a daily time frame screened by a weekly. It's simple in the sense that all it consists of is bars; my PeakOscillator, which helps identify market times; my KaseCD, which is a confirmation indicator parallel to the MACD, my Dev-Stop, which is a statistical exit system and stop system. With this we use simple timing (that is simple, traditional timing indicators) to time in and out of the market once we feel there is a market turn. In addition, the timing system is screened in the higher time frame by my Permission Screen.

The feature that makes it a very good trading system is that it's simple in the sense that it only really has four basic indicators in it. But all of these indicators are based on very rigorous mathematics and statistics and probability theory, and therefore they work quite well and are highly accurate.

I trade the system because I feel very comfortable with it and we've been highly successful with it. Not only ourselves, of course, but our 30 corporate clients, who swear by it.

4. *How long ago did you write your first trading system?*

I think it was about 1987, right around when System Writer first came out.

5. *Remember back to your first trading system. Can you tell us the rules?*

As far as I can recall, basically what I was doing was this: I was looking for a divergence on the stochastics. If we had a good divergence and follow-through—that is, the stochastics falling down below a certain level and breaking through some stops—we would put on one-third of our trade. Now, I will say at this point that we were using a very highly dampened slow stochastic. We were using generally a 28- to 34-period slow stochastic so that my rules were based on a dampened stochastic that basically would stay in overbought territory during uptrends and oversold territory during downtrends and would very rarely break the 70 percent or the 30 percent point unless the trend was moving into a corrected phase or turning. So we looked for divergence on the stochastic with follow-through. If we got the follow-through, we took one-third of our trade.

Then we were using the DMI. I've always used a 13-period DMI, which is a little faster than I think some other people use, and we would take our trade; again, we had more elaborate rules than I am conveying here. In any case, what we did was look for a DI crossover and, generally speaking, we looked for a 5 percent filter on the crossover. If my memory serves me right, it was somewhere between a 2 percent and 5 percent difference between the upper and lower DI to enter a trade. And there were, of course, other things that had to do with this, like the slope of the ADX, the value of the ADX, and some other things that were used. But basically we put the second third on a DI crossover, provided the ADX was confirming the trade. Then, if the market continued to go in our direction, we took the third third on a moving average crossover, and basically the moving average that we used in those days was 5- and 21-period moving average where the 21 was the high and a low, so that we used, in a sense, a high low volatility filter on our moving average. The system worked very well because I started to trade it in the late 1980s into 1990 when we had the Gulf crisis, and the market was so nicely trendy during the Gulf crisis that a system like this, which relied on strong divergences and trendiness, worked really, really well.

6. *What caused you to abandon or modify that trading system the very first time?*

I've always been the kind of person who wants to improve things. I've never just sat on my laurels, so to speak. It's just like saying, you know, why didn't the developers of the PC stop with the AT, or why didn't Henry Ford stop with the Model T? Because it wasn't perfect and because it could be better and because I'm always driven to improve things. What bothered me the most about it was that the math wasn't right. The math in the old traditional indicators is not, generally speaking, based on a sound understanding of the underlying structure of the market; it is based more on empirical observations. Most of the old-fashioned indicators have nothing to do with the math of the market. That bothered me.

For example, if we want to go back and look at exit and stop systems, I was using a volatility stop that I picked out of Welles Wilder's book that he wrote in 1978. This was the volatility system where he used a fixed multiplier times the true range. Now, as I sat next to these smart people at the bank and understood more and more about distribution curves and variance and standard deviations and such, it became obvious to me that an average true range totally neglected to take into consideration any variation around the averages. So that, for example, if you have a market that had an average true range of, let's just say for the sake of discussion, a dollar, and a standard deviation was five cents, three standard deviations above the mean, you needed to take a $1.15 risk in order not to get stopped out on the true range of one bar. If you had a market that had a standard deviation of 50 cents, you would have had to take a $2.15 risk not to be stopped out by one bar. So it was clear to me that this old system was flawed and that it did not take into consideration the variance or standard deviation of true range. It was only taking into consideration an average. That's just a simple example, but if the physics aren't right, the product isn't going to be right. That's basically why I modified my approach.

7. *When you look at another person's trading system, what is the very first thing you look for to tell if it's a good or a bad system?*

There are good systems that are not suitable for me, and there are systems that are good for me that might not be good for somebody else. The key thing is that you have to ask what your objective in trading is. Are you a private trader trading speculatively with your own money, with the capability and freedom to trade any commodity you wish to trade? Or are you a professional trader who is employed to trade a single commodity and who'd better darn well have a view as to what's going on and be trading that commodity and not diversify?

Basically, what I would look for is lack of optimization. I would look for a system that works if you changed some of the numbers. If you have a system with an input variable of 28 in one of your indicators and you're trying to change to 29 and the whole thing falls apart, you have a lousy system. Another thing that I would look for is testing over a relatively long period of time. On intraday bars, I would look for testing over different samples. For example, if I had a five-minute bar in a couple weeks in 1990, I'd look for a five-minute bar in a couple weeks in 1988, a sampling over different types of market conditions. If it was a daily system, I would like to see it tested over, let's say, 10 or 15 years in maybe 10 or 15 different commodities. But the main thing I would look for is universality; that the system works under all kinds of different conditions, that it's not optimized, that you can change the numbers and it still works. The best systems are systems that are adaptive, that automatically adapt to market conditions.

I think another thing that's really important is whether or not there is a good money-management system embedded in there.

8. *What is the least important aspect of a trading system as far as you are concerned?*

I think the least important aspect of a trading system is the details. What I mean by that is, if the system is rigorous—for example, if it has a good solid theoretical underpinning, the math is right, it's adaptive, it's nonspecific—then theoretically, you ought to be able to change one of the parts and it would still work.

9. *In your current work, are you using a mechanical approach, or is there judgment involved in your trading?*

We use a mechanical approach, but there is judgment in our trading. When we are trading, when the market is open, when we are actually executing contracts, our approach is based on a strategy that is set forth and executed on a mechanical basis. However, the establishment and design of the strategy when the market is closed is based on judgment. Our forecasting accuracy over the last two years in the markets that we follow has been documented conservatively at 87 percent. I advise all my clients on my service as to what my market forecasts are. It is my view that if one can become a good strategist—that is, if you can do a good forecast—you can have a very good idea of what to expect in the market, and you can bias your trading strategy accordingly, allowing you to trade much more accurately. It is basically whether you fly by the instruments, fly blind without a clue as to what is going on in the market, or you have a very good idea of what's going on in the market, and you can get a leg up over your competition by understanding what's going to be happening. My approach is to do a rigorous and thorough market analysis and forecast once a week and bias my trading strategy for the week according to my forecast.

For example, if my forecast is up to a particular price level with a high probability of turning at that level, I might take first signals as the market turns down from the level I've called for. Whereas if the market turns from a level that I'm not expecting, I might wait for second signals in order to take a trade. My general rule for this is, you take first signals in the direction of the trend, second signals against. Of course, if you don't have any judgment as to which way the market is going, what the trend is, you can't take first signals in the direction of the trend and second signals against. So our forecast and our strategies are based on judgment. Once our strategies are set, the execution of the strategies is purely mechanical.

The other element that I would say is somewhat judgmental is that our system is highly momentum-based and requires a determination of market divergence. We could say the rule is that if the market diverges we do XY or Z, but looking at the chart and identifying divergence is judgmental because it's generally a visual determination.

10. *Are you currently using TradeStation or System Writer? If not, what software do you use to run your trading system?*

I don't use System Writer anymore. The copy that I have is the one I bought in 1989. I do use TradeStation, and we also have Aspen.

11. *Is your current trading system for sale? For lease? On a fax line? How do you provide this information to clients?*

I don't sell my current system. I don't call it a trading system. We call it decision support system because, as I've just explained, it's not a black box. The trader develops a game plan or strategic approach based on a forecast or market view then, based on the plan, trades.

Let me also just make a comment about my trader support system. My trading system is for corporate clients. We only advise high net worth individuals, who own their own oil and gas companies, and what we are doing is basically helping them manage their oil and gas risk or trade in the oil and gas market in order to enhance their current business. They don't trade 100 percent mechanical systems. It's just not de rigueur, so to speak, in the corporate environment. If you are a professional trader, the reason that you are on a salary, the reason that you've been hired, is to have a view of the market and exercise some judgment and discretion in your trading.

So we don't have a black box system, we have what we would call a trader decision support system. We lease it. We basically have a system that imports as a third party add-on package into TradeStation and Super Charts. We have two systems: one for traders and one for hedgers. Our hedging system is basically a quantitative or statistical package, but it still charts on TradeStation. In any case, our trader decision support system, which we call Kase Analytica, is on a lease basis. Most of our clients are on one-year or three-month evergreen leases.

Again, there is no fax line because this is all basically on a third-party add-on. We do have a fax service, a once a week fax where we do a

market analysis and forecast. And we have a quarterly hedge strategy report, which sets the long-term risk-management strategies for our clients.
So, in essence, we have four different products. We've got our trading decision support system; we've got our hedging system; we've got a weekly
fax; and we've got a quarterly hedge advisory report. Our weekly fax is by
fax, and our quarterly hedge advisory service is about a 100-page report
that goes out by Federal Express.

12. *Can you share the concept behind your trading system, for example,
your main entry technique, your exit if you are wrong, and your exit if you
are right?*

What we look for is a sign that the market might turn. My
PeakOscillator is an indicator that catches market turns that other indicators—for example, the stochastic, the MACD, the RSI, and other momentum indicators—miss because they don't diverge. The PeakOscillator
catches these nondivergent turns. So, for example, if we had a PeakOut
setup, which is a setup signal that the market might be turning and our
PeakOscillator on a daily chart, we would then drop down to what we call
a timing chart, which is a short-term chart, to look to time them into the
market. If we got a timing signal on our timing chart that was permissioned
in a longer term to medium term, that is, if our Permission Stochastic that's
based on our medium-turn time frame gives us permission to enter in the
opposite direction of the short-term time frame, we take half of our trade.
The second half of our trade we would put on after either a pullback and a
new signal on the timing chart or a permissioned signal on the monitor
chart. A permissioned signal is a signal that has been filtered in a higher
time frame. Basically, I'd have to tell you about our philosophy of charts
timing, monitor and higher time frame, but the monitor time frame is usually a fifth to an eighth of a day. The timing chart is a third to a fifth of the
monitor chart. So we've got these three different time frames set up. If we
get a signal on the daily chart that is a timing signal that's confirmed on the
weekly, we can move up to follow the trade on the daily chart. Generally
speaking, most of my clients' and my own bias is not to monitor the market on the daily chart; it's just too long a time frame for my appetite. But if
some of our clients want to hold longer-term positions, we'll move the
trade up to a daily level if it is permissioned on that level.

Basically, what I look for very rigorously is signs that the market
might turn. We look for patterns and use candlesticks quite rigorously. If we
have a candlestick pattern that is coincident with the PeakOut, confirmed by
a KaseCD divergence, we have a very strong sign that the market might

turn. Of course, there's all kinds of different permutations and combinations of this. You can get a candlestick setup with a PeakOscillator divergence as opposed to just a plain PeakOut. In any case, we look for a very strong sign the market might turn.

If the market looks like it might turn, we look to exit the market on a number of different signals. Number one would be a completion of the divergence. Number two would be a completion of the candlestick pattern. The remainder of the exits would be based on my Dev-Stop system; Dev-Stops one, two, and three. If we have a very strong sign the market might turn, we generally pull our Dev-Stop into Dev-Stop one. At this point, we would do an updated, rigorous analysis of the market to determine whether or not we thought the market was going to turn into a major correction or an opposing trend or whether or not we thought we were just going to stall into a correction. If we thought we were going to stall into a modest correction that was going to be short-lived, we would trade it accordingly. And by this I mean we might only trade it in a very short-term time frame for a couple of cents in and out if we just want to kind of scalp it so to speak, or we would wait and take a second signal waiting for a C-wave or a three-wave confirmation. In any case, we would time into the market just as I've described the first timing into the market, but we would take first or second signals, depending on our view. All of these decisions would take place when the market was closed, but we would set the strategy based on our analysis.

So, to summarize, basically our system is using very, very, simple timing signals to time into the market in a short time frame and then scaling up in time as these signals get confirmed. But what we really are looking for, and what my whole system is based on, is identifying market turns based on pattern and momentum, really managing my exit very, very precisely, and then taking a post turn, taking new timing signals—either first signals or second signals depending upon the strengths of the turn signal and the market forecast and outlook that we've developed. Our exit if we are wrong is simply based on our Dev-Stops. Normally, we'll keep our stops at stop level three on our monitor and timing charts, and if just out of the blue, with no sign of a turn, the market just kind of gaps to the opposite direction or just meanders in the opposite direction and takes out our stops, we're out of the market. Again, if we get pattern and momentum, we take 50 percent of our profit or exit 50 percent of our trade on a divergence confirmed by pattern and 50 percent of our trade on stop one if we've got this warning that the market is going to turn. If we just get stopped out of the clear blue, again, we just take equal exits on stop one, two, and three.

13. *If you could advise system developers to do one thing when they are starting out, what would that be?*

The main thing I would advise new system developers is don't try to develop a system. Well, I don't mean that they shouldn't try to develop a system, but basically what people who are trying to code systems should do is try to code a system that's already been developed in real-time. In other words, trade a system profitably. Trade a system and work the bugs out of it and know that it's a good system and then code it.

You know, I'm sure you've heard the story about random versus nonrandom events, that if you give a monkey a barrel with a bunch of letters in it, it is very unlikely that the monkey can take the letters out and come up with a bible or an encyclopedia, for example. So, there is no way that you are going to be able to develop a system just by randomly trying ideas if you don't already have a gut feel for the math and the fact that the system is going to really work. So you've got to get the system to work before you code it. My best advice to people who want to develop a system is to develop it in actual real time, in a real market, trading every day, and then code it. Don't try to develop something out of the clear blue sky.

And sort of a second corollary to that is that the system has to make sense from a logical standpoint. It has to have a theoretical and philosophical underpinning that's sound and based on the way the market behaves, not just on guesses.

14. *Other than yourself, who do you think is the best system developer, or who do you think is the best teacher of system development?*

I think the best system developer is the fellow that wrote *Market Wizards*, Jack Swager. You know, he developed a system that probably cost millions of dollars to develop for; I think it was Prudential Bache. Forgive me if I'm a little off. It is kind of difficult to separate the who from the resources they have. I just read in the *Economist* about a big bank that wrote a system to kind of capture the thoughts of their best trader. I think they spent three, maybe more, million dollars developing this system, which captured the whole thought process of this good trader. Most of my experience with other people's systems is by reputation, not by use, so I kind of have to beg off commenting any further about that. But the question would be, if all of us were given, let's say five million dollars to develop a system, who would be best. So again, to some degree, ability and resources are related.

15. *When you devise a trading system, what time frame do you use most? For example, do you use daily bars, weekly bars, 1-minute bars, 10-minute bars, or 60-minute bars?*

I already alluded to this. Generally I use one-fifth to one-eighth of a day bar for my monitor, my main time frame, and one-third to one-fifth of that time frame to time into the market. I also use tick charts to finesse my trades. Corporate traders often find it very difficult to only trade based on daily bars because of the risk involved. Typical trade size for a corporate trader would be 200 to 1,000 contracts. Some traders even might have books with 5,000 contracts in them. But in any case, if you have an average trade size, let's say of 500 contracts, the risk associated with using a daily bar and sitting through the normal fluctuations in the market in a daily bar time frame are generally too large. So, again, we use one-fifth to one-eighth of a day as our main time frame.

16. *If for some reason they closed every commodity in the world except one, and you were the guy in charge of deciding which one would stay open, which commodity would you choose? Why? What hours would it be open?*

This is kind of a hard question, but I probably would choose something like the S&P simply because it's a nice index for highly traded equities, and in that sense it has a great value. And when you say "closed every commodity" you are talking about regulated exchanges. Certainly, many commodities, like gold, silver, dollars, and yen, can be traded outside regulated exchanges and are quite active.

17. *If you were to choose one commodity you could never trade again and you could never include in a trading system, which commodity would this be? Why?*

These commodities kind of decide for themselves what won't trade again. In other words, if a commodity isn't successful, the exchange will eventually close trading on that commodity.

18. *Where do you get your ideas for your system? A chart? A pattern? Observations? Trades that you have done before? What is your favorite technique for coming up with a trading system?*

I think the best teacher, the best generator of ideas for systems, is just basically our experience. But what I have found to be quite helpful is that from time to time, about twice a year, I hire a financial engineer, someone who knows the numbers, often, for example, a professor from a university, to teach me something. For example, my most recent experience was that I hired a statistics professor from the University of New Mexico to give me a refresher on stochastic processes and probability theory, and we came up with some improvements to the way that random walk is calculated. Without going into a tremendous amount of detail, we dampen out the true range calculation so that it's not so highly erratic and short look-back lengths. So I get a lot of my ideas by hiring experts in particular fields. They might not know anything about trading, but listening to them, talking to them, studying the mathematics a lot of times generates a new idea.

19. *I want you to write a trading system for me. I want you to give me all the rules. I want you to tell me what commodity, what time frame, whether it is daily bars, whatever. What your entry rule is, your exit rule with a profit, your exit rule with a loss. It doesn't have to be a great system. Just give me an idea of something you would look at, something you would test to see if there was any validity.*

This is kind of a hard question to answer because I have a system I'm happy with, and I have no desire to come up with a totally new system. But I will give you an idea of the types of things that we're looking at to develop new approaches and bring our system into new generations. Right now, we're looking at equal volatility bars. I think one of the things that's been neglected in the systems is the data. People tend to focus in on the algorithms that analyze and crunch the data as opposed to the way the data is formatted to begin with. And so one of the things that we're looking at is formatting the data differently, and specifically we're looking at equal volatility bars. People say point and figures are kind of equal volatility in a sense because each box is a range. But I'm talking about going beyond this to where each bar has the same volatility or same range and therefore would have a number of different results. One of the key results is that the standard deviation of range is minimized, is at the minimum value theoretically possible because if all the bars have the same range, the average true range and the range of each individual bar is virtually identical, and therefore you have very little standard deviation in the true range. This means that you can manage risk much more closely. It means that if you have a volatility expansion, you get more bars; if you have a decrease in volatility, you get fewer bars. The bottom line is that in price trades, the price changes proportional to the square root of time, proportional to the square root of volume, but directly proportional to volatility. So if you can look at equal volatility bars, you can maybe get some interesting things happening. We've got a beta version of this that we've designed for TradeStation. So in any case, those are the kinds of things we do.

20. *What's the typical day in the life of a system developer? What time do you start? What time do you end? What is it you do all day long? How are your orders placed? How is your system run?*

I have about six or seven people working for me, so I'm not the only person involved. And our business is not just sitting around and developing systems. We have clients we're advising; we have marketing things we are doing, proposals that we are writing; we have projects that we are working on. A lot of our work is not on a stand-alone basis. In other words, we're not just developing a system; we are developing a whole risk management, trading and hedging, policy and implementation plan for a major corporation, which includes systems that they are going to use. So there is a lot more to it than just sitting around developing a system in isolation. And of course, we have to manage the office, accounts payable, accounts receivable, supplies, personnel issues, helping our people manage their time better. There are a lot of things going on other than just sitting and developing systems. Generally, whenever we do any work on our systems, it's driven by client projects.

In any case, we start at about 8:00, and we end at about 6:00. I don't think there's any kind of description that describes my day. We call our clients; we try to keep in touch with our clients. We have customer contact on the projects that we're working on. We answer new inquiries; we write proposals; we follow up on existing proposals; we work on project documents; we assist our clients in simulations of systems that were developed for them. There's a lot that goes on.

21. *If you could have your system run in any manner, what would be the preferable method? Would you have the person whose money is at risk run the system, or would you have a third party run the system and just arbitrarily take the trades as they are generated, regardless of consequence?*

I think the preferred method in running a system is to let our clients run their own systems with our advice. Of course, that's the best of both worlds for me, because for helping them we get to manage their systems, but we don't have the grunt work of having to stare at the screen all day long.

Our third parties at risk are basically corporations with, on average, maybe half a billion, a billion dollars a year of risk, so they are going to manage their own systems. Big corporations with 10 people in the trading department aren't going to farm out their trading to other people.

22. *Let's pretend I don't have a single book on commodities, and I'm interested in writing systems. Other than your own work, what book would you recommend? Along these same lines, is there anything you would avoid—whether it's software, books, lectures, whatever?*

I think it's George Angell's book *Winning in the Futures: A Money Making Guide to Trading, Hedging and Speculating.*

Basically, books that I would avoid are books by what I would call charlatan traders. I mean, I would want to buy a book or get advice from someone who makes his or her living, not from selling books and getting people into seminars, but from writing systems and from advising paying clients on how to use those systems and/or managing money. I would definitely avoid those people who make their living from writing books and giving lectures.

23. *Do you think it is necessary for a software developer/real-time trader to have tick-by-tick real-time quotes? Why or why not?*

I can't imagine a professional software developer without real-time tick data or a professional real-time trader without real-time tick data. Now that's not to say that when doing research we can't get away with historical tick data, but how you can trade real-time without real-time quotes, I can't even imagine. You know, people could always say, well, we could use historical data, but then you lose the criticality of the integrity of your system because you cannot see forward into the future. You know, whenever we use historical data we can see forward into the future, and we might lose some of the flavor of how the chart looks to a trader in real-time. So I just can't imagine a professional adviser, software developer, or trader without real-time quotes. We basically have three different types of quotes in our office: S&P CompStock, FutureSource, and Telerate, and I like both the TradeStation system and the Aspen system. I don't have a problem with either of them.

24. *What kind of quotes do you have? What kind of software would you recommend? Are there any systems or software that you would definitely not recommend?*

I wouldn't recommend any of the hard-coded old-fashioned systems. I feel that it's nice to have the ability to interface with the data.

25. *How much data do you think is necessary to be tested as far as assessing a day-trade session on five-minute bars? A daily bar system? A 60-minute system?*

I would think that anything over 15,000 data points would be acceptable. If you are testing a day-trading system, you just can't use 15,000 consecutive bars, though. You need to sample different markets and different commodities and different environments. So, my general answer is 15,000 data points, and for intraday data I'd like to see those data points sampled from different years and different market conditions.

26. *Why do some systems consistently perform year after year, and other systems fail or need to be continually optimized?*

Some systems perform consistently because they are universal. They take into consideration how the market really behaves, and they breathe and change and are adaptable. Either they perform consistently because they work well over a diverse set of commodities, or they work consistently because they are adaptable.

Other systems fail because they are particular. They are not tested over a long enough data stream, and they only work because they have been optimized. They're really not rigorous enough systems; they don't hang together because they're not based on how the market really behaves.

27. *How important are drawdowns in your research? How important is average trade size?*

Drawdowns are absolutely key because if a company loses too much money they are not going to use me anymore. If the company loses too much money, the trading manager is going to get fired, the trader is going to get fired, and they are not going to use me anymore. So drawdowns are critical.

As a matter of fact, the losses and drawdowns are more critical than how much money is made. Average trade size is also critical. If you're designing systems for corporate environments, the corporate risk profile and the amount of the commodity that they produce, or the commodity they consume directly impinges on the amount that has to be traded. Therefore, I need to work around the company's dictate.

28. *Do you do portfolio management—linking several commodities of different systems together? Do you do pyramiding? Why or why not?*

No, we don't do portfolio management because all of our clients are basically exposed to single commodity risk. They are either natural gas clients or oil clients or electricity clients or metals clients. Even if we do have a portfolio, it's generally a synthesized set of commodities that has a particular covariance that can hedge a commodity that is not exchanged or traded, for example, hedging electricity by using the copper contract or a number of different metals contracts.

As I mentioned earlier, we do scale up in time; you could call that pyramiding. We do pyramid up in time, and the reason we do it is to limit our risk. If we start our trade at a very low time frame, we have profited the trade by the time we move up to a higher time frame. So it's a way of decreasing the probability of loss and the size of loss. I should say, though, that we do look at covariance of portfolio, or basis risk. For example, if we're trading a natural gas contract but we're using this contract as a hedge or a proxy for physical natural gas and therefore we have basis risk left over, we do look at the covariance of the basis portfolio to see how that impinges on the overall result.

29. *Let's get a little morbid. You've died. You've left a sealed letter to your heirs. It contains the secret of your fortune. It's the secret to allow them to continue the lifestyle to which they have been accustomed. What one sentence is in the letter?*

I would say something like this: Seek first the kingdom of God and his will in your life. Acknowledge with humility any talents or abilities you may have and know you are responsible for the proper exercise of such talents. Have faith, persevere, and things will turn in the optimal fashion for you.

30. *Without giving the secret of life, how would you write an imitation of your system in two lines or less in TradeStation language? For example, I have an S&P system called Buy Monday. "Monday you buy it, put in a $1,400 stop, get out on the close." That's how you write that.*

Well, in practical terms, it would be very difficult to write my system in two lines, but if we wanted to be simple about it we would say that when the probabilities of the market turning are very high, exit your existing trade aggressively and take a new trade in the opposite direction on the simplest of timing signals.

31. *Give us an example of some of your work put in English-type language for a system.*

A thorough and clear explanation of a trading system can be found in my book *Trading with the Odds* (Chicago: Irwin, 1996), pages 111-113. There is no way to skirt around the work that is needed to compete successfully in the markets; however, a careful study of some sample trades will give you valuable insights into trading with a professional approach.

Joe Krutsinger

INTRODUCTION

Joe Krutsinger is President of Krutsinger & Krutsinger, Inc., an Omega Solution provider and software publishing firm that distributes and supports Portana, the Portfolio Analyzer Software developed by Tom Berry and Welles Wilder. He is also the Trading Systems Designer for Robbins Trading company in Chicago and has years of experience developing and testing trade system ideas. He has traveled the country showing traders how to systemize their trading and is the instructor of the popular video series, *Trading System Development*. Joe also is the author of the *Trading-Systems Toolkit*.

1. *Tell me about yourself. If someone were to say, "Tell me Joe Krutsinger," what would you want them to know? Give me a brief biography of you before you got into commodities, and a brief biography of what you have done since you got into commodities.*

Before I was in commodities, I was in the grocery business. I went to Michigan State University, and I was the outstanding senior in food systems, economics and management. Michigan State is a pretty big campus, had 43,000 students, so that made me feel pretty good. I was loading block salt one day, and a farmer dropped a block of salt and mashed my hand; he didn't say excuse me or anything, he just kept on loading. I said to myself, gee, I think I've taken a wrong career path. So with my broken hand, I decided to get into commodities, and I went to look at commodity firms.

As far as what I've done since I've gotten into commodities, in 1978 I became the youngest vice president of Piper Jeffrey and Hopwood. In 1980 I had 16 job offers, all of them in Des Moines, Iowa, to run commodity departments. The commodity field is fairly small, and I think I have done fairly well in it. I have been a broker continuously since 1976. So this is my 21st year in commodities. My complete biography is in the back of the book as author of this book.

2. *Tell me about your technique. What makes it exclusively yours? How did you develop it?*

Actually, my technique is using software developed by others. I've become an expert at System Writer, TradeStation, Super Charts, and Portana. I liked Portana so much I bought the company. I am not a software designer, but I am a very good software user, and basically my technique is to use commercial software.

3. *Tell me about your best current trading system. What makes it tick? What are the features that make it the best trading system? Why do you trade this system?*

The best current trading system I have is actually One Night Stand, and I wrote about it in 1992. It's actually a world famous system. There are over 50,000 copies in circulation. When I wrote the system One Night Stand, I had showed it to *Futures Magazine*, and they put it in their "Trading Systems Special Issue." They printed up 50,000 copies of that special issue and distributed it to about everybody in commodities. The interesting thing about One Night Stand is that I divulged all the rules. The entry, the exit if you are right, the exit if you are wrong, and although it has had wide distribution, the system continues to do well today.

4. *How long ago did you write your first trading system?*

The first trading system I can remember writing was in 1979, called Hi Ho Silver, and basically it's this: If the close is above the 32 day moving average, you're long; if it's below it, you're short. Remember, in 1979, there weren't many people writing trading systems, and in a five year period, that system made over a quarter of a million dollars trading just silver.

5. *Remember back to your first trading system. Can you tell us the rules?*

I just gave you the rules on Hi Ho Silver, which basically is: If the price is above the 32 day moving average, you're long silver; if it's below it, you're short. You're always in the market.

6. *What caused you to abandon or modify that trading system the very first time?*

I decided to look for more complicated trading systems, thinking that surely complication was the key. I used a variation of this system in cattle. In 1983, I had nine losing trades in a row, always reversing, always being on one side of the market or the other in a reversal system, and although the tenth trade was a huge winner, it made me kind of wonder about reversal systems.

7. *When you look at another person's trading system, what is the very first thing you look for to tell if it's a good or a bad system?*

Drawdown. If the drawdown is too big, you'll never trade that system, at least not for very long. That is the very most important thing to look at, the magnitude of the drawdown.

8. *What is the least important aspect of a trading system as far as you are concerned?*

Consecutive winners or consecutive losers. A lot of people put a lot of store in that, but I had a real-time trading system in 1989 that had 42 consecutive winners, and then I had a loser, and 25 percent of my people quit because they thought the system was broken. So consecutive winners or losers don't mean much to me anymore.

9. *In your current work, are you using a mechanical approach or is there a judgment involved in your trading?*

I use 100 percent mechanical systems. My idea of a great system is: A system that once I write it, I never have to touch it again—One Night Stand, Paul Revere. Paul Revere is a trading system for the British pound where you buy at the highest high of the last six days, or sell to the lowest low of the last six days, and use $1,000 stop. I haven't changed the rules for Paul Revere since I wrote it in 1989.

10. *Are you currently using TradeStation or System Writer? If not, what software do you use to run your trading system?*

I use all the Omega products. System Writer, I still think is the very best tool, if you are looking for what combination of systems will work the best, because you can still take several pieces of data and ten or twelve different trading systems, and let the machine sort out the body, so to speak. TradeStation isn't to that order of effectiveness, yet.

11. *Is your current trading system for sale? For lease? On a fax line? How do you provide this information to clients?*

My current trading system is a bond system that I lease for $75 a month per contract trade. The reason I lease it for such a small amount of money is that I want to lease a lot of them, and as people have experience with the system, instead of trading one contract or two contracts, I hope they trade four or five. If a person trades four contracts on my system, he has to pay me $300 a month. And I trade all my systems exclusively at Robbins Trading, where I'm a consultant, so that I can watch my systems and tune them up, and make sure they are being traded correctly.

12. *Can you share the concept behind your trading system, for example, your main entry technique, your exit if you are wrong, and your exit if you are right?*

The rules to One Night Stand, which I think is my best system, are basically this. If the ten day moving average is above the 40 and today is Friday, then buy the highest high of the last four days on the stock. If the ten day is below the 40 and today is Friday, then sell if the lowest low of the last 8 days on the stop. Use $1,000 stop on day of entry, and get out on Monday's opening. The system is so hard to do in real time because no one wants to buy new highs and sell new lows going into a weekend, carry the position and then automatically liquidate. It's very, very difficult to get someone to actually do it.

As far as the current system I'm using at Robbins, it is a volatility breakout system on bonds. It has a day trade module and an overnight module, and the concept is to hold bonds for a very short length of time, but overnight. Hold them for a day or two to make probably ten or twelve trades a month on the overnight system, another eight or nine trades a month in the day trade system and try to make between $6,000 and $8,000 a year per contract traded. That's very good return in bonds, and that is my goal.

13. *If you could advise system developers to do one thing when they are starting out, what would that be?*

I guess the first thing I would tell them to do is read the body of knowledge. For example, look at Larry Williams' work. Larry Williams, I think, is the very best system developer in the world. Look at some of the old work, lessons from the masters. Read the Jessie Livermore book, *Reminiscence of a Stock Operator*, and code some of that into a TradeStation and System Writer and see how well it works today, but don't get myopic looking at your own little thing. Look at other people's material. Code up what they have to say and see if there are things you can use.

14. *Other than yourself, who do you think is the best system developer, or who do you think is the best teacher of system development?*

Other than myself, huh! Well, actually I think the best system developer and best teacher are both Larry Williams. Larry is not only probably the nicest guy in the futures business, but also he's probably the smartest, and he is a very modest person. He is able to communicate at all levels. He's just an excellent, excellent person and system developer.

15. *When you devise a trading system, what time frame do you use most? For example, do you use daily bars, weekly bars, 1-minute bars, 10-minute bars, or 60-minute bars?*

I like daily bars. There are some problems with them, using close stops and some of the things, the intricacies for day trading. But you can get them readily, the data is clean, and you can be pretty sure if you've got a system that you've tested correctly on daily bars without too many parameters in it, you have a good chance of it repeating. One of the problems with small time frame stuff is you can find stuff that works over a three or four month period because of a unique way the market's running. For instance, here it is the first quarter of 1996, and you have a very volatile market in the stock market and the bond market, very high ranges, stuff that you write and make work in this time frame may not work in most time frames.

16. *If for some reason they closed every commodity in the world except one, and you were the guy in charge of deciding which one would stay open, which commodity would you choose? Why? What hours would it be open?*

United States Treasury Bonds, and I would have them open from 8:00 A.M. until 2:00 P.M.

17. *If you were to choose one commodity you could never trade again and you could never include in a trading system, which commodity would this be? Why?*

I guess, if I had to say there is one commodity that I just could do without trading, it would be oats. I think you can fool yourself with oats about as well as anything because it's such a small contract, and it moves in such a small manner, you can sit in a position forever and never really get anywhere. As far as testing, there is not enough volatility. I think it's the kind of contract you could pretty well lead. There's an old phrase in commodities back from the early days that said, "Gentleman don't trade oats."

18. *Where do you get your ideas for your system? A chart? A pattern? Observations? Trades that you have done before? What is your favorite technique for coming up with a trading system?*

My favorite technique is to look at major tops and bottoms and draw out what is going on right before the top or bottom. In other words, patterns. I think indicators can be stressed way too much in most systems. My favorite systems have no indicators. They look at a pattern, and then they do a break out anticipating a trend change. Larry Williams' OOPS! system, when the market opens sharply lower and then comes back to the previous day's low, for instance, is a classic example of the kind of system that I think is unbeatable because you can see the market psychology there at work where the people say, "OOPS! Something is wrong," and they have to go back the other way.

19. *I want you to write a trading system for me. I want you to give me all the rules. I want you to tell me what commodity, what time frame, whether it is daily bars, whatever. What your entry rule is, your exit rule with a profit, your exit rule with a loss. It doesn't have to be a great system. Just give me an idea of something you would look at, something you would test to see if there was any validity.*

One of the things I'd look at is a dual system. A system where it does one thing in choppy markets and does another thing in trending markets. The trending part of the system would be fairly easy. Something like this. Buy tomorrow at the highest high of the last 10 days on the stop; sell tomorrow at the lowest low of the last 10 days on the stop. Then I would also have a condition. And the condition would be if the range of today is less than the average range of the last 10 days, then I would trade System 1. If today's range is above the range of the last 10 days, then I would trade System 2. As far as exit with a loss, I would probably use a money management rule of about $500, and as far as exit with a profit, I would not use a profit target.

20. *What's the typical day in the life of a system developer? What time do you start? What time do you end? What is it you do all day long? How are your orders placed? How is your system run?*

Basically, I'm in the office before 7:00 A.M. to make sure all the data was collected right and all the systems are running. I'm fairly unusual because I have 18 different active trading systems to watch. I have eight TradeStations to monitor so mine is kind of a mechanical life. I want to make sure that those opening ticks come in right and everything is fine. After all the openings are done by 9:30 A.M. Chicago time, I pretty well sit in a room and write new trading systems and work on new work. I'll be interrupted several times a day to help clients and prospects from all over the world tune up their trading systems, or figure out what it is they are trying to do. I eat lunch about 12:30, 12:45, and by 4:30, 5:00, I'm back home.

21. *If you could have your system run in any manner, what would be the preferable method? Would you have the person whose money is at risk run the system, or would you have a third party run the system and just arbitrarily take the trades as they are generated, regardless of consequence?*

I really prefer the system assisted approach that Robbins has; that's why I helped make it come to be. I feel that it's much easier for someone who doesn't have their money at risk, to follow the rules and to follow them correctly without trying to put judgment into the system. I think that's what made System Assist the success it is.

22. *Let's pretend I don't have a single book on commodities, and I'm interested in writing systems. Other than your own work, what book would you recommend? Along these same lines, is there anything you would avoid—whether it's software, books, lectures, whatever?*

I think Larry Williams' book, the Silver Book and the Gold Book are invaluable as are any of his seminar manuals. I think you can learn the most by writing systems, and the way you write systems is to look at other successful systems and build your own building blocks.

As far as things to avoid, I think I would avoid a lot of the black box stuff. The stuff that's out there that you put in the open, high, low, and close and push a button, and it tells you something to do, but doesn't really tell you why. I would avoid that stuff.

23. *Do you think it is necessary for a software developer/real-time trader to have tick-by-tick real-time quotes? Why or why not?*

I do not. I think the daily bar is enough, and I think if you want to back test and do some dual testing on back tick data to make sure that the daily bar acts the way you want, that's fine. But I think that watching the market is not beneficial at all.

24. *What kind of quotes do you have? What kind of software would you recommend? Are there any systems or software that you would definitely not recommend?*

I use Signal and Bonneville quotes. I guess Signal has acquired Bonneville now. And I use TradeStations. If I were just watching quotes and not writing systems, Commodity Quotes Graphics is a tremendous piece of software. I had one of the very first ones in 1983, but since I am a system developer and write lots of trading systems, there is absolutely no platform better, that I know of, than Omega's Trade Station.

I don't think I'd recommend the systems that are the handheld variety. I've heard guys say they take them to the restroom at work and watch their handheld system and make trading decisions. I think that's a poor way to trade.

25. *How much data do you think is necessary to be tested as far as assessing a day-trade session on five-minute bars? A daily bar system? A 60-minute system?*

As far as a daily system, I think you have to have three years of data to show a test and three years of data on a daily system of 750 bars. I think 750 bars is a good length number of bars to test. So in a 60-minute session that would be about 120 days or so, and so forth.

26. *Why do some systems consistently perform year after year, and other systems fail or need to be continually optimized?*

I think the more parameters there are in a system, the more likely it is to fail, and the more likely it is for those parameters to have to be analyzed.

If you have a basic pattern setup such as a higher high today and a lower low today than the previous day, that's an outside day setup. You take that, and then you can use a trigger; if tomorrow's low is below today's low, then sell. I think those type of things that are very hard to optimize to any degree tend to hold up.

27. *How important are drawdowns in your research? How important is average trade size?*

Drawdowns are the most important thing. When I look at total money made if the drawdown is more than 10 percent of the total money made, I don't like the system. As far as average trade size, the average winner or the average loser doesn't mean as much to me as the average trade. The average trade size should be over $150 in most systems. In bonds, I'll take a very small average trade size of $60 to $70 because the bonds have very little slippage.

28. *Do you do portfolio management—linking several commodities of different systems together? Do you do pyramiding? Why or why not?*

Absolutely. The only way to make a lot of money in commodities is to find systems that complement each other. I've done a lot of work on this. I have a program called All In One where I take One Night Stand, my S&P system, my bond system, blend them together and do them all in one. And that's really a huge new area of system development, portfolioing and pyramiding.

29. *Let's get a little morbid. You've died. You've left a sealed letter to your heirs. It contains the secret of your fortune. It's the secret to allow them to continue the lifestyle to which they have been accustomed. What one sentence is in the letter?*

Buy Monday, buy the S&P on Monday, use $1,000 stop, get out on the close. That is the secret.

30. *Without giving the secret of life, how would you write an imitation of your system in two lines or less in TradeStation language? For example, I have an S&P system called Buy Monday. "Monday you buy it, put in a $1,400 stop, get out on the close." That's how you write that.*

That's how I write it too! That's my Buy Monday system.

31. *Give us an example of some of your work put in English-type language for a system.*

I've given several of those, but I think the best thing you can do is take my Buy Monday together with my One Night Stand and then use a volatility breakout in bonds, and I'll give you the volatility breakout system in bonds. Buy tomorrow at the open tomorrow plus 30 percent of the range on the stop. Sell tomorrow at the open tomorrow minus 30 percent of the range on the stop. Use a $500 stop, and get out on the first possible opening.

Glenn Neely

INTRODUCTION

Glenn Neely's approach is different than most of us in the technical field. He uses a very complex idea of Elliott wave, and it's fairly hard to mathematize his method. I think you'll get a kick out of Glenn's ideas, and I think you'll appreciate the system I wrote, Neely 31, at the end of the commentary.

Talking about Neely 31, based on Glenn's idea of rate of change, if the rate of change is positive then buy at the next breakout of yesterday's high. If the rate of change is negative then sell at the breakout of yesterday's low, and we showed a $3,000 stop and other than that it's reversing system. I've also given you a chart that shows the open high-low close on the Japanese yen and in the rate of change expressed as an indicator below. This system, called Neely 31, is written in the Quick System Editor so it can be for Super Charts or TradeStation and basically, it's a very interesting look at rate of change.

1. *Tell me about yourself. If someone were to say, "Tell me about Glenn Neely," what would you want them to know? Give me a brief biography of you before you got into commodities, and a brief biography of what you have done since you got into commodities.*

I'm the president of the Elliott Wave Institute. I founded the company in 1983 and have been spending most of my career focusing on technical market research and innovation, primarily in the field of wave analysis. By focusing for 14 years on Elliott wave I began to evolve an approach far more advanced and scientific. The technique that I use helps to make wave analysis much more objective, and what's been a big downfall of the wave theory for a long, long time is that when you ask one wave analyst or another what their opinion is about the market, you'll frequently get completely different opinions. That's common in the field of technical analysis period, no matter what the approach. So it's been my feeling for a long, long time if technical analysis is to have any validity, its conclusions must be reproducible and as objective and scientific as possible. I don't mean scientific in terms of mathematical formulas; those really don't work when you're analyzing mass psychology. It requires a fractal structuring of mass psychology, which is what the wave theory is all about.

I got involved in this business by purchasing a very expensive gold trading system when I was in my early 20s, probably about 21, and I raised some capital from some local businessmen I knew and started trading the systems and learned pretty quickly that there was a lot more to making money in the markets than just having a good system. Mostly, managing your emotions and risk. From that point forward, I started focusing more on trying to learn about markets and understanding them so I could later successfully trade them. I focused mostly on the analytical side of things and learned about how to forecast, as opposed to starting a money management company.

2. *Tell me about your technique. What makes it exclusively yours? How did you develop it?*

The approach I use is probably the most complex approach to market analysis ever devised. If for no other reason, that makes it, you might say, exclusively mine. The other critical and important factor relating to my approach is that it is based on concepts of logical deduction and what I consider to be a form of vector physics as it relates to the movement of price action. The NEoWave perspective, which is a superset of Elliott wave, takes the foundation of Elliott wave and adds a whole layer of logical concepts, concepts of market force to determine how powerful or how weak the market is at any given time. I conduct a personal training class over the telephone; I've been doing it for more than 10 years. From being forced to come up with logical reproducible explanations of exactly how I come to my conclusions about what the market is going to do on a day-to-day or week-to-week or month-to-month basis has actually allowed me to develop a logical foundation to my approach. This logical foundation can be applied to almost any market at any time, but I've particularly been focusing on the S&P, gold, and bonds (interest rates) as my primary market. Most of the foundation of my approach has been the result of following those three markets.

The development process was very long, at least five to seven years in the making, and it's evolved into a very elaborate approach to market analysis where every single trading approach is conditional based on current market circumstances in the market; I have no preference for any trading time frame. I'm not a day trader or weekly trader or long-term or short-term trader; I don't prefer options over futures or stocks over options. My approach is always dictated by market action. Let's say I am in a market environment that is expected to move a lot in a short period of time; that would be a market in which I'd probably consider buying options or buying futures. If the move is expected to last more than two weeks, my trading would be mostly futures-based; if the move is expected to take more than, say, two months, I would strictly look for stock-trading opportunities. Because NEoWave allows for so much specificity regarding market direction and magnitude, it allows me to determine what kind of trading vehicle is best suited for each particular environment. The larger and quicker the expected move is going to be, the more likely option buying is appropriate. Intermediate term movement is more appropriate for futures trading, and longer term trends are most appropriate for stock trading. NEoWave can spell these things out all specifically: what the range will be, how long it's going to stay in that range, and minimum and maximum price expectations. If it's expected the market is going to go nowhere for a while, I would want to sell option premium, which is called writing options.

3. *Tell me about your best current trading system. What makes it tick? What are the features that make it the best trading system? Why do you trade this system?*

I don't have a trading system in the normal definable sense. Instead of designing an approach that fits all market environments, my approach adapts to each market environment. I've designed a way of looking at markets that tells me the kind of environment the market is in, then I adjust trading to fit that environment. There is no way to specifically describe my trading approach unless you understand all the different market environments. There is no one concept or idea that makes it tick.

What makes it the best trading system is that it is the only one in the world that I know of, have ever known of, that adapts and evolves to all market environments, usually right after the environment gets underway.

So we're not deciding that we're in a consolidation well after it's obvious that we are in a consolidation, which usually means by the time it's obvious it's about to finish. These techniques are designed to let me know, usually within the first or second segment of a pattern, what the environment is going to be. That leaves me with anywhere between two to nine waves to take advantage of in that particular environment. If you are looking at a weekly chart and you see a nice decline and you realize, based on the surrounding evidence, that the decline is the first segment of a long sideways period, you would immediately change and adapt your trading style to fit that new environment to take advantage of nontrending conditions.

To give you an idea of what the environments are that NEoWave helps you identify, the primary environments are expanding, contracting, and neutral, and within those three categories there are subcategories. You can have expanding trending markets, expanding sideways markets; you can have neutral trending markets, neutral sideways markets; you can have contracting sideways markets, contracting trending markets. Those are the primary environments. Each requires a different approach. If your approach adapts to the environment, you are taking the best advantage of the circumstances. For example, a lot of people have a general preference for either breakout trading, trend following, or consolidation trading. Those are three primary categories most systems focus on. If anyone tries to integrate them, it diminishes the usefulness of the approach in any one of those environments. But most people do focus on one of those three approaches.

Let's say you are a breakout trader and the market happens to be in a trending environment. It doesn't really matter whether it's trending neutral, or a contracting or expanding trend; if it's a trending environment, then breakout trading will work relatively fine most of the time. You'll start to run into real serious problems, if you are a trend follower and the market goes into a neutral expanding environment, which means you're breakout trading every new high, every new low, and the market keeps reversing to make new highs and new lows on the opposite side of the range. If you don't have any idea you are in that kind of environment, all the money you may have made during a trending period will be eliminated during this expanding neutral period. It also could happen in a more trending expanding period, but the biggest damage usually occurs for trend followers in an expanding-neutral environment.

If you are a person who likes to sell strength and buy weakness, that kind of trading would do terrifically well in any kind of neutral-sideways, expanding-sideways market. But if you are a consolidation trader who attempts to pick tops and bottoms in a trending market, you are going to get stopped out over and over as the trend continues. It is critical to determine the environment the market is in. NEoWave is the only analytical technology in the world that allows you to determine future market environments almost the minute they begin (instead of after it's finished, which is typical of market analysis). By knowing the environment in advance, you can really fine-tune your strategy to extract the most profit.

4. *How long ago did you write your first trading system?*

I worked on some real simplistic and mostly mathematical approaches to market analysis about 10 years ago or more. I eventually gave up on those, realizing no single mathematical approach ever represented reality. The problem with all back tested and historically tested trading systems, according to wave theory, is that the market is ever evolving; it is never in the same place twice; therefore you can never design a mathematical, mechanical system that will work well continuously into the future. Most technical approaches try to take advantage of repetitious action, which means you are looking at the past to determine the future, and you are expecting the past to repeat in the future. NEoWave theory along with Elliott Wave takes the position markets are never in the same place twice; they're constantly evolving. With NEoWave, your trading style and techniques evolve with the market. Sometimes you may realize you are in an environment that requires following weekly charts or monthly charts, which indicates short-term trading is not appropriate and sometimes the reverse is true.

After giving up on simple mathematical formulas and realizing they didn't work, I moved into the Elliott Wave arena, which slowly evolved into NEoWave. I've never had any other technique of significance that I use to do my research and analysis and trading except NEoWave. From its Elliott Wave beginning, I added more and more features and ideas, creating a growing foundation to the original concept.

5. *Remember back to your first trading system. Can you tell us the rules?*

I can't really tell you the rules for my first trading system because I constantly searched but didn't find the right answers. The rules that make up NEoWave are so extensive, there is really no simple way to explain it.

6. *What caused you to abandon or modify that trading system the very first time?*

It stopped working. It depended on a very volatile sideways market in gold. When that volatility died off and the market started trending, the system no longer worked. It's a perfect example of a system that was designed to take advantage of consolidations; it did not know how to deal with breakouts and trending markets.

The rules were very simple. It was one of the more bizarre systems I've been exposed to. It basically was attempting to grab less profit than it risked. The system made your chances of success dramatically higher and your number of profitable trades greater than you'd get in most systems. You could easily have 80 to 90 percent profitable trades with very little effort. Commissions could eat you alive with this approach because you were having to trade virtually every day. It was basically an on-market-opening system.

7. *When you look at another person's trading system, what is the very first thing you look for to tell if it's a good or a bad system?*

If it's not dynamic and fractally based, then I think it's worthless. For example, if a system regimentizes the time frame, that means if it locks in a time frame so you have a 5-day moving average or a 20-day or a 30-day or moving average it is going to have little true long-term meaning to what's going to happen in the future. A five-day moving average may have worked fine in the past, but it has nothing to do with what may happen in the future. Anyone who creates a system based on a solidified time frame is asking for big trouble. Sometimes market patterns will last 5 or 10 days or 5 or 10 weeks, but then all of a sudden, that behavior stops and a completely different rhythm begins. Patterns might start forming on a 12-month basis all of the sudden, for example. If you are going to design an approach around moving averages, no matter what time frame you pick initially, you need to make sure you have the same kind of approach applied to all time frames. If you are going to apply a five-day moving average to a daily chart, you'd better use the same rules and concepts on a weekly, monthly, and hourly chart. As a general rule, the longer-term should overpower and overrule the shorter-term. When doing your analysis start from a long-term foundation, breaking down to the shorter term. You should never start with the short term to build up to the long term.

One other thing I think is dangerous to have in a system is a standardized, predetermined stop-placement approach. In other words, the stop placement should be determined by market conditions and volatility, whether it is trending or not, expanding or contracting, etcetera. Stop-placement should have nothing to do with any generalized statement, such as, I always put 2 percent stops or five-point stops. Any kind of specified stop-placement approach is a dangerous thing. If your stop-placement approach is locked into a specific style, then you are not going to be able to take advantage of other types of market environments. Just keep in mind that standardized stop-placement approach to all market environments will never work over the long term.

8. *What is the least important aspect of a trading system as far as you are concerned?*

I really don't think there is anything unimportant regarding markets and trading and success. I'm not real familiar with most trading systems because I don't believe in systems that standardize strategy.

9. *In your current work, are you using a mechanical approach, or is there judgment involved in your trading?*

There is definitely judgment used in my approach. It's mostly judgment based on a process of logical deductions. It's more deduction than judgment, and it's not opinion as much as logical proof of what a market should or shouldn't do. Of course, it doesn't mean I'm always right about what's going to happen, but I know exactly when I'm wrong, exactly what needs to happen to make me right, and I know this on a day-to-day basis; I'm not constantly left in the woods about how to proceed or what to think. For example, a lot of systems focus just on the timing of a market; some of them focus on just the price movement of a market. NEoWave focuses on all aspects of market action, so I always have a continuous idea of how long a move can take before something starts to go wrong; how far it needs to go, minimum and maximum, to keep things in good shape; how far it can and cannot go to maintain the proper count. The minute it starts getting off track, I prepare to move stops closer to the market or just liquidate my position.

The mechanical approach I occasionally use for market analysis is called my M.O.A.T. Index, which I use to help me trade and analyze, mostly when the markets are not predictable from a NEoWave standpoint. It's at the extremes in price that most mechanical systems break down, which is when wave theory starts working best. Therefore I tend to use wave theory when the market is approaching the end of a trend or is in the early stages of a trend. I depend on wave theory less as the market approaches the middle of a trend.

10. *Are you currently using TradeStation or System Writer? If not, what software do you use to run your trading system?*

My system is too complicated to computerize; therefore I do all the analysis in my head and by hand.

11. *Is your current trading system for sale? For lease? On a fax line? How do you provide this information to clients?*

You could say my current trading system is for sale if someone is willing to spend several years learning how to do it. It is not sold as a computerized system, and it is not sold as a system on paper. I do have my book, *Mastering Elliott Wave*, which spells out all the technical aspects of my approach. I've focused on the technical realm of market analysis and prediction. Once I started to master that, I wrote *Mastering Elliott Wave*, then I started focusing more on the trading aspects of market analysis, and I've tried to master that part of the equation. Now that I think I have both of them mastered, I'm moving into money management on a relatively big scale.

We have fax services available, so customers who don't want to learn or don't have time to learn can know what I'm thinking and recommending. We have daily and weekly fax services and daily and weekly hotline services. We also do private training courses for clients who want to understand my approach in detail.

12. *Can you share the concept behind your trading system, for example, your main entry technique, your exit if you are wrong, and your exit if you are right?*

The concept behind my approach is that it is based on a logical foundation using inductive and deductive reasoning and self-confirmation pattern limits. That's about as generalized as I can make it. There is no main entry technique, no main exit technique, nothing that can be generalized or standardized to say how I do what I do because it all depends on market environment.

13. *If you could advise system developers to do one thing when they are starting out, what would that be?*

When you are devising a system, you'd better make sure you apply it to all time frames. No matter how you design it, the minute it is designed on that particular time frame—daily, weekly, or monthly—you immediately want to apply it to all other time frames and get a panoramic view of the market using all time frames.

Another critical thing to developing a system is that it be developed using cash market information. If you don't base your systems on cash data, you have to go through all kinds of complex mathematical equations and formulas to deal with deterioration of contracts and connecting one contract to the next. Your patterns aren't as reliable; the behavior is distorted; the data is distorted. It's a very dangerous way to trade markets.

14. *Other than yourself, who do you think is the best system developer, or who do you think is the best teacher of system development?*

I don't spend any time focusing my attention on "system development" or people who trade and work with systems because I've never known anybody who has any system they've used all their life that has continuously worked. I have very low expectations for systems trading. By definition, only the worst systems will be sold to the public.

15. *If for some reason they closed every commodity in the world except one, and you were the guy in charge of deciding which one would stay open, which commodity would you choose? Why? What hours would it be open?*

I would pick the S&P because it is one of the largest futures markets and works best with wave theory.

16. *If you were to choose one commodity you could never trade again and you could never include in a trading system, which commodity would this be? Why?*

Pork bellies, because it has such a short shelf life. Wave theory is not designed to predict the behavior of consumable/agricultural products.

17. *Where do you get your ideas for your system? A chart? A pattern? Observations? Trades that you have done before? What is your favorite technique for coming up with a trading system?*

The ideas that I've gotten for my approach have all come from teaching other people how to do objective, scientific market analysis and trading. Through the process of teaching, I came up with ideas little by little that have created a complex decision tree process. The charts I use make a big difference in my ability to discover new concepts. If I didn't have a more standardized way of plotting and recording data, I wouldn't have been able to come up with so many ideas. If I still used bar charts and futures data, I would have remained in the dark ages as far as my technical knowledge is concerned.

I don't have favorite techniques for coming up with systems because I don't create systems. I just continuously add to the foundation of concepts I call NEoWave.

18. *I want you to write a trading system for me. I want you to give me all the rules. I want you to tell me what commodity, what time frame, whether it is daily bars, whatever. What your entry rule is, your exit rule with a* *profit, your exit rule with a loss. It doesn't have to be a great system. Just give me an idea of something you would look at, something you would test to see if there was any validity.*

There is no way I can quickly give you any kind of trading system that is going to have any reliable results. It may be the way that most people approach markets because they have no better alternatives, but I know from my NEoWave that I have a vastly superior approach to any mechanical trading system or technique. So I never attempt to create mechanical approaches any more. Even my M.O.A.T. Index, which is a mechanical approach I came up with about 10 years ago, has evolved and adapted over time, so it also has become a very complex approach to market analysis, far more advanced than your standard technical analysis approach to the market.

19. *What's the typical day in the life of a system developer? What time do you start? What time do you end? What is it you do all day long? How are your orders placed? How is your system run?*

I spend most of my Mondays, Wednesdays, and Fridays between about 11:00 Pacific time and 5:00 in the afternoon working with clients, teaching them how to analyze markets in a logical, scientific way, showing them how to develop trading strategies around their analysis. I start the day usually around 6:00 or 6:30 when the market opens here. I end my day anywhere between 8:00 at night to midnight, so my typical day is well past 12 hours. On Tuesdays and Thursdays, I generally spend more time writing and preparing new research.

As far as how orders are placed, I generally just go into the market when it's time. I virtually never use limit orders to get in. When it's time to get in, I just get in. I don't worry about penny-pinching and trying to squeeze every nickel or dime out of the situation. When it's time to get out, it's time to get out. I always have stops to protect my position if things do not go as expected.

The system is run all in my head. I basically just study the charts, analyze the patterns, then logically deduce what's possible and what's exploitable from the current circumstances; I figure out what the time frame is, how volatile the situation is going to be. I decide whether I want to trade in the market at all, whether it's too dangerous or not, whether I want to trade options or futures or stocks based on the time frame expected. Then I closely monitor the charts. I usually work with daily, weekly and monthly charts; I don't follow hourlies. Only when I think a trade is really approaching a critical point, will I go to a five-minute or hourly chart. I take a look at the action there and decide if it looks like things are ready to go; that helps me decide. Most of the time, I simply use daily and later time frames to make my decisions.

20. *If you could have your system run in any manner, what would be the preferable method? Would you have the person whose money is at risk run the system, or would you have a third party run the system and just arbitrarily take the trades as they are generated, regardless of consequence?*

I'd prefer it to be completely automated on computer, have it give me all the trades, maybe even give them to someone else to place the orders. I'd make money from that and still be able to run my business. That obviously would be ideal. But since the markets are constantly evolving and changing, for a computer system to work, you've got to constantly evolve and change and write the program to fit the changing environment. That becomes a process that's too time-consuming and too complicated to be worthwhile. Your mind can easily adjust and adapt to the new circumstances, but the computer system can't until you write the extra code. You could spend all your time writing code, never getting around to trading, and never having much success in the long run because you are always going to be behind the changes if you try to computerize everything.

21. *Let's pretend I don't have a single book on commodities, and I'm interested in writing systems. Other than your own work, what book would you recommend? Along these same lines, is there anything you would avoid—whether it's software, books, lectures, whatever?*

There are several books I would recommend to help a person understand markets a little bit better. One of the few that had the most profound impact on me was *Contrary Opinion*, by R. Earl Hadady. It's a very good book on the realities of futures markets: Never can everyone win; there's always got to be a loser, and the losers always have to be a greater number than the winners for the system to work in the futures market. In the stock market, that's not the case because everyone theoretically can win due to growing prosperity in a country. But the futures market is a net sum zero game, so there is always one winning contract for one losing contract, and there is a slight bias toward the losers because of commission.

The first book I read that got me involved with Elliott Wave is *The Commodities Futures Game*. I don't remember if it's a really good book on the subject, especially from a professional's perspective, but it was a good book for me as a beginner. It gives a good overview of lots of different systems and techniques. The Jessie Livermore books, *Speculator King*, and

Reminiscences of a Stock Market Operator, are both good books and are classics.

I would avoid books, for beginners especially, that try to sell a particular mechanical approach to the market. I think people need to educate themselves on the complexities of markets and the fact that the market is an evolving phenomenon. Books that deal more with philosophy and concepts of markets than specific techniques are better. I'd say focusing on trader discipline, learning to take losses, accepting that you will occasionally be wrong, and getting over your ego, books that deal with psychology—personal psychology and trading psychology—are very important like *The Disciplined Trader* by Mark Douglas. Those are the kind of books beginners should focus on. Books on mass psychology and personal psychology are some of the most important keys to becoming a successful trader.

22. *Do you think it is necessary for a software developer/real-time trader to have tick-by-tick real-time quotes? Why or why not?*

Definitely not. For most people, especially beginners, the constant access to information is a distraction. I strongly recommend that beginners not get real-time or delayed quotes. End-of-day quotes are best: Plan all your trades overnight; have everything ready to go the next morning; don't alter your scenario or alter your strategies at all during the day; be prepared to do what you planned from the previous night. One of the worst things that people do is make trading decisions during the day. I can do it now because I've been doing this for so long, but most people can't deal with the emotions. Everything should be spelled out until you get more comfortable with the markets, which for most people takes about 5 to 10 years.

23. *What kind of quotes do you have? What kind of software would you recommend? Are there any systems or software that you would definitely not recommend?*

The quotes I currently get are real-time from Signal. The end-of-day service is probably the best for most people. I have a friend who trades over a hundred million dollars in Laguna Beach, and he doesn't even have a quote system in his office.

Almost any system will work as long as you have a good disciplined trader who can take and limit losses and let profits run. But it takes a long time to learn how to do that. It is easy to say but very difficult to execute in time.

24. *How much data do you think is necessary to be tested as far as assessing a day-trade session on five-minute bars? A daily bar system? A sixty-minute system?*

I don't test my approach except in real-time, so that's a hard question for me to answer. I guess at least a year or more for a day-trading system would be a good time frame to test. But again, I think back testing is a waste of time.

25. *Why do some systems consistently perform year after year, and other systems fail or need to be continually optimized?*

I don't know of any systems that consistently perform year after year. They may work for awhile, but if you catch up with them 5 or 10 years down the road, they usually don't. So, again, I have very low confidence in any kind of mechanical system unless it's a very complex, sophisticated mechanical system, which most aren't. And if it is very complex and sophisticated, we probably don't know about it in the general public, so it's not something we have access to.

26. *How important are drawdowns in your research? How important is average trade size?*

Drawdowns are very important. It's critical to keep drawdowns as small as possible. Anything approaching 20 percent starts to get very dangerous because it's hard to recover from. You should try to keep risk at 1 percent per trade per market. The more money you have, the more it should be 1 percent; the less you have, the more it can approach 5 percent, but that should be the maximum. If you can't keep risk at 5 percent per trade, you really shouldn't be trading that market. You should trade something you can trade with less money and keep your risk parameters in line.

As far as trading size is concerned, I usually ask the broker what is the maximum number of positions I can take. I divide that by two immediately, never taking more than that. If I'm scaling in, I'll divide that into four parts and scale in 25 or 50 percent at a time, making the average trade about one-quarter and no more than one-half of the total allowed position based on margin requirements.

27. *Do you do portfolio management—linking several commodities of different systems together? Do you do pyramiding? Why or why not?*

I don't link commodities together and different systems together. I will pyramid under certain circumstances. You can only pyramid if you are in a trending market as the market is moving in your favor, and you are in profit on your other positions. Pyramiding is fine as long as you are in a powerful trending market and the evidence is increasing that everything is going correctly with your analysis. But it's obviously a very dangerous game if you are not into trend, so you need to know in advance whether you really are trending and whether buying on new highs or selling on new lows is going to work out.

28. *Let's get a little morbid. You've died. You've left a sealed letter to your heirs. It contains the secret of your fortune. It's the secret to allow them to continue the lifestyle to which they have been accustomed. What one sentence is in the letter?*

I'd say hard work. That's the only thing that can possibly allow a person to make a good living as far as I'm concerned. Hard work and good ideas.

29. *Without giving the secret of life, how would you write an imitation of your system in two lines or less in Trade Station language? For example, I have an S&P system called Buy Monday. "Monday you buy it, put in a $1,400 stop, get out on the close." That's how you write that.*

It would be absolutely impossible.

30. *Give us an example of some of your work put in English-type language for a system.*

Well, I would want the system to analyze the structure of the market, which is what wave theory is all about, analyzing the speed of a move. Let's say that a market is near a top or a bottom and you are waiting to see if a new trend starts. The first thing I would want to analyze is the quickness with which the new trend gets underway. Unless the market kicks off a new trend powerfully, it's not going to be the start of a new, powerful, tradable trend. You want to carefully observe price action to try to find that kind of event. Once you've found it, you want to make sure that the move up or down is quicker and larger than any previous move up or down in the same direction during the prior trend to indicate that it really is the start of a new trend. You want it to observe the length of the first move compared to the length of the second when you usually want the second one to be larger; otherwise, you're not in a very powerful trend. You want the retracement of the first move up or down to be less than 61 percent of the first move. You want to make sure that the correction following the first one is not overlapping the first correction. These are all parts of wave theory and what defines a good real trend. There is a lot to it. It would be very complicated to explain all the details, but that gives you some idea of how I would begin designing a computerized system.

Jeff Roy

INTRODUCTION

Jeff Roy has a small consulting company called *MarketSolve* in Chicago. He has been trading and providing trading solutions since 1991. His academic background consists of math, statistics, and economics, which is why technical approaches to the markets have always appealed to him He began writing indicators and systems while in college and continues to do so today. He began his career at Pardo Group Limited, a trading research company in the Chicago area. He is currently consulting for Bressert Investment Group.

1. *Tell me about yourself. If someone were to say, "Tell me about Jeff Roy," what would you want them to know? Give me a brief biography of you before you got into commodities, and a brief biography of what you have done since you got into commodities.*

Before futures trading, I was mainly interested in trading securities. I traded my first stock when I was 16 and knew that financial analysis was my future. I graduated high school with honors and attended Loyola University Chicago. My studies were focused in the fields of economics, mathematics and statistics. Extra-curricular academic pursuits were population modeling and demographic research. While at Loyola, I was lucky enough to have a most inspirational advisor, Dr. David Mirza. He suggested I pursue quantitative analysis within the economics department. I soon found myself in Dr. Mirza's "Introduction to Futures Trading" course where I was able to win our mock-trading contest with the help of trending currency markets and good risk management.

With the help of Dr. Mirza, I took a position at Pardo Group Limited, a trading consulting firm in Northfield, Illinois. I worked under Robert Pardo conducting computerized research on mechanical futures trading systems. I learned a great deal about technical analysis and trading system development. I found that my background in objective and disciplined thinking lent itself to futures trading.

I began trading futures from my dorm room in my junior year of college. I used mechanical systems to trade the currencies, bonds, coffee, cotton, and soybeans. I did very well in the beginning, more than 350 percent return on a $15,000 account in three months and then spent the next five months giving it back. I realized that the systems that I was using had little or no shelf-life, so I worked on ways to develop more robust systems. I found there are a number of ways to do this, and the systems that resulted were very different in character. These robust systems were more generalized and tended to be more conservative, yet more consistent, in their profitability. That was, and still is, a trade-off that I am willing to make.

Since developing methods for robust system design, I have consulted for institutions and individual traders on system development and testing. Joe Krutsinger and I have worked on a number of research and educational projects together, including teaching system development to a private classroom of institutional traders. I have recently started a company called MarketSolve that will focus on trading system sales, leasing, and consulting.

2. *Tell me about your technique. What makes it exclusively yours? How did you develop it?*

I have several techniques, but I think that I have benefited most by developing creative ways to use very basic market measurements. My newest and best system is an S&P day-trader called *Pit Boss* that uses fairly common measurements for intraday support and resistance. The way I actually use the levels is where the real creativity and profitability come in.

My ideas most often begin with chart analysis. I watch the markets very closely and get a feel for very general action/reaction relationships that seem to occur with consistency. I then program the actions and try to develop methods for profiting from the reactions. Once I feel that I have my new observed relationship programmed, I then go back and look at its historical validity. If the performance falls apart, I don't have a generalized system; i.e., the system is in tune with the current market character (on which it was developed) and not with the general market character. This leads me into the answer to the next question.

3. *Tell me about your best current trading system. What makes it tick? What are the features that make it the best trading system? Why do you trade this system?*

Currently, my best trading system is *Pit Boss*, my S&P day-trader. As I mentioned earlier, it trades off of intraday support and resistance using a creative method for confirming entries. The features that make it my best trading system are the same things I was describing in the previous answer. Let me take you step-by-step through my development of *Pit Boss*.

First, I developed the support and resistance levels. These levels have been around for a long time and are simply a function of the previous day's price action. I plotted these levels on my TradeStation S&P charts and watched them real-time for about six months. By this time, I was convinced that the levels were not enough by themselves but were very useful.

Second, I worked out a plan for how to trade support and resistance since I had now defined them. I wrote the TradeStation code to sell every violation of support and buy any subsequent violation of the support, which would then be resistance. I coded it to buy any violation of resistance and sell any subsequent violation of the new support. Once I worked any bugs out of the code and tested it on 15-minute bars, I was excited. The system broke even, right out of the bag! My attention was first drawn by the extremely high frequency of trading. Upon examining the charts, I found that the market tended to oscillate around these support/resistance levels enough that a 15-minute time frame was capturing more noise than meaningful market activity. I made the bars 45 minutes long, and then I was really having a good day. The system made good money and had a reasonable drawdown. My continuing problem, however, was that there were too many trades in relation to the profit the system was generating, or the average trade was too small.

The last thing I did was to realize that many of the trades were very small profits and scratch trades. This led me to the conclusion that, each day, only one or two support/resistance were really important where, originally, I was trying to trade every violation of any of four-five levels. To isolate the more important violations, I developed a pre-buy qualifier and a pre-sell qualifier, which would determine if and how I was to trade each level. Well, I'm sure you've guessed that there was going to be a happy ending. The system was very profitable, the drawdown was less than $5,000, and the average trade was large. The only problem now was that I had only been looking at the September 1995 S&P 500 contract. The real test was to look at the system historically and forward. What I found was something that I had only seen a handful of times in my career. Right out of the bag with no changes, the system performed even better from 1990-93, about the same from 1994 through the third quarter of 1995, and it has worked best on the forward data from the end of 1995 through February 1996.

The features that make *Pit Boss* my best system center around how it was developed. First, the system is simple and has only two main parts: the support/resistance levels and the pre-buy and pre-sell condition. Second, the system is not based on a number of previous bars that need to be optimized like three, five, seven or nine days. The support/resistance levels are based on only the previous day's price data so there is no optimization needed and, therefore, no risk of curve-fitted results. Lastly, the system really just fell into my lap. That is, the elements of the system are simple, and to get good results, I did not have to make a long series of changes and enhancements to the system, which also increase the risk of curve-fitted results. I trade *Pit Boss* because, due to the way it was developed, I know that it has a high probability of continued success in a market that has both good liquidity and an extremely high profit potential.

4. *How long ago did you write your first trading system?*

During my third year at Loyola University, I wrote my first system. I had always been intrigued by oscillators probably because the way they are plotted at the bottom of a chart, under the price, makes them look more like a leading indicator than most of them really are. My first system was on the Swiss Franc and used a detrending oscillator, which for me was simply the difference between price and a particular moving average. Plotted as an oscillator, the value of the detrend indicator oscillated above and below zero.

5. *Remember back to your first trading system. Can you tell us the rules?*

If the 37-day DeTrend oscillator is above 1.00 (in the Swiss Franc), then I buy. If it is below -1.00, then I sell. I used a $1,200 stop-loss, and after the position reached a profit of $1,600, I would only risk 75 percent of the maximum profit achieved during the position. Since any trailing stop has the potential to pull you out of a winning position too early, I developed a re-entry technique. The re-entry was based on the highest high during a long position and the lowest low during a short position. If I was trailed-out of a long position, I would place a buy stop at the highest high achieved during the position. The inverse was true for a sell.

6. *What caused you to abandon or modify that trading system the very first time?*

I haven't abandoned the system and still track it for a long-term approach. The system has good and bad points. One of the bad things about it is that it relies on a moving average, which relies on a specific number of days. We all know that different periods work better at different times. The good thing was that about half of all the periods I tested were profitable and about 25 percent were very good.

7. *When you look at another person's trading system, what is the very first thing you look for to tell if it's a good or a bad system?*

When I look at any system, I first determine whether the system is feasible to trade real-time. If a system relies on market orders, slippage needs to be calculated accordingly. If the system uses limit orders, you have to be ready for those disappointing phone calls from the floor where you hear that your best entry point in weeks was "unable." If the system uses 1-minute bars, you have to be prepared to have different results on different data feeds or even on the same data feed in different locations. If the system satisfies that criteria, then at least you can rely on the historical performance.

The other important thing for me is how the system was developed. Is there a theoretical basis for the system logic? Was the system developed by curve-fitting a bunch of rules and parameters? Does the system have logic for both trending and choppy markets, or does it need a complementary system to go with it?

8. *What is the least important aspect of a trading system as far as you are concerned?*

The least important aspect of a system for me is accuracy, or percentage of winners. If you manage risk well and have a reasonably sound method for entering, you can win 30 percent of the time and still net a lot of money. Systems that have a very high accuracy tend to set small profit objectives and take small wins, while risking a relatively large amount. While the accuracy is high, one loss will wipe out several wins. Since any method can go through a very bad stretch, I would rather be managing risk more tightly and relying on larger wins than to risk a lot on each trade and lose several trades in a short time.

9. *In your current work, are you using a mechanical approach or is there judgment involved in your trading?*

All of my current work is based on mechanical approaches. I have used discretionary trading methods before and have not met with the consistent, reliable success that systematic approaches are capable of. With systematic methods, you have the luxury of being able to test your strategies over as many market conditions as are contained in the historical data. When done properly, this allows you to define your risk as well as your expected gain, which allows you to develop a trading plan. With a trading plan, you can have confidence in your overall trading success and not micromanage each trade. With a plan, you are also able to judge whether your trading plan can be or needs to be enhanced, and that is the only place where judgment is involved in my trading.

The judgment is whether or not a system can or should be enhanced. When trading a system, you inevitably run into situations where you feel the system should have done something that it didn't, or did something that you feel it shouldn't have. However, if you simply change the system each time this happens, the result is curve-fitting to the current data. This reduces the chances of the system succeeding in the future. The correct way to judge whether to make a change to a system is to be very clear about the specific purpose of the system and decide whether the proposed change contributes to the system's goals or acts as an extension of them. Then the final judgment is whether the change enhances the system constantly over time, or merely enhances the current period (the development period) and destabilizes the rest of the performance.

10. *Are you currently using TradeStation or System Writer? If not, what software do you use to run your trading system?*

I currently use TradeStation to both test strategies and trade them real-time. I think it is the most complete and most flexible package out there. My programming experience helped me to get up to speed with TradeStation programming. Since then, I have been able to program and test hundreds of ideas.

11. *Is your current trading system for sale? For lease? On a fax line? How do you provide this information to clients?*

My current systems are for sale and lease. I provide the TradeStation program for my systems to purchasers of them. My systems are also available on a lease basis through Robbins Trading Company.

12. *Can you share the concept behind your trading system, for example, your main entry technique, your exit if you are wrong, and your exit if you are right?*

The concept behind *Pit Boss* is intraday support and resistance. My entries first require a pre-buy or pre-sell condition to be established by intraday price activity. If we are in a buy mode, we buy violations of resistance and tests of support. Inversely, if we are in a sell mode, we sell violations of support and tests of resistance. Once we are in the market, we set a stop large enough to withstand volatility around our entry point. In the S&P, this is usually $1,200 to $1,500. After we have been in the position for a period of time, we move the stop loss to $700 to $1,000. Throughout the position after the initial bar of entry, we use a next bar trail based on the maximum profit in the trade so far minus $900 to $1,200. *Pit Boss* is a day-trader so it exits profitable trades either on the trailing stop or on the close of the day.

13. *If you could advise system developers to do one thing when they are starting out, what would that be?*

I would advise new system developers to study and trade successful systems to arrive at a benchmark for their own research as well as an understanding of the transition from development to real-time trading. This will usually save a new developer from making the same costly mistakes that others have already made. I would advise new developers to have a clearly defined purpose, or set of goals, for their system. Many developers try to catch every swing in the market. Not only do I consider this impossible, but systems developed like this usually end up to be loose collections of ideas all trying to work together to accomplish different goals. Under those circumstances, it is not clear which element(s) of the system are really contributing to the success of the trading system.

14. *Other than yourself, who do you think is the best system developer, or who do you think is the best teacher of system development?*

I would have to say, honestly, that Joe Krutsinger has been my biggest influence over the years. We have worked closely on a number of projects, and Joe's ideas are great. I find his systems so valuable for the same reasons I mentioned earlier. They are usually simple ideas with a theoretical basis and not a myriad of unrelated parameters mixed and matched until profitable. I think that systems like these have the highest chance of success and the longest shelf-life.

15. *When you devise a trading system, what time frame do you use most? For example, do you use daily bars, weekly bars, 1-minute bars, 10-minute bars, or 60-minute bars?*

It has been my experience that the time frame used for a system should be directly in line with the purpose of the system. If your system is trying to take small pieces out of the market like $500 in the S&P, you should probably be looking at 1-minute or smaller bars. If you are trying to trade the major trend in the yen for large moves, you should be looking at daily, weekly, or even monthly intervals.

I think that some bar sizes contain more and different information than others. For instance, I find that a weekly or monthly bar is more useful than a two-and-one-half-week bar. By the same token, a 15-minute bar will capture a lot more market "noise" than a 45-minute bar. That is, essentially, why *Pit Boss* uses 45-minute bars. Also, because I feel that the trading session should be evenly divided by the intraday bar you use, I don't like to use 30-minute and 60-minute bars in the S&P as much as I like to use 15-minute and 45-minute bars. With 30 and 60-minute bars, all the bars don't contain the same amount of information; that is, the last 30-minute bar really only contains 15 minutes and the last 60-minute bar really only contains 45 minutes of market activity.

16. *If for some reason they closed every commodity in the world except one, and you were the guy in charge of deciding which one would stay open, which commodity would you choose? Why? What hours would it be open?*

The market to keep would have to be the S&P. I like the S&P best because it is liquid enough to trade effectively, and the average daily movement is much larger dollarwise than other markets. The stagnation periods in the S&P are short and infrequent.

17. *If you were to choose one commodity you could never trade again and you could never include in a trading system, which commodity would this be? Why?*

I don't have much use for cocoa, but I feel that one of the most important keys to trading success is diversification among markets and strategies. For that reason, I would keep the rest of the markets to diversify my portfolio.

18. *Where do you get your ideas for your system? A chart? A pattern? Observations? Trades that you have done before? What is your favorite technique for coming up with a trading system?*

At the beginning, I touched on how my trading systems usually start as action/reaction relationships observed on a chart. My favorite technique, then, is to observe a particular price reaction and be able to link it to a well-defined previous action. Usually, if it draws my attention, it is because I have seen it before; therefore, it is worth testing. I write a TradeStation program that identifies the action and trades the reaction, and then I test it.

19. *I want you to write a trading system for me. I want you to give me all the rules. I want you to tell me what commodity, what time frame, whether it is daily bars, whatever. What your entry rule is, your exit rule with a profit, your exit rule with a loss. It doesn't have to be a great system. Just give me an idea of something you would look at, something you would test to see if there was any validity.*

Let's go through the rules for my first system, using the detrend indicator. First, we calculate the indicator. DeTrend is equal to the close minus the (37 day) moving average. The value oscillates above and below zero. When the value goes above 1.00 (for the Swiss Franc), we buy the next day's open. We set a $1,200 stop-loss and after we make $1,600, we only risk 75 percent of the maximum equity achieved. If we get out of the long trade and go flat, we set a buy stop at the highest high achieved during the life of the long position. We do the inverse for sells.

20. *What's the typical day in the life of a system developer? What time do you start? What time do you end? What is it you do all day long? How are your orders placed? How is your system run?*

I'd like to be able to monitor all the markets all the time that they are trading. I would get up at 7:00 CST. Unfortunately, I do not have the luxury of being able to always be in front of the TradeStation. I have most of my systems traded by Robbins Trading Company in their *System Assist* program. With them monitoring every system, every trade, I don't have to worry about missing anything and can spend most of my day doing research. I do, however, monitor and chart the intraday market activity both real-time and with historical data. This is where I have made the market observations that have led to the development of my best systems.

21. *If you could have your system run in any manner, what would be the preferable method? Would you have the person whose money is at risk run the system, or would you have a third party run the system and just arbitrarily take the trades as they are generated, regardless of consequence?*

As I mentioned, I prefer to have Robbins Trading Company trade my systems. They take every trade arbitrarily and execute them properly. Sometimes my gut says that a trade that the system dictates is not the right thing to do. I have learned over the years that if you're going to trade a system, you *trade* the system. That is, if you begin to take some trades and not others you will change the whole risk/reward outlook of the system. With Robbins trading the system, I don't have to worry about this issue at all.

22. *Let's pretend I don't have a single book on commodities, and I'm interested in writing systems. Other than your own work, what book would you recommend? Along these same lines, is there anything you would avoid—whether it's software, books, lectures, whatever?*

Many books tell you about good system ideas but don't tell you how to use them systematically. Some books show you system code but don't explain how the idea came about or why it works. One book that does both and does them very well in a concise, down-to-earth manner is Joe Krutsinger's *The Trading System Toolkit.* Joe's book was very inspirational to me, and I think it is a good, straight to the point way for someone to begin learning trading systems. Joe's ideas have the benefits of both simplicity and theoretical backing. I also have studied material from Larry Williams' seminars, and I found that his ideas were some of the best and most robust that I have studied.

One the other hand, I would encourage beginning traders to apply what they are learning as they learn it. When studying the material, it becomes more and more abstract the deeper you get into it. You need to see and experience how good systems behave to make the learning material concrete. You need to apply the methods you are learning or have someone test/monitor them for you.

23. *Do you think it is necessary for a software developer/real-time trader to have tick-by-tick real-time quotes? Why or why not?*

This goes back to my discussion of time-frame. If a trader is going to look at an intermediate term or long term trading strategy with reasonable sized stops, then daily data is adequate. If the strategy is shorter term, the trader should consult intraday data. The trick with intraday data is that you must have a very clear idea of the purpose of the system. This is important because the size of the bars you use need to reflect the price activity that you are trying to capture and not the "noise" that clouds the real picture. With intraday data, you also must keep in mind that the smaller the size of the bars, the higher the chance that your bars will not be formed exactly as the same bars on a different data feed or even on a different computer with the same data feed.

24. *What kind of quotes do you have? What kind of software would you recommend? Are there any systems or software that you would definitely not recommend?*

I would definitely recommend TradeStation for the serious real-time trader/system developer. I would say that Super Charts does a great job for someone who wants to do any level of charting and simple system testing. I use at least two different data feeds and have experience with several. The data feed that you choose is very important, and they come in several flavors. Some feeds are faster and some are slower but more accurate. Some feeds are higher priced, and some are better values, and with each fee, there is usually a choice of reception type. I would be happy to discuss, over the phone, any data feed issue as well as the products out there that have shown to be ineffective.

25. *How much data do you think is necessary to be tested as far as assessing a day-trade session on five-minute bars? A daily bar system? A 60-minute system?*

I look to my statistical background when deciding whether I have tested a system over enough data. I think that the time frame of the data is not as important as the number of times the logic was tested. That is, number of trades determines the validity of the test. The number of trades should be sufficiently high in relation to the number of rules in the system. In statistical modeling, the validity depends on the number of cases in the study in relation to the number of variables in the equation that is supposed to *model* the phenomena. In trading system development, the number of cases is the number of trades, the number of variables in the equation is the number of rules in the system, and the phenomena we are all trying to develop a model for is price action. For example, if a system tested on any time frame,

5-minute or weekly bars, and the system has 20 rules for trading and only four trades in the test period, the test is not a valid one in my book.

If a system can take several stabs at beating the market and consistently make money all the time, then you really have something. Even the best system will go through periods where the market is not offering much opportunity. The important thing is that the system keeps on chugging and takes the opportunity that is in line with its purpose when the opportunity exists. You want a system that isolates a market characteristic that is persistent, and then your drawdowns tend to be smaller and shorter in duration.

26. *Why do some systems consistently perform year after year, and other systems fail or need to be continually optimized?*

I started on this point at the end of the previous answer. If a system isolates a very changing characteristic in the market, then the system needs to be changing or continually optimized. A system that isolates a very persistent and consistent market characteristic will tend to have very persistent and consistent success without the need for optimization. As I mentioned earlier, the system needs to be developed soundly and not curve-fit in order to have a long, static shelf life.

27. *How important are drawdowns in your research? How important is average trade size?*

Drawdowns are all important in my research and should be an important consideration in anyone's research. Drawdowns do not, necessarily, determine whether a system is good or not. They do, however, help to determine the size of the account needed to begin trading the system. That is to say drawdowns are more important in determining if the system is right for the trader who will potentially use it. I have seen great systems go untraded because the drawdowns are too much for a particular size account or for a particular trader's stomach, but it doesn't change the fact that it is a good system.

Average trade size is to be considered when trying to determine if the system is feasible from an operational standpoint. Average trade size helps to determine whether the system will be able to overcome commissions and withstand some slippage.

28. *Do you do portfolio management—linking several commodities of different systems together? Do you do pyramiding? Why or why not?*

I do portfolio management always. When deciding on which combinations of markets and systems to trade in an account, it is very important to select markets and ideas that complement each other. If all the components drawdown together, you are not getting any reduced risk by trading them together. A good portfolio will have a drawdown that is 70 percent or less of the sum total of the components' drawdowns. That means that you are achieving reduced risk through trading the components together. A good piece of software that I use for testing portfolio combinations is *Portana*.

There are many more ways to pyramid unsuccessfully than successfully. I don't tend to pyramid aggressively, but have more strict criteria for adding contracts. Once contracts are added, I have proportionally loose criteria for scaling back. A good system can benefit from a sound method for pyramiding, but even the best system can be hurt by bad pyramiding methods. When given the choice, I would almost always add a different market to my trading than add another contract to one market.

29. *Let's get a little morbid. You've died. You've left a sealed letter to your heirs. It contains the secret of your fortune. It's the secret to allow them to continue the lifestyle to which they have been accustomed. What one sentence is in the letter?*

Assuming that they want to pursue systematic trading with the same zest that I do, I would tell them to buy a good system or develop a good system and stick to it. I find that the number one reason that someone does not succeed with a system is for lack of follow through in trading the system. When you learn of the risk parameters of a system, namely drawdown, and decide to trade the system, you must *actually* be prepared for that drawdown. Many people will see a small fraction of the maximum drawdown, and no matter what they committed to at the outset, they abandon the system. Drawdowns occur throughout the life of any system, and if we abandon a good system at any point during a drawdown, we never realize the new highs in equity that follow the drawdown.

30. *Without giving the secret of life, how would you write an imitation of your system in two lines or less in TradeStation language? For example, I have an S&P system called Buy Monday. "Monday you buy it, put in a $1,400 stop, get out on the close." That's how you write that.*

I will show a small component of a system that has good potential. In the S&P, we could use yesterday's low and high as today's support and resistance. On 45-minute bars using a function called DailyLow, you would let the market trade for one bar and write:

If Open[0]> DailyLow(1) and Low[0]<= DailyLow(1) + 1.00 and Low[0]>= DailyLow(1) - 1.00 then Buy at Open[0] stop;

You would need to build in some reasonable stop like $1,000 or perhaps a reversal on a new low for the day.

31. *Give an example of some of your work and put it in English-type language for a system.*

To describe the previous code in English, I would say that if the market opens above yesterday's low and trades within a reasonable range around it, I would consider it potential support and place a buy stop at a reasonable distance above the low or, in this case, at a key pivot point like today's open. If we then got long, I would use a reasonable stop-loss like $1,000 and possibly a reversal at a new low for the day, which would turn our previous idea of support into resistance.

INTERVIEW 11

Richard Saidenberg

INTRODUCTION

Richard Saidenberg is a commodities trading advisor and an independent futures trader. He has fifteen years experience trading his own account. Initially, Rick traded stocks (from the long side only), then moved to stock index options before graduating to futures. Now he concentrates entirely on the S&P Index. Rick created R-Breaker and R-Levels, two systems for day trading the S&P futures contract. Both systems have shown excellent performance since their release in 1993.

After receiving a B.A. degree in Economics from the University of Michigan, Rick worked on the floor of the American Stock Exchange as a specialist clerk and an arbitrage clerk in the Major Market index options pit. Rick got his first exposure to mechanical systems trading there. For several years, he diligently kept track of his trading systems with a notebook and a calculator. To speed up the research and development process, Rick became an accomplished computer programmer. For the past three years, Rick has provided custom programming of indicators and trading systems to users of TradeStation and SuperCharts (technical analysis software packages from Omega Research Inc.) In addition, Rick develops and trades mechanical systems from his office at home. In my opinion, Rick is one of the best TradeStation developers in the country.

1. *Tell me about yourself. If someone were to say, "Tell me about Rick Saidenberg," what would you want them to know? Give me a brief biog-*

raphy of you before you got into commodities, and a brief biography of what you have done since you got into commodities.

I've been trading since I was in college, starting in 1981. Basically, I started trading stocks to the long side only. I used the Value Line Investment Survey which ranks most stocks on a scale of one to five for two categories, timeliness and safety. I picked stocks that were ranked one or two in both categories. I got lucky. There was a strong bull market for stocks right through my college graduation in 1986. I made quite a bit of money. Since then I've been bitten by the trading bug, and I've never wanted to do anything else.

Right out of college, I went to work on the American Stock Exchange floor. I was a clerk in the XMI (Major Market Index) options pit. I was working with the options specialists. One of the jobs I had there was called the wheel. I kept track of the positions in the wheel account. The wheel account was only short options, both puts and calls. The wheel stayed delta neutral, so it had no market risk. That taught me that the way to make money in options was to be net short, earn the time premium, and take no risk relative to the market movement in the underlying index; although as soon as the market moves, you have to scramble to adjust your position in order to remain delta neutral. Being delta neutral means you have no risk from market movement—net short both puts and calls enables you to earn the time premium.

I worked on the floor for about a year, and then I left to trade my own account. I set up real-time quotes on a PC with MasterChartist software. I was using space in my brother's computer consulting office, and I helped with his business as I began trading S&P futures for my own account. I really like trading futures better than other trading instruments, like options or stocks, because trading futures gives much cleaner and cheaper execution.

I started reading Gerald Appel's newsletter, *Systems and Forecasts*. I also read Appel's Scientific Investment Systems Research Group (SYSRG) reports. Appel's work gave me my first exposure to trading systems. In 1987, I bought Time Trend II, a system that Mr. Appel was selling (now it is Time Trend III). At the time, it was $2,000. I still use that system. I think it was a great deal. My systems trading went well, but my discretionary trading, using conventional technical analysis, went poorly. So, I became a systems trader. In any case, in 1992, I got TradeStation (a charting and system testing software package from Omega Research Inc.). Since I was already following mechanical trading systems, I quickly became very good at programming in Easy Language (TradeStation's built-in programming language) so I could test and track my own trading ideas.

As other traders learned of my TradeStation programming expertise, I found that my skills were in demand. That's how I began consulting for TradeStation users—programming custom systems and indicators and helping traders develop and test their own systems. Since then, I've been trading my own account, selling R-Breaker and R-Levels S&P systems, and selling code packages for TradeStation and SuperCharts users. In April 1995, I started working with SoundView Advisors. Now, I am the head trader for the SoundView Advisors Managed Futures Account Program.

2. *Tell me about your technique. What makes it exclusively yours? How did you develop it?*

My technique for S&P day trading is 100 percent mechanical. I developed my technique by looking through S&P Futures price history and making guesses for concepts which might work, then programming a concept and testing it to see whether or not it works. Is anything that I've done exclusively mine? Well, I've learned from studying books and going to seminars. I'm not a creator of ideas, but I am a great synthesizer of ideas. So I synthesize ideas I've learned from others, and that's how I make something exclusively mine.

Developing a system for me is like taking a stab in the dark. I try things. When it seems like it's going to work, I go with it. I try to be careful and honest in my testing, so I'm not deceiving myself in creating a system that's just worked in the past and won't work in the future.

3. *Tell me about your best current trading system. What makes it tick? What are the features that make it the best trading system? Why do you trade this system?*

The current system that I sell, R-Breaker, is my best system in terms of the total net profit that it is able to generate. It's an S&P day trading system that trades frequently and takes advantage of the dynamic intraday range that the S&P Futures shows. Due to the dynamic range, the S&P offers day trading opportunity. Other futures contracts don't show the same intraday range that the S&P does. R-Breaker uses stop orders for entry and stop orders or market on a close for exit.

R-Breaker has three types of entries. The first is the breakout component: Place a buy stop in new high territory to go long, and place a sell stop in new low territory to go short. The second is the reaction component: After the market moves into new low territory, place a buy stop inside today's range to go long as the market moves back up; after the market moves into new high territory, place a sell stop inside today's range to go short as the market reacts and heads back down. The third is the reversal component: After losing money on the first trade of the day, stop and reverse the position. The reaction component is pretty unusual because it takes trades by placing stops that are inside today's range. Most systems either use stop orders outside the day's range for breakout trades, or use limit orders or indicator rules for reaction trades. My technique for generating reaction trade stop levels that are inside today's range is something that is unique about my system.

Why do I use R-Breaker and also the other systems that I trade? I trade them because I've proven that they work in historical testing, and in real-time testing. Frankly, I'm not a great reader of what's going on in the market at the time, but I am an excellent researcher, and I know how to accurately track a system and attempt to make my actual account perform just like the system's hypothetical performance. If my system's hypothetical performance is profitable, my account will be profitable.

4. *How long ago did you write your first trading system?*

That's hard to remember, but I would say probably in 1988, which is eight years ago. I wrote a system for the S&P futures that used the Relative Strength Index (RSI) on half-hour bars. You could use this system on any time frame, but I was tracking it carefully on half-hour bars.

5. *Remember back to your first trading system. Can you tell us the rules?*

The rules are as follows: Use a nine-bar RSI on 30-minute bars. The RSI has to go below 30 (the oversold level) and make a bottom. When it goes below 30 and makes a bottom and comes back above 30, I store the lowest level that the RSI got to. Then I need a successive bottom in the RSI that has to occur within 45 bars of the first bottom, and the second bottom in the RSI must be between zero and 10 RSI points above the first bottom. It doesn't matter whether the prices are below or above the first bottom in prices that correlate to the first bottom in the RSI as long as you have a rising double bottom in the RSI and the second RSI bottom is within 10 RSI units of the first bottom, but not below the first bottom. After the second bottom is in place, I wait for one bar where the RSI turns up, and then I go long. I also have a fail-safe buy rule to handle a rising market when the double bottom pattern does not materialize. I find the highest RSI value for the last 45 bars. If this RSI value is less than 70 (the overbought level), then I buy an RSI upcross of 70. If this RSI value is equal to or greater than 70, then I buy when the RSI makes a higher high. This system is "always in" the market, long or short, but never flat. The rules for going short are an exact mirror image of the rules for going long. It is possible for this system to have multiple buys or sells in succession. Often the system would buy, and then buy again at a lower level, and then buy again at a lower level. But in my trading, I was always in one contract, long or short, including holding overnight. Following my half-hour system worked pretty well. I made good money on it. I've programmed my first system in TradeStation and still track it.

6. *What caused you to abandon or modify that trading system the very first time?*

When I finally got TradeStation, I programmed the 30-minute RSI system. It was my first difficult programming task. The code is six or seven pages long. It is capable of handling complex double bottom and top patterns. For example, if RSI makes one bottom at 10, then a second bottom at 28, and then a third bottom at 12, as long as the bottom at 12 is within 45 bars of the first bottom at 10, it would still allow a buy even though there is an intervening bottom. When I finally was able to computer backtest this system over my six years of historical data, I did see drawdowns that were near $45,000. Even though the system was a reasonable system, making about $150,000 on the six-year period, the drawdowns were too high to take. So, it started me on the search of systems that were less risky in terms of the amount of drawdown they would incur.

7. *When you look at another person's trading system, what is the very first thing you look for to tell if it's a good or bad system?*

The first thing I look for is the frequency of trades. Most often, people want to trade the one-minute or the five-minute charts entering and exiting several times each day. These systems just trade too often and can't possibly make enough on an average trade basis to justify offsetting commission and slippage costs.

The second thing is to see if the system has some sort of original or interesting idea.

Good systems generally use stop orders for entry, trading breakout style. So, systems that don't use stops for entry are probably not going to be too good.

If a system has a large drawdown, I don't necessarily say that it's a bad system. I like to compare the system's maximum drawdown to the system's average yearly profit. It's very unusual for a system to have a maximum drawdown, which is less than the average yearly profit.

8. *What is the least important aspect of a trading system as far as you are concerned?*

Percentage of winning trades is not too important because a system that only has 30 percent winners still could be a profitable system if the winners are much larger than the losers. I prefer profit factor (net gain divided by net loss) rather than percentage of winning trades to determine whether or not the system is going to be a winning system.

9. *In your current work, are you using a mechanical approach, or is there judgment involved in your trading?*

On my day-to-day trading, I use a 100-percent mechanical approach. I follow my systems totally to the letter. I try to make sure that my actual account performs as closely as possible to the hypothetical performance for the systems that I use to trade my actual account. I want my real performance to match my hypothetical performance. That's my goal. The judgment involved comes once every year. This is when I set my plan for the next year. It's a very difficult thing to do, to set a plan and then follow it strictly for an entire year. I do the best I can in following my plan. My plan includes threshold levels for when I increase my position size as well as cutoff levels and fail-safe levels for when to abandon a particular system. Also, my plan involves trading multiple systems. I follow each system independently as if I were a different person trading each system.

10. *Are you currently using TradeStation or System Writer? If not, what software do you use to run your trading system?*

I use TradeStation. I think TradeStation is just grand. I've gotten totally adept at making it do just about whatever I want. I really have a love affair with it. It's just great.

11. *Is your current trading system for sale? For lease? On a fax line? How do you provide this information to clients?*

Frankly, I'm not interested in holding the hands of individual clients; so my system, R-Breaker, is for sale. I sell it as a manual, and I include the TradeStation code. I require the purchasers to sign an agreement that says they will not reveal the rules to anyone else, they will not copy the manual, and they will not trade it for somebody else's account. For R-Breaker, I charge $3,000. I also have another system, R-Levels, which is a component of R-Breaker. R-Levels sells for $2,000. When you purchase R-Breaker, you get both R-Levels and R-Breaker.

12. *Can you share the concept behind your trading system, for example, your main entry technique, your exit if you are wrong, and your exit if you are right?*

There are two parts to R-Breaker. First, there is the breakout, which involves placing stops in new high and new low territory. Second, there is the reaction: To go short, I wait for the market to go up and then I place a sell stop inside the day's range; to go long, I wait for the market to go down and then I place a buy stop inside the day's range. If I'm wrong, I have a $1,000 money management stop. The exit stop for the first trade of the day is a stop and reverse. The stop and reverse is my second trade, and it also has a $1,000 money management stop. If the market moves in my direction, I exit MOC (market on close). In R-Breaker, I also have the late exit, where at 3:30 P.M. Eastern time, the stop moves closer to the market. The best trades are always exited MOC.

13. *If you could advise system developers to do one thing when they are starting out, what would that be?*

I would advise them to start out with other people's ideas that they think are good and try to adapt the ideas to make them their own. I would also advise against curve fitting, neural networks, expensive black boxes, and various types of market advisories where you don't know the entire trading rules. The most important thing is to know the strategy you are trading, and how it is put together. Otherwise, you won't have confidence in your strategy, and you won't be able to trade it for yourself.

14. *Other than yourself, who do you think is the best system developer, or who do you think is the best teacher of system development?*

I think Gerald Appel's books and newsletter, *Systems and Forecasts,* are just great. Also, he has written a whole series of reports called the *Scientific Investment System Research Group Reports* where he talks about systems and trading methods. His approach of looking at the markets is simple and sound. I strongly recommend to anybody who is not aware of Mr. Appel to look him up and check out his newsletter, *Systems and Forecasts*, and check out the things that he's written.

15. *When you devise a trading system, what time frame do you use most? For example, do you use daily bars, weekly bars, 1-minute bars, 10-minute bars, or 60-minute bars?*

I use 30-minute and 45-minute bars. I call them big-time-frame intraday bars. They are more reactive and can catch more of the overall price movement than a daily bar can, but they are not too short like the one-minute or five-minute bar, which has too many blips and dips which make a trading system take too many trades and have an average trade that is too small. With 45-minute charts, I can have many trades in a short timespan, but my average trade is still big enough to justify trading by offsetting the costs of slippage and commission.

16. *If for some reason they closed every commodity in the world except one, and you were the guy in charge of deciding which one would stay open, which commodity would you choose? Why? What hours would it be open?*

I trade the S&P and currencies, but I exclusively day-trade the S&P, so I would want the S&P to stay open. The hours that it is open now are just fine, so I'd keep it that way. I think maybe I'd like to move to Colorado so I could follow the market from 6:30 A.M. to 2:15 P.M. and then spend the rest of the afternoon skiing. That sounds like a perfect lifestyle that maybe I'll get to soon.

17. *If you were to choose one commodity you could never trade again and you could never include in a trading system, which commodity would this be? Why?*

I like testing systems on all commodities. I think it's a flaw to expect a system to perform well on every commodity because some have distinct characteristics. Some are, by nature, more trending. The currencies seem to be the most trendy. Others are more flat. Less trending and nontrending commodities can still be good for systems trading if you are using a reaction style system. So I don't want to eliminate any one particular commodity.

18. *Where do you get your ideas for your system? A chart? A pattern? Observations? Trades that you have done before? What is your favorite technique for coming up with a trading system?*

I love to look at charts and throw up concepts for indicators or calculations. My indicators aren't typical indicators. They are usually calculations that come up with a price level and may stay horizontal for a while and then jump to a new price level. I put things up on a chart, and I scroll through the chart and see how the price action interacts. From there, I get ideas for systems. Generally I go to the programming language and put the system into code. First, I make sure the code does what I expect it to do. Then I test the system. One thing I like to do when a system is completely terrible is try the reverse system by replacing the buy orders with sell orders and the sell orders with buy orders. I'm willing to try anything to come up with a system. If it works and proves itself historically and in real time, let's trade it.

19. *I want you to write a trading system for me. I want you to give me all the rules. I want you to tell me what commodity, what time frame, whether it is daily bars, whatever. What your entry rule is, your exit rule with a profit, your exit rule with a loss. It doesn't have to be a great system. Just give me an idea of something you would look at, something you would test to see if there was any validity.*

Let's start with daily bars on the Swiss franc futures. Let's take a three-day moving average and a 15-bar standard deviation of the close, multiply that standard deviation by two, add it to the three-bar moving average for the upper band, and subtract it from the three-bar moving average for the lower band. Take these bands and shift them forward in time for 10 days. Now, use the lower band for the sell stop level; use the upper band for the buy stop level. If the prices go through the lower band, go short and stay short until the prices go through the upper band. If the prices go through the upper band, go long and stay long until the prices go through the lower band. Note that you reverse your position when there is a breakout of the shifted standard deviation band. This system is "always in" the market, long or short. Every day, you place a stop order to reverse your position. I'm willing to bet that this system's going to be profitable, probably have around 40 percent profitable trades and the average winner will probably be three-and-a-half to four times the size of the average loser. Let's have a go, see what it does.

20. *What's the typical day in the life of a system developer? What time do you start? What time do you end? What is it you do all day long? How are your orders placed? How is your system run?*

I don't keep regular hours. Often, I work late into the night (or the next morning) doing programming and research. However, I always know my position, and I always have my orders placed correctly so as to take every trade (entry and exit) properly. Even so, sometimes I make a trading error. But as soon as I discover my mistake, I immediately correct it and make sure my position is correct.

21. *If you could have your system run in any manner, what would be the preferable method? Would you have the person whose money is at risk run the system or would you have a third party run the system and just arbitrarily take the trades as they are generated, regardless of consequence?*

I like the idea of arbitrarily taking the trades as they are generated, regardless of consequence. However, in S&P day trading, there are times where TradeStation gives the beep and then one second later you've got to have your position on. So it's important that the person trading not be a computer or just following signals as they beep. The trader has to know the system and know when these situations are going to occur, so he can be on the phone with the floor ready to do a market order at the exact time. This is part of making your account perform just like the hypothetical system performance. A trader who just follows the signals generated by a "black box" will not be able to handle all situations as well as somebody who knows the system's trading rules and can anticipate what the system will do. Anticipation helps the trader achieve consistent and clean execution. Still, it's most important to keep your position right by taking all the trades as they are generated.

22. *Let's pretend I don't have a single book on commodities, and I'm interested in writing systems. Other than your own work, what book would you recommend? Along these same lines, is there anything you would avoid—whether it's software, books, lectures, whatever?*

One book that I think is great is called *Technical Traders Guide to Computer Analysis of the Futures Market* by David Lucas and Charles LeBeau. The book covers several systems and analysis techniques. The authors approach market analysis from a system trader's point of view. This book is not like so many other "how to use indicators" technical analysis books, and I like that.

I would avoid black boxes or systems when you don't know the complete rules. Just be careful about spending a lot of money for something that's not going to help you out. If you are going to buy a mechanical system, make sure it's profitable. Make sure it's tested and tracked by Futures Truth or some third-party tester. Don't believe the vendor's performance reports. If you are going to buy a methodology, know that you

are buying a methodology and not a mechanical system. Make sure it is
something that you want to learn about. You should not expect to be able
to learn another trader's methodology and make money with it right away.
A methodology is something you'll have to spend much time learning. I
don't recommend methodologies; I prefer mechanical systems. It is possible to buy a mechanical system and trade it correctly right away. Again, be
careful; there are bad systems for sale.

23. *Do you think it is necessary for a software developer/real-time trader
to have tick-by-tick real-time quotes? Why or why not?*

If you are going to day trade or make trades during the day, it's important to have tick-by-tick, real-time quotes. I know one guy who day
trades the S&P getting his quotes using the CNBC ticker on cable TV. If
he can do it, more power to him. But for me, I like to have real-time
quotes. If you intend to trade using daily bars and placing orders which
are good for the day, then real-time quotes are not required.

24. *What kind of quotes do you have? What kind of software would you
recommend? Are there any systems or software that you would definitely
not recommend?*

I have BMI real-time quotes from the CME, and that gets me the
S&P quotes I need. I also keep track of other commodities. I paste them
into my TradeStation. I have a close friend nearby who gets everything, so
I update my database for research and testing purposes. But currently, for
real-time trading, I just have the CME quotes.

Are there systems or software that I definitely would not recommend? Sure, there are lots of them. I don't want to put those names in a
book, but I'd be happy to talk to people if they've got questions about any
system that's for sale. I've seen an awful lot of them, and most of them are
not so good.

25. *How much data do you think is necessary to be tested as far as assessing a day-trade session on five-minute bars? A daily bar system? A
60-minute system?*

My answer for all these time frames is the same. Test all the possible
history that you can. The key to testing is to make sure that your system
performs consistently over an indefinite time period. I like to study the
most difficult periods when the system is struggling. I want to know how
tough it will be to trade the system. In real-time trading, I will have to endure difficult times and continue following the rules of the system, so I'm

there when the good times come around. I don't want to limit the amount of testing. I have been shown the greatest system on earth. It trades the five-minute chart and made $50,000 over the last three months with virtually no drawdown. First of all, big drawdowns are not likely to show up during highly profitable times. After running this system over five years, I found one three-month period where the system lost $50,000. Also, the average trade was under $85 before subtracting slippage and commission. Can you trade that? I don't think so.

26. *Why do some systems consistently perform year after year, and other systems fail or need to be continually optimized?*

This probably has to do with the logic used to create the system. If a system is created from a concept of how the market moves, that system is going to continually perform year after year. While other systems are curve-fit systems, using specific parameter sets that test well historically, but when you change the system's parameters, the system no longer performs well. These are the systems that are going to continually need to be optimized and will continually fail.

27. *How important are drawdowns in your research? How important is average trade size?*

You guys hit the nail on the head with this question. Drawdowns are probably the most important thing. You have to make sure that your account has enough capital to handle the largest historical drawdown and more. In real trading, I plan to withstand up to two times the maximum historical drawdown. I've seen traders throw out a system when the real-time drawdown surpasses the maximum historical drawdown. This is a mistake. The biggest drawdown is always in the future.

How important is average trade size? This is a key statistic. If your average trade is not big enough to offset slippage and commissions, you can't trade the system. If you make a system trade very often, it's going to have a small average trade. If you make a system trade long-term, the average trade gets pretty big and it's pretty easy to trade. The trade-off is that long-term systems will likely have larger drawdowns and require longer time periods to recover from a drawdown.

28. *Do you do portfolio management—link several commodities of different systems together? Do you do pyramiding? Why or why not?*

I do portfolio management by combining systems. I trade multiple systems, all in the S&P. I test these systems in combination to see that the drawdowns occur at different times. When you are trading multiple systems, the individual drawdown of each system can be offset by profitable periods in other systems. So your combined drawdown is not as big as the sum of the drawdowns of all the individual systems; but your combined total net profit is equal to the sum of all the individual system's total net profits.

As far as pyramiding, I don't pyramid in an ordinary way. I trade multiple systems. Sometimes only one system is doing something in the market, so I'm trading one contract. Other times, multiple systems are doing something in the market at the same time, so I am involved in multiple contracts. Again, I treat each system independently, as if I'm a different person trading each system. If all of my systems have triggered, I have one contract for each system in a trade. In addition, I have some systems with rules for multiple contacts. If a system is long three, then I have three contacts on for that system.

29. *Let's get a little morbid. You've died. You've left a sealed letter to your heirs. It contains the secret of your fortune. It's the secret to allow them to continue the lifestyle to which they have been accustomed. What one sentence is in the letter?*

That's a real whammy. I don't know. I wish I could think of something here. Actually, I wouldn't expect anybody else to have the same desire to follow the markets that I have.

30. *Without giving the secret of life, how would you write an imitation of your system in two lines or less in Trade Station language? For example, I have an S&P system called Buy Monday. "Monday you buy it, put in a $1,400 stop, get out on the close." That's how you write that.*

I don't think it's possible to write an imitation of R-Breaker with two lines or less in TradeStation language. I'll try just the breakout component. Place a buy stop at yesterday's high plus two-thirds of yesterday's range and place a sell stop at yesterday's low minus two-thirds of yesterday's range. Use a $1,000 stop and reverse. Take a maximum of two trades in a day, exit MOC. The other stuff is too complex to put in two lines. These rules probably would come out profitable on their own. There would be some hefty drawdowns and long waits before you make new highs in equity, but you could trade it.

31. *Give us an example of some of your work put in English-type language for a system.*

I think what I just did in the previous question qualifies.

Randy Stuckey

INTRODUCTION

Randy Stuckey is the designer of Catscan, and he's offered a unique offer to people who buy this new book for Catscan and Catscan II. So if you are interested in Catscan and the offer, call Randy Stuckey directly and make sure that you mention that you have purchased this book.

1. *Tell me about yourself. If someone were to say, "Tell me about Randy Stuckey," what would you want them to know? Give me a brief biography of you before you got into commodities, and a brief biography of what you have done since you got into commodities.*

My background is actually in the manufacturing world. I spent about 25 years there, starting out as a quality engineer and eventually working my way up to quality manager of a fairly large manufacturing plant. From there, I was promoted to corporate headquarters as division quality manager and eventually spent my last few years as a corporate quality director. Along the way, I learned a fair amount about statistics and learned how to discern enough about a manufacturing process that one could control that manufacturing process. This obviously was very important to me as a quality manager; I wanted the highest quality products to come out of our manufacturing process.

There's an interesting side note. Later on I'll talk a little about overoptimized commodity trading systems. What many people in the commodity field probably don't know is that overoptimization could apply to just about any process. I'll give you an example. I once worked for a large composites manufacturing company that made honeycomb for the aerospace and aircraft industry. One of those honeycombs was made out of a paperlike DuPont product called Nomex. With my newfound knowledge of statistics, I did a complex multiple linear regression of a whole bunch of DuPont Nomex test results versus the mechanical properties of our honeycomb. I found an incredible correlation between the raw, Nomex fiber paper and our finish honeycomb properties. Based on my report, DuPont embarked on a major R & D project to change the properties of Nomex to give us better properties in our honeycomb.

The bad news is what I had really done was create a system with eight optimized parameters. It would be like taking a commodity trading system that has eight parameters, all individually optimized for one commodity and one commodity only. You can imagine what the results were. They took a couple of years to modify this paper, and it didn't work worth a darn because what I had done was not really discern anything about the inherent nature of our manufacturing process or theirs, but had simply come up with a mathematical equation or curve fit to a set of back data.

2. *Tell me about your technique. What makes it exclusively yours? How did you develop it?*

My technique is probably unique in the entire commodity trading industry, and it's because of my manufacturing background. There is a rather sophisticated technique called the Taguchi robustness concept of processes invented by a Japanese fellow by the name of Taguchi. He developed this methodology by which you could make a manufacturing process more robust. Let's say you had a machine that was making some product and somebody came along and accidentally bumped one of the machine settings. Well, normally, that would immediately generate a defective product. But after using this Taguchi robustness approach, specifically the Taguchi orthogonal array designed experiment, you could select a set of machine parameters that were extremely robust. Somebody could come along and bump one of the settings, and it really wouldn't matter a whole lot. It still produced a quality product.

It struck me that the commodity market is one giant process, which brought up the question: Why couldn't we use the same technique to develop a very robust commodity trading system? And that, in fact, is how the basic engines of my Catscan system came to be. It turned out that the methodology worked extremely well. I'll give you an example of its robustness.

The Catscan system has one optimized parameter for each commodity. From the orthogonal array experiment I knew the parameter would be robust. But even with this experiment, I didn't realize just how incredibly robust it would be. I actually had the Futures Truth Company do the optimization. Because I didn't want a horrible overoptimized mathematical equation over a set of back test data or prices, I gave them instructions, "Don't do hundreds and hundreds of tests and find that magic parameter value that works only on the back test data." Their orders were to only do 21 optimization tests for each commodity. Well, I got a call from Futures Truth after they had done the first three commodities and they said, "We've got a problem. The problem is that on the first three commodities, all 21 tests were profitable! Now what do you want me to do?" Of course, that was wonderful news because that said that the parameter was very robust. That's important because if I, for example, had picked a value of 50 for that parameter and it really should have been 40 or 60, it really doesn't matter very much because all three of those should make money.

3. *Tell me about your best current trading system. What makes it tick? What are the features that make it the best trading system? Why do you trade this system?*

I'm going to talk about Catscan a little bit, my trading system. Prior to developing Catscan, I had purchased about 10 trading systems, paying up to $5,000 for some of them. All 10 of those systems looked great during back tests and just horrible in real-life trading, and so it was really kind of out of self-defense that I got into the systems development business. All of the 10 systems that I purchased were trend-following systems, as I think most commodity trading systems are. That's great, and they did pretty well when markets were trending. The problem was that 75 percent of the time the markets were not trending, and they got beat up pretty bad. So the basic premise of Catscan is that actually it's two systems in one. It is a trending-market trading system, and it is a choppy-market trading system for use during those time periods when markets are not trending. The system then has a choppiness index in it that attempts to measure whether the market is trending or whether the market is in a choppy mode. Then the system automatically switches back and forth between being a choppy market trading system and a trending-market trading system. In very simple words, that is the basic concept of Catscan. I'll even tell you what that one optimized parameter that I mentioned a bit earlier is. It's simply the cutoff limit for the choppiness index, where the system switches back and forth between being a choppy-market trading system and a trending-market trading system.

Just prior to developing Catscan, I contacted the 10 people that I had purchased trading systems from that didn't work in real life, that looked so wonderful in back tests, and I found out what approximate time period they had used to develop and optimize the system. I then tested it in a time period other than that and, sure enough, all 10 of the systems fell apart. Some of them, very, very badly, which of course tells me that they were just grossly overoptimized to a set of back test data.

Catscan was released in October of 1994, and during its first year of post-release performance it actually performed a little bit better than it did during back tests on average. I think the reason is because it is not severely optimized. It has just that one parameter that has to be set for each commodity.

In October of 1995, at the request of several Catscan owners, I released Catscan II. Catscan II was developed primarily because several Catscan owners traveled a lot; in many cases, Catscan requires the opening price of the day to generate its stop orders, and they wanted a system where you had the stop order value the night before. So Catscan II is basically a Catscan system that has its stop values the night before.

The interesting thing is I had to go to two optimized parameters per commodity. I hate doing that, and so after I developed Catscan II, I held it for several months, checking it in real life. I also had people trading it in real life before its release to see whether it was just an overoptimized mathematical equation of some back test data or whether it continued to truly discern something about the process of commodity pricing. So far, it has performed quite well in real life in what you might call a post-back-test test, or an out-of-sample test. When I developed Catscan and Catscan II, I intentionally had them tested over a time period that left some data untested. For example, I used 1983 to 1993 prices to develop Catscan and Catscan II. Then when everything was finalized, I tested it on pre-1983 prices because I knew darn well Catscan and Catscan II have never ever seen those prices, and I also tested it on post-1994 prices. Both came through with flying colors. That's interesting because it's the test I had given those other 10 systems, and they had all failed that test. Catscan has been very successful in real-time trading so far and to my knowledge is one of the very few systems out there that Futures Truth has tested that immediately jumped to the top of the charts.

4. *How long ago did you write your first trading system?*

Actually, I've only been involved in systems research and development for about four years now. I got into it, as I mentioned earlier, kind of out of desperation and exasperation, after purchasing system after system that did not work.

5. *Remember back to your first trading system. Can you tell us the rules?*

I vividly remember the very first system I wrote and actually traded for two months; it was a wonderful learning experience. The first thing I did was take one of those 10 trading systems I had purchased and I optimized the heck out of it. Of course, now I realize how terribly stupid that was, but nevertheless that's what I did. I had four or five parameters individually optimized for each commodity. I traded the system for two months. The market told me that this was a bad, bad, bad idea and removed a considerable amount of money from my bank account. Then I stopped, and for the next year and a half no system came out of Randy Stuckey. I simply did research on what makes a good trading system and basic research on things like prices. For example, one of the basic studies that I did was a correlation analysis of today's price to yesterday's price. Very simple. I did it on 30 different commodities. The commodity that came out most random, pretty much a 50-50 coin toss in the very, very short term, was the S&P 500. Because of that, when I developed Catscan I didn't even test it on the S&P 500. Like most good systems Catscan needs a tiny amount of nonrandomness to take advantage of. So many people asked me if they could trade the S&P 500 with Catscan that I finally tested it. I was right. It does not do well on the very, very random S&P 500.

So my first trading system was a grossly overoptimized thing that had five parameters, individually optimized for an individual commodity. It was a mathematical curve fit to a bunch of back test data.

6. *What caused you to abandon or modify that trading system the very first time?*

What caused me to abandon and modify the trading system was simply that it did not work. And since then I have learned even more. I've learned to use the Taguchi orthogonal array designed experiment to generate robustness, and I have taken to generating three-dimensional graphs, surface response graphs that kind of look like topography maps, where you vary any two parameters and see what effect it has on a third result, for example, profits or drawdown or some ratio of profit to drawdown.

The combination of the Taguchi concepts plus—and this is really important—the visual impact of looking at a trading system in three-dimensional space has told me a lot about trading systems in general and, of
course, Catscan and Catscan II specifically.

7. *When you look at another person's trading system, what is the very
first thing you look for to tell if it's a good or a bad system?*

Any time I look at a trading system, the very, very first thing I do is
test its robustness by running a 3-D graph. I vary its two most important parameters and see what effect that has on the ratio of profits divided by drawdown. If I see a very, very spiky type of response surface—for example,
let's say we varied one of the parameters from 20 to 80, and at 34 you get a
big spike of profits and everywhere else you get little or no profits—I would
throw that system in the garbage can immediately. That would be the kiss of
death to trade because trading systems are squirrelly. They have a tendency
to move around on you. This month, using that same example, 34 might be
a wonderful parameter value to use for trading system X. Six months from
now, 50 might be a wonderful value to use on that same parameter.
Unfortunately we don't know that in advance, and so if 50 produces losses
during the back test, it most likely will do the same in real life. On the other
hand, if you have a nice, smooth hill of profits all the way from 20 to 60,
you're probably going to be in pretty good shape if you set the parameter
somewhere in the middle of that hill, and even when this squirrelly process
of commodity prices moves around a bit, it won't hurt you too much.

After looking for robustness, the other thing that I look at is whether
it works on more than one commodity. I have a strong feeling, and I'm
sure that a lot of people do not share this, but I have a strong feeling that
a system that works on one commodity only is probably just an overoptimized piece of junk. If it works on multiple commodities, and you are
very fortunate, perhaps it discerns some small piece of that process known
as commodity pricing.

8. *What is the least important aspect of a trading system as far as you are
concerned?*

Just about everybody talks about drawdown. Of course, they also
talk about profit, and both of them are quite important. But profits and
drawdown and win-loss ratios and percent wins and all this stuff, none of
it is critical to me. The important thing is obviously that the expectation of
winning needs to be greater than the expectation of loss.

9. *In your current work, are you using a mechanical approach, or is there judgment involved in your trading?*

I believe in a mechanical approach to trading. Judgment has no place in my particular systems. I'm not saying that some people don't have good judgment; I'm sure they do. But I think there are very few people out there with the judgment ability to perform well in the commodity trading market, as evidenced by the fact that most everyone loses money, and not everybody is using a mechanical approach to trading.

10. *Are you currently using TradeStation or System Writer? If not, what software do you use to run your trading system?*

I started out using Super Charts to evaluate systems. I immediately saw that I needed more than that and purchased System Writer. I love System Writer even though it's not a Windows-based program; I still occasionally use System Writer. It has some inherent flaws, such as it doesn't keep track of the discount points. If you set, let's say, a $2,000 money management stop, and you put in multiple contracts with rollovers and if you have $10,000 profit and you then roll over to a new contract and for a short while the market goes against you on that trade and you are down to $8,000, System Writer will stop you out. It will say, oh, you lost $2,000. Of course, you didn't. There are several flaws like that, but System Writer in general is a very, very fine piece of software.

I also purchased TradeStation, and recently I bought Futures Truth's Excalibur software for the PC. Excalibur is by far the trickiest and most difficult to learn, but it is also by far the best system development and testing software that I have seen. I'm using it almost exclusively to do my systems analysis and development work because it generates so much information when you test a particular system or run through a series of optimization tests, and it does all of it pretty much automatically. There are a whole series of files you can look at either from within Excalibur or by exporting them to something like Excel or Lotus 1-2-3. It has very, very few flaws. Certainly, it has corrected all of the flaws of System Writer. It uses actual contracts, rolls over just like you would in real life. So I primarily use Excalibur now, and I use Excel to create three-dimensional tables, if you will, two parameters versus a result. I then generate three-dimensional graphs using a brand-new software package called Harvard Chart XL. It's very reasonably priced, and it does an astounding job of generating three-dimensional surface response graphs in beautiful color.

11. *Is your current trading system for sale? For lease? On a fax line? How do you provide this information to clients?*

Both Catscan and Catscan II are for sale. I don't believe in "black box" systems. All of the system rules are fully disclosed in a thorough manual. We've also written code that adds Catscan into TradeStation or Super Charts. It's very unique in that it also prints out your orders for tomorrow on your printer each evening. Both systems are tracked by Futures Truth Company. As you probably know, they are the "consumer's report" of commodity trading systems. Since Catscan's release in 1994, Futures Truth has ranked Catscan as the number one T-bond system in the world. It is also almost always the number one or number two crude oil, D Mark, cotton and coffee system in the world.

12. *Can you share the concept behind your trading system, for example, your main entry technique, your exit if you are wrong, and your exit if you are right?*

I already have, but I'll talk a little bit more about it. You know the basic concept of the system, but let's talk about entry techniques. Catscan is primarily a reversal system, so it's in the market 90 to 95 percent of the time. It has multiple entry techniques. Part of the entry techniques relate to price-channel breakout, such as the old Donchian price-channel breakout. Part of it is volatility based, and volatility-based breakout, and of course the most unique attribute is its ability to switch back and forth as you go from a trending market to a choppy market. In a trending market, for example, if Catscan declares it a bull market, it will only take long trades. Bear market, only short trades. In a choppy market, it will take either. It holds trades quite a long time in trending markets, and holds trades a very short time in choppy markets.

The exits, as I said, are usually reversals but not always. There's also a money-management stop in the system. I put that in there more for psychological benefit to me and everybody else than for any other reason. It's just there because I don't ever want to lose a large amount of money on any one trade. It also has a profit based exit.

13. *If you could advise system developers to do one thing when they are starting out, what would that be?*

The best advice I could give to any system developer would be do not, do not, do not develop a system that works on only one commodity that has more than three optimized parameters. You can have more parameters than that; sometimes, you really do need them. In addition to the one parameter in Catscan that is optimized by commodity, there are a few additional parameters. For example, it looks back over the last 30 days to figure out whether the market is in a trending mode or a choppy mode, but it does that same thing and it uses that same 30 days for every commodity in the world. My advice to system developers would be to keep it super, super simple. I know Joe Krutsinger is going to agree with that. Don't make things extremely complex.

There are a lot of indicators out there that measure, or attempt to measure, whether markets are trending or whether they are in a choppy mode. Some of them use extremely complex formulas, logarithms and all kinds of complex stuff. Mine is astoundingly simple. When I test Catscan with one of those extremely complex choppiness indexes versus my simple one, Catscan works just as well with my simple one.

The other thing I would advise them is be very careful if they discover that an idea of theirs works on one commodity and one commodity only. A good example of what I think is short-sightedness is price patterns. People that develop trading systems that are based on a price pattern almost always find that that price pattern applies to one commodity and one commodity only, and they say, well, see, I didn't really optimize anything; it's just this one little pattern. Well, the truth of the matter is it probably is a grossly overoptimized solution even though they didn't in their minds optimize anything. If you think about it, if you try 500 price patterns on 20 commodities, you are bound to find, just through sheer luck of overoptimization, one price pattern fitting one commodity for that historical price data. It has nothing to do with discerning something about the true nature of that market. It is just an overoptimized curve-fit solution. So, you have to be really careful, I think, with price patterns. Too many people fanaticize that because they don't see lots of parameters there, it couldn't be an overoptimized curve-fit solution. They are wrong. If they trade it, they will be poor and wrong.

14. *Other than yourself, who do you think is the best system developer, or who do you think is the best teacher of system development?*

I don't know of all of the systems developers out there. I do know that most of them are really, really bad. Most of them use severe overoptimization. Most of them come and go. John Hill, the president of the Futures Truth said, Randy, I think you are going to be around a long time because you are using a simple, basic, solid, robust approach.

Joe Krutsinger is a good example, I think, of an excellent systems developer. Maybe that's because he shares my view that a very simple system is the best. But, then again, some simple systems are pieces of junk. A good example of that is the simple moving average system, which I think is pure trash.

Who do I think the best teacher of system development is? I honestly don't know. I have Joe Krutsinger's book, *Trading System Toolkit*. I have 30 other books. I guess I learned a little bit from each of them but not a whole lot from any one of them.

15. *When you devise a trading system, what time frame do you use most? For example, do you use daily bars, weekly bars, 1-minute bars, 10-minute bars, or 60-minute bars?*

I'll tell you what I always use: daily bars. I think the person who develops trading systems for 1-minute bars, 10-minute bars, 60-minute bars, whatever, intraday trading systems, I think those people are primarily, I hate to say it, doomed to failure. I think in short-term day trading, the floor trader has it all over you, and will just eat your clock. Pure and simple. So I don't care how beautiful you design a trading system, I'm not sure you can design one that works very well on an intraday basis. You're just up against the giants, and the giants are going to continue to win. So I have only developed daily bar systems so far. I may even look into weekly bars, but probably won't look into intraday.

16. *If for some reason they closed every commodity in the world except one, and you were the guy in charge of deciding which one would stay open, which commodity would you choose? Why? What hours would it be open?*

I don't have one commodity I favor. Any commodity that trends well is fine with me. Even Catscan, which takes advantage of trends or choppiness, performs better during trending markets, so why not pick something that trends? You could say, well, the S&P is great because it really has trended. Well, yes, it has; the last 8 to 10 years it has had a phenomenal bull trend, no doubt about it. On a shorter-term basis, though, it starts to get real, real random and squirrelly again.

18. *Where do you get your ideas for your system? A chart? A pattern? Observations? Trades that you have done before? What is your favorite technique for coming up with a trading system?*

I develop trading systems differently than some people. I know several system developers who just try things one after another after another. They try hundreds or even thousands of things. I don't develop my trading systems that way. I do kind of the reverse process. I do a lot of thinking. I look at charts. I think. I create an indicator. I think some more. I start from a concept or an idea and, from there, develop the trading system as opposed to developing a trading system without having a concept or idea. I feel real uncomfortable about a trading system where the person can't explain why they think the system works.

I certainly would use the Taguchi orthogonal array designed experiment to generate some robustness. I would confirm that robustness with three-dimensional surface response graphs.

19. *I want you to write a trading system for me. I want you to give me all the rules. I want you to tell me what commodity, what time frame, whether it is daily bars, whatever. What your entry rule is, your exit rule with a profit, your exit rule with a loss. It doesn't have to be a great system. Just give me an idea of something you would look at, something you would test to see if there was any validity.*

I'll write a trading system for you right now that is a fairly good trading system. As a matter of fact, a piece of it is a part of Catscan. The rule is very simple. Buy on the open tomorrow if the close today is higher than the highest high of the last 40 days. Sell if the close today is lower than the lowest low of the last 40 days. It's the old Donchian price channel breakout. It works well on multiple commodities. In three-dimensional graphing, it produces a very smooth response curve. You can gussy it up with all kinds of different exits, but just using it as a pure and simple reversal system with maybe a $2,000 money management stop is fine.

The way I would test it would be to see what kind of profits it generates on each commodity over a 10-year time period. There's only one parameter, the 40 days. I would vary that parameter a little bit, maybe 20, 30, 40, 50, 60 and 70. Then you can generate a 3-D graph even though it only has one parameter. The way you do it is to treat time as the second parameter. In other words, you generate a whole bunch of equity curves and graph them, treating the price channel days as variable A, the time as variable B. The Z axis could be profit or drawdown or the ratio profit divided by drawdown.

20. *What's the typical day in the life of a system developer? What time do you start? What time do you end? What is it you do all day long? How are your orders placed? How is your system run?*

My typical day starts about 8 o'clock. I usually spend the morning doing research. In the afternoon, I try to clean up correspondence and requests for information on Catscan. Often, in the afternoon and evening, people who have just purchased Catscan spend some time on the phone with me because I want them to. I'm just the opposite of some developers. I like to talk to those people. I want them to be totally confident that they are using Catscan correctly and that we are getting exactly the same signals each day. Once we are getting exactly the same signals, they're on their own. It's tough enough to make money in the commodity market; it's just plain impossible if you are doing something wrong. So that kind of covers my evenings.

Orders are all placed in the morning before the open except on Catscan, which requires the opening price. If you have the type of broker that'll take it, you can place a buy on the open plus X amount type of stop.

My system runs on Super Charts, TradeStation, System Writer, or Excalibur software, or you can even do it manually; it's rather a simple system. You can do it with a calculator each evening.

21. *If you could have your system run in any manner, what would be the preferable method? Would you have the person whose money is at risk run the system, or would you have a third party run the system and just arbitrarily take the trades as they are generated, regardless of consequence?*

It might be wise to let a third party trade the system. Fear and greed drive most traders. Of the two, fear is usually the stronger force. I recently had a call from a Catscan owner, who proudly announced that he had just closed out a coffee trade with a $4,000 profit. I asked him why he had closed out the trade since Catscan was still in that coffee trade. He said he was afraid Catscan might give back some of the profit, so he closed it out. Eleven days later Catscan closed out that trade with a $13,000 profit.

22. *Let's pretend I don't have a single book on commodities, and I'm interested in writing systems. Other than your own work, what book would you recommend? Along these same lines, is there anything you would avoid—whether it's software, books, lectures, whatever?*

I can recommend two. Pardos' *Design Testing and Optimization of Trading Systems* and Joe Krutsinger's *Trading System Tool Kit*.

I found Larry Williams' seminar to be valuable, not so much for what he handed out, but for some of the ideas that I was able to slip into my notes by tapping his mind. He's been around quite a while, seen a lot of stuff, has some interesting observations on the nature of markets, which I think is the right way to approach developing a trading system, understanding something about the nature of a market.

23. *Do you think it is necessary for a software developer/real-time trader to have tick-by-tick real-time quotes? Why or why not?*

I do not think it is necessary for software developers and traders to have tick-by-tick real-time quotes. The reason is, I do not believe that the average person can beat the floor traders, so they shouldn't be trading these crazy intraday systems. Therefore, there is really no need for tick-by-tick or real-time quotes. One of the most knowledgeable day traders is Gary Smith. He told me that out of several thousand off-the-floor day traders, he only knew two who made money.

24. *What kind of quotes do you have? What kind of software would you recommend? Are there any systems or software that you would definitely not recommend?*

I use an end-of-day service. I happen to use CSI; I've also used Genesis and several others prior to that. That's all I need. I need end-of-day prices, open high low close, plus volume and open interest.

It hurts to say this, but there are an unusually large number of crooked system vendors out there. Some even falsify their systems performance statistics. Other make the results look good by using continuous contracts. That way they don't have any rollover trade costs. I include over 1,000 rollover trades in my Catscan performance reports. I take a $75 commission and slippage hit for each rollover trade. It hurts profits, but that is the price of truth. Other vendors like to report only closed trade drawdown as opposed to the worse, but more honest, closed plus open trade maximum drawdown. Another con is to make sure that their system has some subjective rules in it. You can just see the sly grin on their face. What a neat con. They can claim any outrageous performance. When challenged, they then say it depends on the person trading the system. One thing is for sure. You're not the one that made ten zillion dollars trading the system. But wait a minute! If it really depends on the person, of what possible use is the "200 percent profit" or "10 million dollars" or "94.6 percent accuracy" statement these vendors make?

I've finally concluded that if any system is not tracked by Futures Truth, you should <u>not</u> buy it. I've noticed that the systems not tracked by Futures Truth are usually the ones that don't perform well and the system vendors don't want you to know it. Some vendors even lie and say Futures Truth can't track their system because it requires 15-minute bar data. Futures Truth can test using 5, 10, 15, 30, or any other time period bars. I should note that I have no financial arrangement of any kind with Futures

Truth. It's just that the system vendors business is <u>long</u> overdue for some truth in advertising.

25. *How much data do you think is necessary to be tested as far as assessing a day-trade session on five-minute bars? A daily bar system? A 60-minute system?*

I don't have a clue how many five or 60-minute because, again, I don't believe you can make money day trading unless you are a floor trader.

Daily bar system? Ten years of data reserving any data prior to that and after that for out of sample testing once you've finalized the system.

26. *Why do some systems consistently perform year after year, and other systems fail or need to be continually optimized?*

Systems fail primarily because they haven't really discerned anything about the true nature of the commodity market. If they need to be continually optimized, it simply means that they aren't real to begin with, and you're only optimizing them to make the past look better, which means they are overoptimized. So really, this question relates specifically to overoptimized systems. That's why they fail; that's why they have to continually be optimized.

27. *How important are drawdowns in your research? How important is average trade size?*

Important, but not real important. Some of the systems that I've purchased showed fabulous profits with extremely low drawdowns during back testing, but it simply wasn't real. Catscan, for example, does not have super low drawdowns, but it works in real life so far. What does that tell you? I think that tells you that drawdown is important. But if it's extremely low, I would worry, just the opposite of most people. I would consider that potentially bad. I would consider that a forewarning that maybe this system is grossly overoptimized.

I'll give you a good example. Catscan over the last 10 years or so trading the Swiss franc makes around $100,000 profit with about $10 to $12,000 maximum drawdown. Just for the fun of it, I took all six Catscan parameters and I optimized them just for the Swiss franc. I got $200,000 profit with $1,000 drawdown. But it ain't real folks. I would never, ever use that system. That's simply a mathematical equation of those 10 years of prices that I used.

Average trade size, on the other hand, is somewhat important. I guess it depends on how often your system trades as to whether average trade size is critical. If it trades a lot, average trade size can obviously be smaller than if it trades infrequently, in my view. Because if the mathematical expectation is positive and it trades a lot, even with a small profit, you can generate quite a bit of money over a year's time.

28. *Do you do portfolio management—linking several commodities of different systems together? Do you do pyramiding? Why or why not?*

I am right now researching portfolio management and linking commodities together and doing intercorrelation analyses of different markets and pyramiding, and I haven't drawn any conclusions yet. I will, but everything that I do is pretty carefully researched, and since it's not researched enough yet I'm not going to comment further on it.

29. *Let's get a little morbid. You've died. You've left a sealed letter to your heirs. It contains the secret of your fortune. It's the secret to allow them to continue the lifestyle to which they have been accustomed. What one sentence is in the letter?*

It would have to be a long sentence. It would go something like this: Take 15 percent of your money and follow the advice of Hulbert's number-one rated newsletter with at least an eight-year track record and let the number-one Barclay rated commodity CTA manage 15 percent of your money and put the remaining 70 percent in ten-year German government bonds. The end.

30. *Without giving the secret of life, how would you write an imitation of your system in two lines or less in TradeStation language? For example, I have an S&P system called Buy Monday. "Monday you buy it, put in a $1,400 stop, get out on the close." That's how you write that.*

In Easylanguage code it would be: Buy tomorrow at open [0] 0 + 0.50 * Average(Range,5) stop.

31. *Give us an example of your work put in English-type language for a system.*

Buy tomorrow on the open plus 50 percent of the average range of the last five days. Opposite of that for a sell. That's it.

Gary Wagner

INTRODUCTION

Gary Wagner is President of International Pacific Trading Company and helped develop the "Candlestick Forecaster," a highly-acclaimed software-based trading application. By combining Western technical indicators with Eastern technical charts, he has created a new and exciting way of looking at the markets. Gary is a registered commodity broker and CTA with more than 11 years of trading experience.

1. *Tell me about yourself. If someone were to say, "Tell me about Gary Wagner," what would you want them to know? Give me a brief biography of you before you got into commodities, and a brief biography of what you have done since you got into commodities.*

Currently, I am a registered CTA (Commodity Trading Advisor) and a market technician. I began my trading back in 1983. I was trained classically in the fine art of western technical analysis. About 5 years ago, my partner, Brad Matheny, and I co-developed a software-based trading application called the Candlestick Forecaster® (a registered trademark of International Pacific Trading Company), which processes both Western and Eastern technical analysis through an expert system. The output is then processed by means of a neural network using rule-based parameters so that it can issue, buy and sell signals based upon this synergistic method. We have constantly been involved in researching Japanese candlesticks, which is the bulk of the trading application that I'm speaking of. Our research has allowed us to write one book published in 1994 by John Wiley, *Gallep Trading Applications of Japanese Candlestick Charting*. We've also written numerous articles for financial publications, nine articles for *Technical Analysis of Stocks and Commodities*, as well as an article for *Futures* magazine and *Traders World* magazine. We have had articles written about us both in *Worth*, Leo Faciss in *Investors Business Daily Publication*, and other well-known publications, such as *Financial Trader*.

Currently, we are pretty much working full-time developing the Candlestick Forecaster® Master Edition. As traders, we use these techniques daily. We are not simply developers in the market. We are developers who actually use these techniques and trade our own personal accounts in hopes that the results of our efforts will be fruitful not only for our end users but for ourselves.

We have been speaking internationally from Asia and Western Europe. In the United States, we are frequent speakers at the Futures International Conferences, which are held both in Burbank, California, and in Chicago. We have had a video produced and published by *Futures* magazine. The video, which came out in 1995, is an advanced trading application of Japanese Candlestick Charting. We are honored to be a member of the All Star Traders Hotline. End users and traders around the country and around the world can call up on a daily basis to hear our actual buy and sell recommendations. By the way, those buy and sell recommendations are based on the same program that we market internationally.

2. *Tell me about your technique. What makes it exclusively yours? How did you develop it?*

The technique or style that we've developed is very interesting. In essence, what we've tried to do is combine the best of Eastern and Western trading techniques. One must realize that in the 1600s, the first futures exchange opened, the Dojima rice exchange: its primary purpose was to trade rice. You have to realize that at that time, rice was Japan's single most important commodity. In fact, Samurai warriors were paid, not in gold, not in dollars, not in yen, but in rice. The creator of this technique is a gentleman named Sokyu Honma, a family member of the largest rice holders from Japan. He began to buy and sell rice and study price activity or movement. Honma believed that there was a method, mathematically based, that could pinpoint reversals or pivotal points, or more importantly sense market psychology. In other words, this method allows one to sense the direction of price movement over time in terms of where it would go in the future, which was quite a feat. The technique is now known as the Sakata Five.

The Sakata Five are a group of five sets of laws or pattern groups. The name Sakata comes from his home city. It was this Honma who back in the 1600s began what we call candlestick charting. Candlesticks is the western term. The Japanese term, translated, means footprints. As a man walks through the sand, he leaves footprints. By following those footprints, you are following his movement over time. These charts are footprints of the market. By following the past price activity and structure of a market, one might have an indication of where that market will go.

The easiest definition of what candlesticks are, or what this form of Japanese technical analysis is, is a mathematical equation of market sentiment. On its most basic level, there are particular candle formations or particular scenarios that will develop, which a high percentage of the time, will give the trader advanced notice as to a potential reversal, key reversal, pinpoint or continuation, or stagnation of a current trend. The fact that these techniques reveal potential reversals prior to any activity indicative of that move lends itself to be a leading indicator.

When we take a look at our basic western technicals, whether it be oscillator based or moving-average based, we are comparing past price activity and comparing that price with the past, i.e. averaging that activity and then making comparison upon the average in an average-based technical study and a current close, and in an oscillator-based study comparing that close to whether it's the highest highs in end period of days or lowest lows in end period of days, such as in a stochastic, or variations of both. Of course, it gets more complex. But my point is that it is always based upon past price performance and comparing an average or a slowing down, so to speak, and so therefore, so that we can derive a direct signal from a western-based technical indicator. Let's assume we're moving in an uptrend. The market has to move to the uptrend, hit a top, and then begin to break; in other words, a short-term moving average crossing over a long-term moving average would then pinpoint a bearish reversal. The key in that particular scenario is the market had to hit a top; then, as it reversed, the technician was able to identify it.

What we have done to develop this technique to make it effectively ours, but not exclusively ours, was to combine many techniques that we found worked well together. By finding certain methods that work well together, we increase the probability of our success. We call that a synergistic approach to trading.

We've tried to term the technique in which we trade STA, Synergistic Technical Analysis. What we've done is as follows. We've explained a little about the fact that we work with Japanese candlesticks and that Japanese candlesticks are a <u>mathematical interpretation of market profile or sentiment</u>. Now there are certain patterns or certain formations that tend to appear a high probability of times just subsequent to the key reversal moment. One example would be the most simple of patterns, which is an engulfing bullish. To explain an engulfing bullish, I'm first going to need to talk a little bit about the distinctions between a bar chart and a candlestick chart. The bar chart is a single vertical line. We draw the open as a horizontal slash. That's placed to the left of the line. To the right of that vertical line, is another horizontal slash, and that represents the close. Simply take the open and close and draw a rectangle around it. If the market is closed higher, we call it an empty candle, and it's left white. If the market closes lower, it's called a full candle, and it's drawn classically in black.

This is simply the first step. There is a third type of candle we'll want to really hone in on called the Doji. The Doji is simply when the open and close are either identical or very, very close together, so we're talking one, two, three ticks maximum. The key in that type of candle is that the open and closing range were never able to move very far apart. Now, typically, if we want to say that a market is in an uptrend, there is a succession of higher closing—let's assume it's a daily chart—succession of higher closing days, then visually what happens on a candlestick chart is these happen to white candles. So you see a succession of white candle after white candle making higher highs and higher lows.

The opposing scenario is a bearish market, which can be defined as a simple succession of lower closes, and these don't have to be consecutive, of course. Visually, on a candlestick chart, you are going to see a lot of black lines moving down, down, with lower lows and lower highs. What makes this technique unique is that visually you are able to take in a whole lot of data. That's not even a segment of the visible part of the iceberg because the Sakata Five is a series of four groups of patterns, and these patterns describe all of the scenarios that are possible to discern whether the market is continuing in a trend or is in a narrow consolidating area, or if it had been in a defined uptrend or downtrend and is about to reverse.

The gentleman who created the Sakata Five is Honma, and in fact he was one of the most prosperous and respected traders of all time. He actually was honored with the rare distinction of being called a Samurai for his training experience in the face of his adversaries. The work he created during this early period was passed down through the generations in two books he wrote: *Sanminoden* as well as *Sakata's Constitution*. These are where he laid down his doctrine of the Sakata Five. Because this is only a portion of our technique; we are going to try to cover it fairly briefly, but it is very important that we understand where these Japanese candlesticks developed from and the beauty of it or the mysticism behind it.

The Sakata Five method consists of four specific pattern types. The interesting thing is that they are all based on the number three. The number three is a very mystical number. The Japanese believe that number three has divine power. The number four in Japanese is analogous to the word death, so you are not going to find a whole lot of patterns that are based on four. These basic patterns that are based on the number three can be broken into the following types: Sanku, which is translated as three gaps; Sanpei, which is known as three parallel lines; Sansen, which is three rivers; and Sanzan, which is three mountains. Now the fifth is an actual trading technique that deals with money management. It says that as one wins 100 pounds of rice, its neck trade, one should pull back 50. If one takes a losing trade after so much, one should exit the market, take a break, and reenter. Sounds very similar to money-management techniques that have been developed by the modern trader, as well as stops and scale buying. Back in the 1600s, these techniques were first beginning to be developed.

The three gap patterns are found when you have three gaps (a price void) that are formed by four candles that move in the same direction. Assume that we have an up day and it closes at a dollar: on the following day, it opens at 105, creating a gap. The Japanese call that a window; simply defined to a western trader, it's a price void. On the following day, it opens at 105 and closes at 2. The following day it opens at 205, closes at 3; the following day opens at 305, closes at 4. I think you get the picture. Now, once you have three windows Japanese style, or three price voids western style, the belief in this pattern is that that represents a possible market consolidation exhaustion, and it is three gaps and four very bullish candles that determine a bearish reversal. That's one of the patterns that most fascinated me because here they are deriving a reversal point simply based on the number of gaps and the fact that if there is a high probability when the market has moved filling those price voids, whereas we western technicians always look to go back and fill the gaps.

The next set of patterns of those three gaps are called three parallel lines. They work very much in the same way. This is a scenario where a market opens at $1, closes at $2, and the following day, let's say it opens at 50 cents and it closes at $1.50. The subsequent day, it would open at $1 and close at $2. As you can see, they are all going within the bodies in the same direction, all closing higher. That pattern is known as three soldiers. That's indicative of a market that should show a continuation of trend. So here we can have three candles or three days that had a relatively similar open to close, and because of the placement between each other, they actually reveal completely opposite results. So, as I said, three gaps and parallel lines are very interesting patterns. The Sansen pattern type implies three rivers and these are patterns that those who have become familiar with some of the basic candlestick patterns are really going to find this is where they fit it. This is the three river evening star. Three river morning star. These are indicative of tops or bottoms of markets. The last one is Sanzan, which implies a type of mountains or top formations. The first mountain type is analogous to our head-and-shoulders formation. The second type is analogous to our double top, and the third is a rounded top. By the way, we call it a head-and-shoulders; they call it three Buddas. Obviously they have some very beautiful ways to use the language. Now, this is really just the beginning of the technique we utilize.

We found that when we computerized all of these patterns and ran them through statistical tests, the results were not much better than flipping a coin or any other poor technique. Although the reversals were deadly on the top, the frequency of them being found midrange or at inappropriate times was unacceptable in terms of having a profitable system. The technique we developed was composed of two parts; the first step was to take these candlestick patterns and then begin to code them into a massive library. Then we developed some computer algorithms that attempt to mimic the human mind. In other words, we are setting up a system of rule-based parameters that will attempt to delineate or determine at what point in the market's activity a pattern has been found.

Here's an example. A market has been moving $3 a bushel; it's been moving from 3 to 2 and is sitting at $1.50. As a trader, you have the ability immediately to know that market's been in a downtrend. Now, you might even be able to go and pull up a weekly chart at that point and look back in history to see if it has ever been at $1 or $1.50. When was the last time it was at $3? How did it react in any of those cases if either of them were true? In other words, you are determining if these patterns occur at a contract high or a contract low. Are you trading after to find uptrend or downtrend? Lastly, you look at the amount of time it took to reach those price movements, and we have an accelerated price to climb or an accelerated price advance. So that when one would actually analyze candlestick patterns to derive market signals, it was not simply using these patterns that gave it its effectiveness. What gave it its effectiveness is the fact that you could apply filters or other similar and different technical approaches. When combined, this technique would give one the ability to determine the frequency or probability of success which could be achieved. It was this method of combining indicators which created a profitable trading system.

The way that we went about developing our application is interesting. I've been trading since 1983. I started trading using a pencil and a piece of paper, not a computer. I used my eyes to determine where to draw trend lines. During the mid and late 1980s, some computer programs began to display price movement without bar charts that we've been looking at all our lives. The bar chart was replaced with a Japanese technique. Blumberg, I believe, was the first to use Japanese candlesticks in 1990. At the same time, Steve Nissan had published a few articles in *Futures* magazine on candlesticks, and a seed, which would change the technicians' world, was planted.

There was a very logical reason why this seed was planted in the late 1990s. During the early 1980s, the Japanese began to enter our market with phenomenal amounts of capital. The incredible thing was that they had a consistently higher success rate of profitable trades and good bottom lines than their American counterpart. Any trader will tell you that we all are looking for an edge. So this is where that interest began to generate. I looked at these charts, and for the life of me I could not determine what they meant. I had an idea of how they were drawn, the difference between a black candle, a white candle, and a doji. I had no clue as to what interpretations and market signals, if any, could be made. I was fortunate in that as I studied this technique, I spoke with a client of mine who understood how to apply this method. He mentioned that he had just picked up a book, called the *Japanese Chart of Charts*, written by one of the foremost authorities in Japan, in fact, currently one of the members of the main exchanges over there, Seiki Shimizu. I said, where do I get my hands on this book? This is something I have to have. My client was kind enough to send me a copy of it. Now, I must admit it was one of the more difficult books, if not the most difficult book, I have ever tried to digest. Besides the complex ideas found within, the translation from a Japanese to an English text is very, very difficult. One must realize that the Japanese use kangi, or word pictures, whereas we use syllables. After about three or four reads though, I began to notice some amazing things. I became astounded at the potential that candlesticks hold as a market forecasting method. As I began to incorporate candlesticks into my trading system, I found that my trading was enhanced. One day, while I was sitting looking at a futures source chart, I had a client in the office and I was trying to explain a candlestick pattern and its meaning. For the life of me, I couldn't attempt to describe what I knew. Then the idea popped into my head; a computer could be used to identify candlestick patterns. One could create some sort of computer algorithm that at the push of a button would run through a library looking for a pattern match, and if it found it, it could identify and interpret the meaning to the end user. So the initial idea that we came up with in developing our system was to develop an on-line tutorial to teach people about candlestick analysis. It grew into one of the most magnificent trading systems we've ever used and changed my life in every single way.

3. *Tell me about your best current trading system. What makes it tick? What are the features that make it the best trading system? Why do you trade this system?*

My best current trading system is the one that I'm working on now. As a co-developer of a software-based trading application, both my partner Brad and myself look at this system as a breathing, living entity. We are constantly testing and training it. Because this system is a neural network; it has the capacity to learn. This means that what we consider to be our best today, we are hoping will be a little bit outperformed by the system we develop next month.

In terms of what makes this system tick and what features make it the best trading system: first of all, we are children who sit in our own candy stores. We are traders and programmers so that we have been incorporating the ideas that we believe will work the best. Through trial and error, we find that not all of the things we think will work do work. Because we have the tools and the ability to test out any given system, any parameter, any change, any optimization, we simply integrate that into the computer code we're working on and run some statistical research, and at that point we can delineate that this is enhancing or giving value-added results to our system or that it is simply an idea that we should discard it.

Why we trade this system is quite simple. We've been using it for six years, and it's been working for six years. My mother and father gave me some great words of wisdom: If something isn't broken, one should not try to fix it, but one should always try to make it better. In other words, we have been working to enhance a system over the last five years, but the reason we trade the system is that it is the best system we have available for ourselves. If there is a better system out there, we're trying to develop it. If ideas are presented to us, and many of them come from our end users, we pay close attention, and we do the statistical research. If we find that it does add value and a higher success rate, we credit the person within our next documentation and thank our end users who really realize what our program is all about. The reason we will never trade any other system is that we will always be enhancing this system.

What makes our system tick, the Candlestick Forecaster®, is the fact that we've taken and developed probably the definitive library of candlestick patterns. We have over 1,350 patterns within the current master edition, and that's the edition that we use each day. These patterns range anywhere from 2 to 30 cycles in length (a cycle can be composed of intraday data or daily data).

Once it finds a pattern—and let's go back to our first example, a typical buy signal—it will run through the rule-based parameters in the expert system using oscillators and moving averages to determine if this pattern has been found after the market has been in a defined trend, be it up or down, or in a narrow defined range, or if it had just been in a downtrend and then is beginning to move up. In other words, it will ascertain where price activity currently is in relation to most current and then further-out past movement. Now, this is quite a task in and of itself. Then we couple that with Thomas R. DeMark's sequential, which is also a pattern, and look for points in which both the candlestick patterns—the Japanese Technical Analysis, Thomas R. DeMark's work—and the western technicals—which are ascertaining or mimicking what we would mimic in terms of trying to figure out what the human mind would do in terms of looking at where that pattern was found.

Now what makes this system tick is identifying a pattern then combining it with a unique set of technical indicators developed by DeMark, the consummate trader of the 20th Century in my opinion and in the opinion of many. We are fortunate that Tom has allowed us to use these techniques within our system and to run it through some simple expert-based rules.

What makes it tick is that it combines all of these things together to create kind of a triple-filtering system that tends to have a high probability of success in markets universally. We market the program to commodity traders and equity traders across the country. That might not be strange. We have large followings in Malaysia, Korea, all through Asia, Germany, all of western Europe. And all these markets, none of which were around during the Dojima rice exchange formation, track exquisitely. So what makes our system tick is that we've combined the old with the new and created a system that allows us to effectively trade the global markets that are available to use trades today.

4. *How long ago did you write your first trading system?*

In terms of technical analysis, I began using some of the more commercially available but available for the broker programs such as the IDA, Intraday Analysis by Computrac, Future Source, and things of that nature. When I began trading technically in 1985 and 1986, we used variations of MACD and stochastics.

5. *Remember back to your first trading system. Can you tell us the rules?*

The trading system, or the focus that I attempted to take, I developed from a gentleman who came into the office. In fact, this gentleman was the former minister of economics of Iran during the Shah's regime. He was kicked out of the country with the Shah, and he supported his family by trading the markets in our office. I noticed he had a very good success rate. He would set up a series of stochastics on the S&P market. He would use a three-minute stochastic, a five-minute stochastic, a seven-minute stochastic and a nine-minute stochastic. And when he would get our basic signals, meaning under 20, and they crossed for a buy signal of 3, he would not take the signal until the 5 or the 7, one of these outer signals hit. His rationale was that although the 3 would give the quickest jump in the market and most certainly hit most of the correct calls, it almost inevitably has what we technicians call noise, or many times in which it fails. He felt that by double filtering it through time cycles, one would have an approach.

Now, this was back in about 1986, and the rules that were developed were quite simple. We would find a stochastic oscillator based on the S&P in which we would use time cycles in an attempt to filter out the noise by only taking two calls.

6. *What caused you to abandon or modify that trading system the very first time?*

It simply was a variation on a stochastic oscillator; it didn't incorporate many of the variables that we also were looking at, and although when it had a frequency of success it was great, it also had large periods of time in which we would witness drawdowns.

7. *When you look at another person's trading system, what is the very first thing you look for to tell if it's a good or a bad system?*

When we look at other trading systems out there, the first thing we do to determine its validity is to historically back test it to see what kind of performance it has generated hypothetically. Of course, hypothetical performance doesn't guarantee future performance, but I have very rarely seen a system that performs poorly hypothetically that does exceptionally well in real-time.

In terms of telling if it is a good or a bad system, one would simply have to take the rules, take the system itself, and track it on a real-time basis, accounting for slippage, of course, and thereby not have the luxury of looking at it in hindsight for possible optimizations and changes.

8. *What is the least important aspect of a trading system as far as you are concerned?*

As far as I'm concerned, the least important aspect of a profitable trading system is how the signals themselves are generated; in other words, whether they use a neural network, a series of western technicals, a series of eastern technicals, any sort of a combination, or complete fundamental analysis. The most important aspect of a trading system is how it was accomplished if it has poor results, so that the bugs can be worked out. If it has good results, that becomes the most important thing. Technique itself is part and parcel of results. So it has to be weighed within results.

9. *In your current work, are you using a mechanical approach, or is there a judgment involved in your trading?*

Currently we're using a 100-percent mechanical approach. It's always been said that trading is as much of an art as a science. Our system will generate a buy-sell report. The judgment involved is whether or not we actually take the trade or pull the trigger. Once the trigger has been pulled, though, we do trade by the book. In other words, we use the mechanical system, stop-placement equity rules, and things of that nature to keep us on track and to have some sort of control; this way, if we do make a change in the system, we can be fairly certain that the actual work we did in the system had the effect and not any judgment calls within it.

10. *Are you currently using TradeStation or System Writer? If not, what software do you use to run your trading system?*

We're one of the few fortunate developers who, instead of using something as excellent as TradeStation or System Writer, which in our opinion are the best on the market, run our trading system on the software we developed. It's a proprietary system, contains over 100,000 lines of code. It's been written over the last year by Brad Matheny, Gary Westerland, and me, along with two gentlemen that we are adding to our programming team. We are quite proud of being one of the few traders that is allowed to develop a proprietary system in order to achieve its goals.

11. *Is your current trading system for sale? For lease? On a fax line? How do you provide this information to clients?*

The system that we are talking about, of course, is the Master Edition. That is our state-of-the-art end-of-day. We also have a real-time system. We have been marketing the program for over five years in terms of straight sell and for the real time on a lease basis. We have no fax line available, but in terms of providing the information to the clients, we offer them the direct ability to utilize the same program that we do, as well as in conjunction with *Futures* magazine. As I said, we are quite honored and fortunate to be a part of their All-Star Traders Hotline.

12. *Can you share the concept behind your trading system, for example, your main entry technique, your exit if you are wrong, and your exit if you are right?*

We've explained that it's a synergistic approach, but in terms of entry and exit techniques, they are put quite forward. It is a straightforward mechanical system. The mechanical system will determine and actually issue a buy or sell signal, an entry point. At that point, it initiates a stop-loss placement. The first given scenario is that if we make the assumption the market is moving up, we take the call the stop is hit. So the exit point is simply on an initial-stop basis. Getting out of a trade that we're fortunate enough to have going with us is determined in one of two ways. If the trend continues in the anticipated direction, our system will move stops up automatically, and will actually suggest stop-placement parameters. If the market continues to go up, and at some point begins to retrace, and let's assume it's a buy signal, and begins to come back down, we will be stopped out and, of course, stopped out at a profit.

The third possible exit point is one in which we have a buy signal. Secondly, we're fortunate enough to be correct in the anticipated direction of the market, and then we get a sell signal. The sell signal causes us either to (A) put our stop up incredibly high or (B) do a net long reversal. In other words, if we had a long position, we would sell two for every one. So in some circumstances, the technique itself will work as a net long or a short in the market at all times, and at other times you will simply be stopped out initially as a stop loss with a loss or, in the instances where we are correct, as a trailing stop.

13. *If you could advise system developers to do one thing when they are starting out, what would that be?*

The one thing I would advise is extreme dedication and focus. That comes from a love or a desire of the vocation, but one has to have some intrinsic bent for something going on, some idea, some clue, some theory or formula that needs to be tested; then the persistence, the focus, the ability to do the research, the tools necessary to accomplish it, and the persistence to see it through is the one and only determining factor whether or not the system that you are anticipating is having potential, will or will not in terms of straight statistical work.

14. *Other than yourself, who do you think is the best system developer, or who do you think is the best teacher of system development?*

Naming who we think is the best system developer or the best teacher of system development would almost make me feel at odds to name one in hopes not to name the other brilliant minds that have been in the industry that we've studied over the last decade and a half. Thomas D. DeMark is the consummate trader of our time. There has never been a gentleman who had unique ideas and the flavor, the drive, the aptitude, the foresight, the insight, the uncanny ability to take an idea and pursue it as though he was playing multiple games of chess until he comes up with the consummate answer. I could not even begin to count the other great minds of our time; there's Larry Williams, Jake Bernstein. And in system development, how far do we take it back? W.D. Gan, of course, Honma, and a gentleman named Takahiro Hikita from Japan.

The best system developer in not so much a name, as a gentleman who has a focus that is unique and brilliant and who is able to take the excellence and the work that has been passed on from generation to generation and see an entirely new global dimension; in other words, a person who is able to take it to the next step, an Einstein of sorts within our industry. And once again, there is only one man, and that is Tom DeMark.

15. *When you devise a trading system, what time frame do you use most? For example, do you use daily bars, weekly bars, 1-minute bars, 10-minute bars, or 60-minute bars?*

In terms of the trading system we've devised, the time frame is applicable almost across the board. When we first began trading, we were very aggressively oriented into the intraday market analysis. In fact, trading the S&Ps, I'd use 3-minute, 5-minute, 7-minute, 11-minute, 13-minute, 17-minute, 19-minute, and 23-minute charts. The one good thing about an intraday approach is that we always go home flat; we feel pretty good about it. The bad news is the risk reward can never be as conducive as one of what we call breakout channels, which is of course what Paul Tutor Jones, Richard Dennis, and many of the greats devised to accumulate millions. In other words, the trend is your friend if you can maximize that position. We have found that if a market has good volume, good open interest is a tradable market. The system that we would develop will work equally well on daily bars, weekly bars, 1-minute bars, 10-minute bars, or 60-minute bars.

16. *If for some reason they closed every commodity in the world except one, and you were the guy in charge of deciding which one would stay open, which commodity would you choose? Why? What hours would it be open?*

I've got to give you a bad answer: CRB. Why? Because it is a composite of everything that we look at. What hours would it be open? Twenty-four hours in global.

Commodities serve a dual-hedged purpose. The primary purpose is to protect the hedgers, the commercial players, the ones that require price stability within our economy. Within our economy, we have the other half of the quotient, the speculators, and the two together provide the liquidity along with the beauty of the exchange. The only one because of that fact and because there is an interrelation between commodities; I mean, if I said corn, how could we not regulate the price of wheat? Wheat and corn and soybeans have something in unison as precious metals, as the financials do. So the only possible market that could stay open, that would have any validity, would be a CRB extended to be a basket of all the commodities players have to choose from. Now, how would the hedgers be able to control that? Well, that's another deciding question.

17. *If you were to choose one commodity you could never trade again and you could never include in a trading system, which commodity would this be? Why?*

There are quite a few that come to mind, but I have never traded them. Any illiquid market, any thinly traded market. A market where the best technical system in the world does not give you the ability to get in at the right time or out at the right time because of lack of buyers and sellers, so liquidity in the market is one in which the best performing system can only work to the ability of the liquidity in the market, so thereby since we are dealing with a systematic approach to increase our probability of our success, we would never want to choose a market that by its nature would decrease that same goal.

18. *Where do you get your ideas for your system? A chart? A pattern? Observations? Trades that you have done before? What is your favorite technique for coming up with a trading system?*

Where does one get any idea for a trading system? The system that Brad and I have been working on has been an ongoing scientific approach in terms of our computer analysis for 5 years and in terms of my analysis for 13 years. In terms of where one gets an idea, I think inspiration is a precious commodity. Inspiration comes from many places. From my tendency it tends to be observation; in other words, seeing something from a particular point. It is a new focus to see a problem in a unique way, maybe from a different angle, through a different set of circumstances. The other thing is trial and error. Trial and error is the most empirically sound, mathematical way that one can ascertain in whether a system works.

So in terms of how we develop our systems and how we refine our system and what inspires us to do something, it is usually something that we observe, or it is something within our system as we back test it that we find is a weakness of the system, because all systems have strengths and weaknesses. If we can hone in on the weaknesses and improve them, the overall effect of the system will be enhanced much more greatly than honing in on the things that are already fairly well-tuned.

19. *I want you to write a trading system for me. I want you to give me all the rules. I want you to tell me what commodity, what time frame, whether it is daily bars, whatever. What your entry rule is, your exit rule with a profit, your exit rule with a loss. It doesn't have to be a great system. Just give me an idea of something you would look at, something you would test to see if there was any validity.*

For the sake of simplicity, we are going to write a simple trading system. What you need to know is what commodity, what time frame, whether it's daily bars or whatever. The first thing that I probably would want to choose is a commodity with some sort of seasonal tendencies. That immediately attracts me to the grains. In terms of the commodities, let's go with soybeans or wheat or corn. Now in terms of the time frame, we began trading the intraday.

So, with that in mind, the trader system that we're going to want to use is going to use a longer time frame. We're going to be using weekly charts. Now, in terms of our entry rule, we are going to set up a parameter of say, 15 particular candle patterns in which we'll issue a buy signal. We are going to issue, let's say, 15 candlestick patterns that would issue a sell signal. Within that, let's take the example of a buy signal, we would set up a series of rule-based parameters so that if we got a buy signal, we would make some first determinations about our oscillators. If the buy signal was located near the lowest lows of a recent period or the highest highs. The rule that we would develop is we would be looking for a buy signal after a downtrend in consolidation or after a straight downtrend. That would be our entry rule. We would always have an exit rule for our loss. The key to successful trading is having risk reward.

Risk reward to me must be three to one, two to one to be acceptable. In other words, if we say that if we buy silver at five and it goes to seven, we'll make money, and it's a two to one risk reward, we have a totally unrealistic risk reward. If the market in silver is trading from 5 to 530 and the low has been about 485, 490, you can see we've intrinsically got about a two to one. That's the first thing. We have to have one of our signals generated through candlesticks; it has to fit the criteria of western rule-based parameters; that's our entry rule.

Our exit rules with the profit are the same as our system. We would have an algorithm that would simply look for series of lows a week and two weeks prior that we would consider to be support levels. We would place them a percentage under the support level; the percentage under would be a factor of that point times what we consider to be a volatility level. And in terms of what it would have to look like to see if the tests were valid, we would basically pull up the system that we have, the Candlestick Forecaster®, and run a watch using some more complicated scenarios in that setup of P & L statement. We could set it up on a spreadsheet like Excel, but it would be a simple rule-based parameter that could be written into TradeStation, MetaStock, System Writer. It would be an empirically testable system.

20. *What's the typical day in the life of a system developer? What time to you start? What time do you end? What is it you do all day long? How are your orders placed? How is your system run?*

The beauty is that there really isn't a typical day. We have routines, but the beauty of being able to be in system development is the opportunity to, at some point during the day, play a chess game. And the magnificent part is to test our ideas each morning when the market trades. It is here that we have an absolute categorically defined judge that gives no grey marks and makes no mistakes, is simply black and white. The system works when we make money over time; it loses when we cannot.

We begin our day usually around 7:00 California time, and that day will usually start with us analyzing the markets. As developers and traders, we are very interested in how the markets are opening up, depending upon on what markets we're trading. Quite honestly, I have the rare fortune that as a CTA I only handle one account, and that is my own. Since I am only responsible to myself, when I do trade with stops, I'm able to wake up about 6:00, 6:30. I keep a system at home. I do a good amount of grain activity. One of the reasons is that it starts at a beautiful point of the day here, at 7:30, finishes up before noon, and is something that I like.

In terms of how our orders are placed, we use a simple mechanical system on an end-of-day basis, which will generate buy or sell signals. We will place those orders market on open in the morning, or we will run the system about a half an hour prior to the close of the day. If we generate a signal that we feel strong about, then we will actually try to have a jump on the system, which of course is more aggressive, more risky, but therefore potentially more profitable. What we will do is place that order market on close the day prior because we have a high probability within 90, 95 percent that that signal will actually be generated on the close. We also use intraday charts for entry and exit points to get more exact timing, and that seems to be a point we are honing in on. But as for the basics of this system, the orders are placed market on open, market on close, and when you are stopped out.

In terms of how our system is run, we've developed a system to run on an IBM base. We interface directly with signal data feed and future source data feed for our real-time data feed. We are affiliated with about 25 end-of-day data feeds so that our system runs on just a 486 66. It has a minimal amount of RAM. It's got 8 meg, VGA screen, a mouse, and a printer. The data feed we utilize for it is a real-time data feed even though it is for an-end-of day, but we can just as easily run it. End-of-day of course is the real time systems allow us to update the charts periodically throughout the day to catch some sort of a jump into the market.

21. *If you could have your system run in any manner, what would be the preferable method? Would you have the person whose money is at risk run the system, or would you have a third party run the system and just arbitrarily take the trades as they are generated, regardless of consequence?*

Optimally, one should trade without emotions. This is easier in principle than in practice. Regardless of whether a third party or the trader whose money is at risk runs the system, all steps must be taken to remove emotional attachment from the trade. If the trader whose money is at risk can accomplish this goal, then he will be able to maximize the potential of any trading system. The key is removal of emotion. Whoever can accomplish this task is the one who should place the trade.

22. *Let's pretend I don't have a single book on commodities, and I'm interested in writing systems. Other than your own work, what book would you recommend? Along these same lines, is there anything you would avoid—whether it's software, books, lectures, whatever?*

There is a multitude of books, but the first book, absolutely, positively, bar none, is John J. Murphy's *Technical Analysis of the Futures Markets*. This gives an overview on all the technical studies available and how the formulas are made. Along the same lines, the other book that I probably would look at is *Computer Analysis of the Technical Market* by LaBoe. That's an exceptional book because it shows you, Murphy shows you, what these technical studies are and LaBoe and Lucas' book really hones you in on how to apply it to a computer based trading application.

23. *Do you think it is necessary for a software developer/real-time trader to have tick-by-tick real-time quotes? Why or why not?*

The main system that we use, the Master Edition of the Forecaster, is an end-of-day system. In terms of it being necessary for a software developer or a real-time trader to have tick-by-tick real-time quotes, from my history as a broker for 13 plus years, I could not conceive of being part of the market without seeing it tick. However, the system that we trade with is based on end-of-day data. The real-time system we developed that works with intraday analysis and day trading has a requirement that it have a dedicated line to a real-time quote system. Another question we're asked is, what do we think about tick-by-tick delayed real-time quotes, and my philosophy is that if you are involved in the market to such a degree where minutes count by the time you have gotten any kind, excuse me, it's a step above end of day; but if you are going to be an intraday trader, to trade with delayed quotes is kind of attempting to trade with two hands tied behind your back, your mouth tied, and the phone off the hook. You simply cannot react to it in time, and in my opinion is completely uncalled for. Now, what do I recommend to our traders who are using a position trading system but watching the market? Delayed quotes are beautiful.

24. *What kind of quotes do you have? What kind of software would you recommend? Are there any systems or software that you would definitely not recommend?*

We use Data Broadcast Company, Signal Data Feed, and Future Source, which is also our real-time data feed. We also have end-of-day data feeds, TC 2000, Profit, and Information Services, which provides access. Because our programs read 25 different data formats, we find that we at least have data files on all of them and accessibility to go on-line on any of them. It's very important to us.

As for software, you have to imagine yourself as a carpenter: Some carpenters are masonry carpenters and some are finish carpenters, some put up the frames of the house and some put up the drywalls of the house, and some dig the foundation. The hammer that I would recommend for you if you were a mason carpenter would bust the wall of any drywall that you had to go into and finish. That would not allow you to get too many more jobs. What I am trying to say is that the software you need is the one that best suits your particular trading style, because software applications are simply tools that allow you to perform your task.

There are systems that I've heard don't perform well. Since these are not systems that I've seen work, and I have not been able to qualify them, I have no comment on them. But the way that I think that the question should be approached is this: If, in fact, these technical packages are simply tools, the ones that I definitely do not recommend are ones that simply don't fulfill the needs of your trading style. For example, if point in figure is not in any way incorporated in your personal methodology, then a system that specializes in point and figure is something I would not recommend. If you are looking at a system that is based on being able to customize formulas and have complete control over them, you would look to TradeStation or MetaStock. However, if you wanted a package in which you are using predefined indicators, there are a lot of other ones available.

25. *How much data do you think is necessary to be tested as far as assessing a day-trade session on five-minute bars? A daily bar system? A 60-minute system?*

In ascertaining validity of any day-trading system, the more data available the better. Daily charts, I believe, require a minimum of six months; however, one year would be optimal for a minimum. Each year on a daily chart will contain approximately 200 trading days. You can use this 200 cycle as a minimum for all time frames. This would include five-minute as well as 60-minute intraday charts.

26. *Why do some systems consistently perform year after year, and other systems fail or need to be continually optimized?*

In the beginning of an article that I had written for *Futures* magazine in July of 1994, I said that although systems have changed over time, two things will always remain the same. First, systems that have validity, that have universal truth, that have merit of working, will consistently perform year after year, decade after decade, century after century. Second, systems that fail or continually need to be optimized do not have that universal quality. They might have the ability to perform well in given circumstances, under set parameters, because of a given environment. I'm not going to say it's a fluke of luck. It's just that the system is highly defined for a particular set of circumstances.

We just finished doing a statistical study on a cotton chart. We went back eight years and found that it performed about $88,000 based on a one-contract lot. This was about a month ago. Right now, it's down to about $77,000. Looking at it year by year, we saw that what tended to happen was that the drawdowns were small; and when it hit these ferocious moves, the risk rewards were great. So in terms of the consistent performance year after year, we have to break it down even further. The performance has to be profitability, but if we have a system that performs well year after year, we analyze it and find that 80 percent of the longs provide 90 percent of the profits. We obviously have a clue as to what to hone in on, whether we simply don't take the short calls or we redefine the short calls.

27. *How important are drawdowns in your research? How important is average trade size?*

How important are drawdowns to research? Just as important as they are to my own trading account. How important is an average trade size? I take this all very personally. We base our research on one-lot trades. We want to know that based upon that one-contract trade, this is how it is going to perform. Now in terms of the importance of drawdowns, drawdowns are a fact of life. Theoretically, we know we can go into a casino even at 48 percent odds and flip a coin, lose, double down, flip a coin, lose double down, flip a coin, lose, double down, and so forth. Theoretically, it works. In reality, it doesn't because we are not a bank. There's a point at which we will run out of money. In terms of drawdowns, we call that money management. Money management means doing a few things first of all. These sound like cliches, but if we can get them to work, they will help. One, maximize upside potential, minimize downside potential. Two, create a mechanical system in which drawdowns are predetermined based upon sound research that on a position trade has a minimum of two to three to one realistically. That is critical.

28. *Do you do portfolio management—linking several commodities of different systems together? Do you do pyramiding? Why or why not?*

In terms of portfolio management, we scan and analyze every single commodity there is. We put that into a portfolio manager and have a theoretical portfolio for our hotline as well as our personal accounts, and we do link several different commodities into our system together.

In terms of how we do work it with this one lot, we don't really pyramid, but we do scale in. In other words, if a market has been in a defined downtrend and it gives us a buy signal, we enter that market. Two days later, we get another buy signal; we add one position. We do not believe in pyramiding. Upside-down pyramiding has an opportunity to work and by that I mean you buy 10, then you buy 5, then you buy 4, 3, 2, 1, so that, of course, when that market turns around—as Volcker said, "Trees do not grow to the sky, never have, never will"—we have the least number of our best positions at the worst possible price. Scale buying, maximizing winning positions, is just as important as trend following.

29. *Let's get a little morbid. You've died. You've left a sealed letter to your heirs. It contains the secret of your fortune. It's the secret to allow them to continue the lifestyle to which they have been accustomed. What one sentence is in the letter?*

One, follow your dream. Two, have the persistence to live it out. Three, have the foresight, the knowledge, and the wisdom to realize when you are right, when you are wrong, and how to deal with both situations.

30. *Without giving the secret of life, how would you write an imitation of your system in two lines or less in TradeStation language? For example, I have an S&P system called Buy Monday. "Monday you buy it, put in a $1,400 stop, get out on the close." That's how you write that.*

The system we have developed would be impossible to write in two lines of code. We have developed a system that has over 300,000 lines of code. So writing something like buy on Monday if this did this, and do this and get out, would simply not be profitable. We have spent five years developing 1,300 patterns, a genetic algorithm that has combined a half a million computations and come up with extreme amounts of variations. I guess the one line I would have to write is learn how to play four games of chess at once; follow them closely, and make sure you win them all.

31. *Give us an example of some of your work put in English-type language for a system.*

Systems of validity that work, be they eastern or western, have a universal quality. They can mathematically define market sentiment. So if we can find certain given scenarios in which the market sentiment is revealed, we can have a clue to the market. The market's moved up for the last three days, for example. It closes at $3. On the fourth day, it opens higher. But at some point during the day, the psychology changes and the price begins to move into the body (range) of the prior day and then closes below the midpoint. In fact, it looks like a dark cloud cover over a white candle. That, simply put in an English-type language, is the definition of one of the most simple patterns, a dark cloud.

32. *People ask us, "Where did you come up with these questions?" We asked a lot of prospects and clients of Robbins Trading what they look for in system developers over the last couple of years. We also posted in the Internet, talked to people at seminars, talked to other system developers, and asked their ideas for questions.*

My philosophy has always been this: I became fascinated in candlesticks because I always had a great affinity, desire, to learn about eastern studies, the culture of Asia. I was also a staunch technician. Many times, new clients, when I used to take them on, would ask me, well, what market should they trade? And I would say, what do you do right now, are you semi-retired? One of them said, yes, in fact I'm semi-retired. Well, what did you do, I asked him. Well, I used to be in real estate. I said, so you are telling me you have a fairly good feel for interest rates, right, you work with mortgages, of course. I know mortgages, he said, but I heard wheat is really hot. I said, do you own a farm, and he said no. Do you have an uncle that owns a farm, he said no. I said, have you ever lived in a farming community, and he said no. And I said, well, why don't you go buy a farm, live in a farming community, get to know those people, get a feel for that and then think about trading wheat. But we could also take an easier route. Take from your life experience. We all have had the beauty and the opportunity to learn about certain avenues. Take that intrinsic knowledge that you have, that fundamental basis, so you have a feel for the market you are looking at, and from that, begin to search the experts out. Learn the technical systems. Learn the systems that have proven over time can give people a higher probability, but most importantly, take the wisdom that you have already learned, the wisdom that we are all searching for and let it point you in the proper direction, so that you can walk down the path of financial success. I think that past learning experience is the single most important thing that you should add and consider when you want to know what questions you need to ask and how you need to go about developing your own system.

This has been Gary Wagner. It has been quite a pleasure speaking with you and I hope that in some small way, the words of wisdom, the mistakes that Brad and myself have made, and hopefully the benefits that we've added to the technical trading community, at large, has helped. Most importantly, we are very proud and grateful to be considered to be part of this community. We thank you very much. It is my wish that you find the wisdom you seek, and that wisdom allows you to reach your financial goals. Good trading.

Bill Williams

INTRODUCTION

Dr. Bill Williams is one of the most interesting people in the commodity business today. He has many interests, and he's good at everything he does. Bill has taken a very complex area, fractal research, and turned it into a symposium seminar where you can go one-on-one and learn about fractals and learn how to apply fractals in trading. If you have the chance to spend a week with Bill, I suggest you do so. I think you'll find it to be a very interesting and educational time.

1. *Tell me about yourself. If someone were to say, "Tell me about Bill Williams," what would you want them to know? Give me a brief biography of you before you got into commodities, and a brief biography of what you have done since you got into commodities.*

I began my career as an engineer with an emphasis on physics. After doing a stint in the Air Force and flying commercially for a while, I went back to graduate school to obtain a doctorate in psychology. While practicing psychotherapy part-time, I was also the executive vice president of what was at that time the world's largest manufacturer of carpets on a square yardage basis. While serving as the executive V.P., our stock went on the New York exchange, underwritten by Merrill Lynch. Our stock appreciated over 13,500 percent in less than two years.

I then received a research grant from the University of Miami Medical School and Nova University to do research in the brain/mind/body connection. An outgrowth of this research resulted in the establishment of the Soma Institute, which still teaches these techniques to medically licensed students. The Institute is currently teaching classes in the state of Washington and in Frankfurt, Germany.

I started trading in 1959 and am currently in my 37th year of trading stocks and commodities. Trading has been my full-time occupation for the past 15 years. During this time, I have traded over 500 managed accounts and been a consultant to a number of foreign banks, large traders, hedgers, and commercials.

I have conducted trading workshops for over 22,000 traders in 14 different countries. In 1986 I began training traders in private tutorials and have trained over 600 individual traders who are now successful independent speculators.

My research in trading has centered around the science of chaos and the underlying structure of the market as displayed by the "fractals" in five different dimensions of the market. Today, my main occupation revolves around trading my own funds, doing further research and conducting a limited number of private tutorials.

2. *Tell me about your technique. What makes it exclusively yours? How did you develop it?*

I believe that our approach is the first successful and practical application of the science of chaos to trading. What makes this approach unique is that we do not use any of the usual linear techniques, such as stochastics, RSI, ADX, DMI, ADX, neural networks, market profile, and so on.

This approach was developed using a Cray mainframe computer with the assistance of two Ph.Ds in theoretical math and computer science. We spent three years converting the computer output to simple visual and tradable pattern-recognition indicators.

From our research, we believe that the market consists of at least five different dimensions as opposed to the usual two (price and time). Our approach looks at the market from price, time (space), mass (volume), momentum, and energy. This approach allows much better entries and exits. Our aim is to take 80 percent out of a trend move, and often puts us short at the bottom of the top bar and long at the top of the bottom bar.

Our belief is that price itself does not cause the market to move. Price is the effect, and what changes before price is momentum, and what changes before momentum is volume, and what changes before volume is millions of us traders making irrational decisions about what to do in buying and selling the market. Therefore, we do not use price-based indicators. Stochastics, RSI, and similar indicators compare price to price and are of no use in our analysis of the market.

Another unique aspect of our approach is the speed of analysis. Using our materials, one can analyze any chart of any time frame and know exactly what should be done on every bar—where to add on, pyramid, stop and reverse, or just get out of the market—in ten seconds or less.

Our approach is based on the market being the big teacher that will show any trader how to handle not only trading but also money management, spreads, and selling options.

3. *Tell me about your best current trading system. What makes it tick? What are the features that make it the best trading system? Why do you trade this system?*

Our best approach is to look at the market from five different dimensions, with each dimension offering buy and sell signals. Our strategy is to take each signal going in one direction and add on to the position on a repeat of that signal or any one of the other four indicators and exit the position or stop and reverse to go in the opposite direction when the first signal in the opposite direction is hit. This approach makes trading low stress and makes it easy to follow the clear, unambiguous signals the market provides.

4. *How long ago did you write your first trading system?*

It was in 1962.

5. *Remember back to your first trading system. Can you tell us the rules?*

Buy new highs, sell new lows using 13-, 21-, 34-, or 55-bar breakouts.

6. *What caused you to abandon or modify that trading system the very first time?*

Two things: It wasn't consistent, and I developed a more sensitive approach.

7. *When you look at another person's trading system, what is the very first thing you look for to tell if it's a good or a bad system?*

I make it a point *not* to look at other's systems.

8. *What is the least important aspect of a trading system as far as you are concerned?*

Market price.

9. *In your current work, are you using a mechanical approach, or is there judgment involved in your trading?*

All five dimensional indicators are absolutely nonambivalent and nonambiguous, and there are places for traders to make what I call executive decisions. So judgment does play a part in such matters as which time frame to trade, how many contracts, how aggressive, and so on. The most important ability any systems trader can have is to know when to take the system's signals and when not to.

10. *Are you currently using TradeStation or System Writer? If not, what software do you use to run your trading system?*

I use TradeStation, CQG, CQG for Windows, DTN, and Teletrac. Some of our indicators can be programmed on TradeStation, and all of them can be recognized on any retrieval equipment.

11. *Is your current trading system for sale? For lease? On a fax line? How do you provide this information to clients?*

It is available in two different forms. We do not sell a "canned" system but rather a complete educational program for successful trading. Our Home Study Package includes our book *Trading Chaos*, a 330-page trading manual; a chaos workbook outlining exactly what to do each day of the 90-day training program; 12 video tapes including actual examples (winning and losing); eight audio tapes designed especially to aid traders in relaxing while trading; and three computer disks, which include TradeStation indicators, an S&P day-trading system, and a computorial disk that walks one through the indicators.

After one completes the home study portion, we have private tutorials where the trader comes into our trading room for four days of learning and actual trading. After that, we stay in close touch via fax or phone or both to make sure the trader not only understands but is successful in using our approach. We feel that once a trader attends our private tutorial, it is our responsibility to make sure that he or she is successful.

In fact, we have a written guarantee that if a trader finds any system that is more successful in the same markets than our technique, we will cheerfully refund the purchase money.

The November 1995 issue of *Technical Analysis of Stocks and Commodities* contains a product review of this material.

12. *Can you share the concept behind your trading system, for example, your main entry technique, your exit if you are wrong, and your exit if you are right?*

We take a nonlinear, natural approach to trading the market, as opposed to an economic, fundamental, technical, or mechanical approach. We trade the underlying structure of the market, as opposed to the current price.

13. *If you could advise system developers to do one thing when they are starting out, what would that be?*

Study and learn from the market itself. It is always 100 percent right, and a willing teacher. Don't copy other approaches; learn from Mother Market herself.

14. *Other than yourself, who do you think is the best system developer, or who do you think is the best teacher of system development?*

The work and research of two traders stand out in my mind. Those are Joe Krutsinger and Tom Joseph. Joe has made great strides in finding out what does and doesn't work and made those techniques available to the average trader. Tom Joseph's seminal work with the Elliott Wave has added precision and predictability formerly not available to Elliottians.

15. *When you devise a trading system, what time frame do you use most? For example, do you use daily bars, weekly bars, 1-minute bars, 10-minute bars, or 60-minute bars?*

I use all time frames. One of the underlying principles of the science of chaos is the concept of self-similarity, which means that if a fractal formation does not work on the monthly, weekly, daily, and all intraday time frames, it is not a fractal.

16. *If for some reason they closed every commodity in the world except one, and you were the guy in charge of deciding which one would stay open, which commodity would you choose? Why? What hours would it be open?*

Currencies, because they are the most trending markets. It would be, as it is now, a 24-hour market and include the entire world.

17. *If you were to choose one commodity you could never trade again and you could never include in a trading system, which commodity would this be? Why?*

Lumber. It is controlled by too few traders and therefore is not a rational trading situation.

18. *Where do you get your ideas for your system? A chart? A pattern? Observations? Trades that you have done before? What is your favorite technique for coming up with a trading system?*

Basically, I get my ideas from nature. My deepest belief is that the market is a natural phenomenon. I look for repetitive patterns, which are determined mathematically through nonlinear feedback calculus. My favorite and most profitable techniques come from getting close to the market and living with it without preconceived ideas. I am best when I can empty my mind and just listen to the market with no input from any other source.

19. *I want you to write a trading system for me. I want you to give me all the rules. I want you to tell me what commodity, what time frame, whether it is daily bars, whatever. What your entry rule is, your exit rule with a profit, your exit rule with a loss. It doesn't have to be a great system. Just give me an idea of something you would look at, something you would test to see if there was any validity.*

I would look at my main concern, which is the market's reaction to incoming volume. Raw volume is important since the market requires new volume to start a trend run. I would take the price excursion (high - low or range) and divide that by the volume. This gives me the "tick mileage," or how much price change each volume tick accounts for. This creates a facilitation index. I want to move with the greater facilitation. So as this index goes up, I will go in the direction of the market and stay in that direction until the index turns (the price changes direction) and the facilitation index increases. I would stay in the market and simply go with the direction and the facilitation index.

20. *What's the typical day in the life of a system developer? What time to you start? What time do you end? What is it you do all day long? How are your orders placed? How is your system run?*

I live in the central time zone. I get up at 5 A.M. and spend the first 45 minutes writing down my thoughts, including my plans for the day and insights of the past 24 hours. At 6 A.M., I go to the gym for an early morning workout. I return around 7 A.M., have a quick breakfast, and go to the trading room around 7:15 A.M. At that point, I call the brokers with my orders for the day.

I make it a point not to get bogged down staring at the screen all day. I place alarms at all the entry/exit points and check the monitors once every couple of hours or when the alarms are triggered.

21. *If you could have your system run in any manner, what would be the preferable method? Would you have the person whose money is at risk run the system, or would you have a third party run the system and just arbitrarily take the trades as they are generated, regardless of consequence?*

I prefer to run the system myself, with my money at risk. I am paid by the market to take risks and would not delegate that responsibility or enjoyment to anyone else. Win or lose, I am willing to take the results without blaming anyone else.

22. *Let's pretend I don't have a single book on commodities, and I'm interested in writing systems. Other than your own work, what book would you recommend? Along these same lines, is there anything you would avoid—whether it's software, books, lectures, whatever?*

Joe Krutsinger's book. I would avoid most common indicators. I would also avoid system writers who brag about their "20 best systems." If you have a good system, you sure as heck don't need 20, now do you?

23. *Do you think it is necessary for a software developer/real-time trader to have tick-by-tick real-time quotes? Why or why not?*

Yes, because that is the real lifeblood and heartbeat of the market.

24. *How much data do you think is necessary to be tested as far as assessing a day-trade session on five-minute bars? A daily bar system? A 60-minute system?*

The amount of back data would depend on the individual markets. Markets change all the time. The S&P does not act as it did two years ago. If someone came to me with a system they claim has worked consistently for 20 years, I would not touch it with a 10-foot pole. I know it won't work in the future. Think back to the early 1980s with those hundreds of black box systems that sold for $3,000 each or more. None of them are in use today. Why? *They don't work* because they are not based on the real underlying structure of the market.

25. *Why do some systems consistently perform year after year, and other systems fail or need to be continually optimized?*

I don't know of any totally mechanical system that has worked over the years. My belief is that unless the system is based on the underlying structure, it cannot change with the market.

26. *How important are drawdowns in your research? How important is average trade size?*

Quite important. They must be low to withstand a series of adverse trades.

27. *Do you do portfolio management—linking several commodities of different systems together? Do you do pyramiding? Why or why not?*

I do portfolio management, again letting the market allocate my assets based on market action. I absolutely pyramid with increasing aggressiveness when it is confirmed that I am in on the right side of the trend. I add on, add on, and add on until I get the first negative signal, and then I either dump them all or stop and reverse. I pyramid because the market only trends about 15 to 30 percent of the time, so I feel I must be very aggressive during this time.

28. *Let's get a little morbid. You've died. You've left a sealed letter to your heirs. It contains the secret of your fortune. It's the secret to allow them to continue the lifestyle to which they have been accustomed. What one sentence is in the letter?*

Learn and be one with the market—*go with the flow and let go!*

29. *Without giving the secret of life, how would you write an imitation of your system in two lines or less in TradeStation language? For example, I have an S&P system called Buy Monday. "Monday you buy it, put in a $1,400 stop, get out on the close." That's how you write that.*

Trade the momentum, not the price. Let the momentum determine direction and load.

30. *Give us an example of some of your work put in English-type language for a system.*

There really is a Holy Grail, and it is "Want what the market wants."

All our disappointments and upsets with the market come from having *expectations* that were not met. "I thought the bonds were going up, and they went down." What if we traded *without* any expectations? Our approach allows us to check our trading acumen every second the market is open. The secret question is "Do I care which way the market moves next?" If I can honestly say that I don't care which way it moves, I am trading well. If I feel, "I wish the bonds would go up," I know I am out of synch with the market.

Larry Williams

INTRODUCTION

Larry Williams is simply the best. I know of no other system developer
who does better work, more original work, and more volume of work than
Larry Williams. I've been a student of Larry's since 1978 and very proud
to say that most of what I know that works is derived from Larry Williams.
In Larry's tape you will find it's given in his speaking style, so don't be put
off by grammar. Take a look at the content because there's more content in
these few pages than in many, many text books on commodity trading.

The system I wrote from Larry Williams' notes is called Williams 19.
It's based on the channel breakout technique of buy the highest high of the
so many days, stop, sell the lowest low of the so many days, stop, but it does
have a twist. And that twist is definitely using his projected highs and projected lows. I wrote instead of using the highest high, it's the highest projected high, and the lows of the projected lows, and we used a 16-bar length.
We did it in the Quick Editor, which means it can be done in Super Charts or
TradeStation, and as you can see, the results for the British pound in a pure
reversal system with no money management stop is very, very good.

1. *Tell me about yourself. If someone were to say, "Tell me about Larry
Williams," what would you want them to know? Give me a brief biography
of you before you got into commodities, and a brief biography of what you
have done since you got into commodities.*

I guess I'd want them to know that I'm somebody who has spent the majority of my life, the last 32 or 33 years, trying to beat the markets, and I've found that it is sometimes very easy and it is sometimes very difficult. I got in the market because it looked like a rather easy way to make money. It looked like it was easier than robbing banks, and that there was a potential there to make a huge amount of money if one were good at it. What I found out was that that is partially true. There is the potential for making huge amounts of money, and I've done that. But it is not easy work. It is by far the most difficult work that I can imagine when you are wrong. But when you are right, it's easier than having the combination to the bank vault. The problem is, nobody in this business that I've seen in the last 30 years has been able to identify the difference between those two time periods. In other words, the old adage that money is hard to come by is true in this business as it is in any business. It takes a lot of work, a lot of effort; you just don't come into town, fall off the turnip truck and make money. This is a tough, high-risk business.

As far as my brief biography goes, I've traded, I've written a couple of books, I've published a newsletter on commodity timing, and I've taught courses on trading. I've had some successes in trading along the way. The most notable one, of course, was the 1987 Robbins World Cup Trading Championship, but it wasn't the first time that I've made a big score in the market. The first time was in 1970 when I wrote *How I Made a Million Dollars Trading Commodities Last Year*, so I've been fortunate to have had some hits along the way.

2. *Tell me about your technique. What makes it exclusively yours? How did you develop it?*

Well, my techniques are technical and fundamental. What makes it exclusively mine? Well, I don't know that anybody has exclusivity to these techniques. I would say what is unique about mine is that, unlike most technicians, since 1970 I've focused on commercials, what the larger interests in the marketplace are doing, and investor sentiment, to see what the public's in, because they are usually wrong, and then I've tried to overlay technicals on top of this. In other words, if I can establish commercials and investor sentiment as a quasifundamental background to tell us what should happen, then we'll place the technical stuff on top of that. So I'm not strictly technical. I would say that is the big difference, one of the demarcations in terms of developing; I've spent years and who knows how many hours developing this stuff, and it seems like so much of my stuff I see other people doing. Fortunately, some of them give me credit. A lot of them don't, but obviously what's mine isn't exclusively mine. I think that I've made two or three big technical contributions. The first was the accumulation distribution index majors, which stood the test of time in 1969 and were responsible in determining accumulation distribution in stocks and commodities and that continue to call market highs and lows quite well. Here we are, some 27 years later. I developed that by looking at the price relationship between openings and closes as opposed to closes and closes.

Another major contribution I think that I made was the concept of volatility breakout. It literally wasn't done until the early 1980s. I think my first seminar on volatility breakout was 1979, where we added a volatility amount percentage of yesterday's range or the average range of the last few days to a value, a center point, a close and opening, whatever, and then bought at that price level. That was arrived at from my study of accumulation distribution because we found with accumulation/distribution the close to opening relationship was terribly important. We also found that the opening is the most important price in the market place, but what's even more important is the markets tend to move in cycles of blasts up and blasts down, and once you get a big blast up you continue going higher. For years, I bought weakness, but I found out that it is a little bit easier to buy strength. That is when the market starts moving past some point, you want to jump on the bandwagon. Another unique technique that is highly popularized now is my day of the week study. We were the first ones to start using it in commodities in probably 1986 to 1987, and that has been highly popularized now. Also my pattern, which has been ripped off by everybody in the world and has been used quite successfully by them. I would say that that's another unique exclusive Larry Williams study. Another one I popularized was zero balance, but that wasn't really mine. It was developed by Dr. Ralph Heiser 45 years ago, but he disappeared, and I've kind of carried on the tradition of that. And finally, pattern analysis. From maybe 1985, 1986 I started getting into specific price patterns for markets higher today than four days ago or that have an up close, down close, two minus closes, and an up close.

3. *Tell me about your best current trading system. What makes it tick? What are the features that make it the best trading system? Why do you trade this system?*

I don't know that I have any one best current trading system. I think trading systems are evolutionary in that you are always learning and adding to them, so I can't say here's one be-all end-all system for the market because I think the market's changed. The hours the bonds trade are different now than they were 10 years ago. The margin is different on the S&P now than it was five years ago. You have to be aware of things. A system will help you trade, but you've got to be awake and aware. I don't think you can just have a black box that sits down and makes money. I think the essence of my systems, though, is what makes them successful. I tend to buy strength. I tend to wait for the market that's set itself up in some fashion either by commercials or by patterns or by seasonals.

Now back to why I trade this system. I trade it because I think it offers the best potential rate of return. It is a system that I know fits my temperament—that might be a better answer. It fits my temperament, and I find as I'm getting older and my temperament changes, my approach to the market probably changes too.

4. *How long ago did you write your first trading system?*

Oh, probably in 1966 or 1967.

5. *Remember back to your first trading system. Can you tell us the rules?*

For stocks, it was based on a moving average and an overbought indicator. My concept was that when the market was overbought and then a short-term moving average would be broken for a sell signal, when the market was oversold and then a short term moving average turned to the up side, you had a buy signal. That was really the first trading system and those are the rules. I think I was using for an overbought indicator a 14-day overbought rate of change and then I was using a three-or-four-day moving average.

It worked very well. I mean I started a newsletter trading stocks, Williams Reports, a pre-newsletter back in those days. One of the very few stock market letters at the time and that was a trading system. It was backed up by using analysis of the advance/decline line to see if the market was particularly strong or weak at these junctures and that led me to think about accumulation/distribution. In other words was there something else that could tell us as we entered these oversold areas and we're getting a little rally, a buy signal, is it a false one or a good one, and accumulation distribution advance decline line gets better or worse. And our long term approach to the market at that time, I used a system that a guy named Gil Haller developed; he was the first person to my knowledge to ever write about the impact of yields on stock prices and he used some advance decline work which was absolutely brilliant.

6. *What caused you to abandon or modify that trading system the very first time?*

The ironic thing is that we abandon these systems because we get infatuated with other ideas. Research scientists continue doing research; that may be an unfortunate thing. I would probably be more successful as a trader if I just did one system and never turned on a computer or thought about the markets again in that sense, but my research is expanding and I'm still learning things about the market so any modifications were really trying to make better what you've got and I never really abandoned it. I used that trading system in the stock market from 1966 to when I sold the newsletter to some other people who continue using it in 1973 or something like that.

7. *When you look at another person's trading system, what is the very first thing you look for to tell if it's a good or a bad system?*

The average profit per trade. The first thing I look at is the average profit per trade and the second thing I look at is the risk reward ratio. If the average profit per trade is small, it probably will be tough to make money with it. For example, I saw one the other day in bonds; the average profit per trade was about $97. They deducted $15 for commission and slippage. That's not enough. You're trading on thin ice because you're going to get slippage; that's part of that system. The good part though is the risk/reward ratio wasn't bad, but I also want to make certain that my risk/reward ratio in relationship to my percentage of accuracy are in balance, which means that I need to have a higher percent of accuracy for the lower risk/reward ratio system and I can get by with a lower accuracy for a higher risk/reward ratio system. This is the average profit divided by the average loss.

8. *What is the least important aspect of a trading system as far as you are concerned?*

I don't know if there is a least important aspect of a trading system.

9. *In your current work, are you using a mechanical approach, or is there judgment involved in your trading?*

I use a mechanical approach with some judgment in it. The system that we use for Commodity Timing is basically everything that I know about the markets and trying to apply it in some reasonable fashion. I don't if you are going to use this question later on or not, but I'll try to answer it here. There are good long term trading systems for sale; the problem with them is their accuracy. They are very low at 30 percent and drawdown high so what you try to do is take that basic perimeter and improve it and with some judgment and contemplating.

10. *Are you currently using TradeStation or System Writer? If not, what software do you use to run your trading system?*

I am currently using TradeStation and System Writer and as you guys know, I love them immensely.

11. *Is your current trading system for sale? For lease? On a fax line? How do you provide this information to clients?*

No, I don't do any of this. I do the Commodity Timing Newsletter, I do a daily hotline, and I do a seminar maybe once or twice a year where I teach what I know, how I trade. I'd rather do that so people know what to do. I want to work with people who want to know this stuff. I don't want to just have a system, sell it and say good bye and let the person think that that is going to be all he has to do the rest of his life. It's not that way, and I don't want to associate with people like that. I want people who, like me, love the market and are infatuated and want to learn and then can take my stuff and continue learning on their own. 迷志

12. *Can you share the concept behind your trading system, for example, your main entry technique, your exit if you are wrong, and your exit if you are right?*

I think I have already gone over it. Usually patterns, volatility expansion, day of the week, time of the month, time of the year, seasonals and all these things is what I look at but of course, the Commercials, open interest, I look at it all.

Your exit if you're wrong . . . it's simply a dollar stop. I determine a dollar number almost all the time that I'm willing to lose, then that's it. Your exit if you are right . . . is some market configuration; the market has done something. It isn't just an absolute price target. One of the studies I did in the early 1970s, showed that in any system you hurt the system by taking a profit of a fixed dollar amount. That still is true today. I don't think I've ever seen a system in all these years forward that's been able to be improved upon by having an automatic price target.

13. *If you could advise system developers to do one thing when they are starting out, what would that be?*

I would advise them to be honest. We all get carried away with our system, and we develop systems that we think are great that later turn out not to be great. I think that we just have to give people a fair shake and say hey, this is my best effort, this is what I found, this is what I noticed, and let them know there is still risk involved. Just because you've done the research for your system doesn't mean it's going to make money for people. And to divulge, to reveal what you are doing so people can make a judgment of yes, I can trade on this, I can change it, whatever. I think too many people think that they are so smart they are going to make a black box and hide it from the world, and I think that is just terribly sophomoric and immature.

14. *Other than yourself, who do you think is the best system developer, or who do you think is the best teacher of system development?*

Well, those are way together two different things. In terms of system developer, Tom DeMarks has done a lot of stuff. Joe Krutsinger has done a lot of stuff. Tom's is highly creative. He may not get it all put together in a concise little format but in terms of his creativity, I can't think of anybody who has been any more creative. And there are so many people now. I mean, in the old days, it was Jake Berstein, and I, maybe Tom; who else would be there? In terms of stocks, Marty Zweis and Ned Davis are just legendary and their work has been extremely helpful in the commodity markets as well. I mean, what these guys have done is phenomenal. I could go on and on. John Hills made his contribution. Bruce Babcock, Welles Wilder, Joe Stowell, and Gerry Apel would be up there too. I admire all the guys who have hung around all these years and are still there today: people like George Angell.

Who is the best teacher of system development? Now that's a whole different question. There are a lot who I learned from: Bill Meehan, Gil Haller, Gerry Apel and Jake Bernstein.

15. *When you devise a trading system, what time frame do you use most? For example, do you use daily bars, weekly bars, 1-minute bars, 10-minute bars, or 60-minute bars?*

Well, I like to use a daily time frame because I don't want to have to watch 1-minute bar charts. So the time frame I'm comfortable with is daily bar charts, and that's what I most always use.

16. *If for some reason they closed every commodity in the world except one, and you were the guy in charge of deciding which one would stay open, which commodity would you choose? Why? What hours would it be open?*

I would probably choose the bonds because the margin is low. If I could lower the margins on the S&Ps, I'd choose the S&Ps but otherwise we'd choose the bonds and we'd have the bonds start trading about 7:00, 7:30 California time and closing at 1:00, 1:30 California time. There would be no night session.

17. *If you were to choose one commodity you could never trade again and you could never include in a trading system, which commodity would this be? Why?*

Oh, I'd probably make this commodity maybe cattle or orange juice, one of these thin choppy markets that there is nothing wrong with them, they are just so illiquid it is hard to get in and out of them.

18. *Where to you get your ideas for your system? A chart? A pattern? Observations? Trades that you have done before? What is your favorite technique for coming up with a trading system?*

Yes, I get my ideas from charts and observations of charts. From thinking and looking and looking and thinking and contemplating. I'll be out fly fishing sometime, and I have my attention really more on a concept of the market. When I run, I do a lot of running (40, 50 miles a week), I'll think about concepts and then I'll go to the computer to test the minutiae of the concept, but new trading system ideas start with a concept that should be logical. That's my favorite technique for coming up with trading systems.

19. *I want you to write a trading system for me. I want you to give me all the rules. I want you to tell me what commodity, what time frame, whether it is daily bars, whatever. What your entry rule is, your exit rule with a profit, your exit rule with a loss. It doesn't have to be a great system. Just give me an idea of something you would look at, something you would test to see if there was any validity.*

You want me to write a trading system for you, huh? Great. Okay, here's a trading rule. We'll buy the British pound at the highest projected high of the last fourteen days and sell short at the lowest projected low of the last fourteen days. A projected high is arrived at by taking the high plus the low plus the close, divide by three times two, subtract the low; that gives me the projected high for the day. And to get a projected low for the day, you take the high plus low plus close and divide by three times two and subtract the high and that will give you the projected low. Okay, then we'll take the highest of those projected highs for the last fourteen days, the lowest projected low for the last fourteen days. I will be a buyer at the highest projected high, a seller at the lowest projected low. Once long, I'll stay in that trade until I'm stopped out by going back to the other side of the equation, the lowest projected low. That's just an idea of a system. I might want to check dollar stops so that when I get tagged for a loss I may have a position where I go flat because I just lost too many dollars and then I would be in Neverland waiting for either a re-buy signal or a new sell signal and often it's in the same direction as the last trade!

20. *What's the typical day in the life of a system developer? What time do you start? What time do you end? What is it you do all day long? How are your orders placed? How is your system run?*

I get up at about 5:00 A.M., go to work, plug in the computer, start playing around, place market orders and in my case, answer the phone and talk to commodity traders or subscribers who have questions. I end the day about 5:00 P.M. At some point during the day I take off for a run, usually anywhere from 5 to 12 miles. The orders are placed depending on where I trade, and they are placed in different ways. Either by me or they are automatically done on the computer. I don't break for lunch; I stay in the office. I guess that's it.

21. *If you could have your system run in any manner, what would be the preferable method? Would you have the person whose money it at risk run the system, or would you have a third party run the system and just arbitrarily take the trades as they are generated, regardless of consequence?*

I think the easiest way to trade a system is to use a third party. Give it to them on a computer floppy disc and let them trade it while you watch it. If you have confidence in the system, that's probably the easiest way of doing it.

22. *Let's pretend I don't have a single book on commodities, and I'm interested in writing systems. Other than your own work, what book would you recommend? Along these same lines, is there anything you would avoid—whether it's software, books, lectures, whatever?*

I don't think I could I put it into one book. However, Joe's book, (*The Trading System Tool Kit*, Chicago; Irwin, 1994) is helpful in learning how to write a system, but in terms of getting the ideas for systems, maybe Welles Wilder's book, the *New Ways Book,* is helpful because there are a lot of interesting ideas in there. It presents you a way of thinking about trading systems.

I would avoid buying all this software and junk out there. I think you need TradeStation or System Writer or some old chart books and that's about it. I mean, you can do a lot of this stuff on your own.

And in terms of lectures and all that stuff, I think you have to pay attention to all of them; you never know where a good idea might come from.

23. *Do you think it is necessary for a software developer/real-time trader to have tick-by-tick real-time quotes? Why or why not?*

I don't think so. Again, it depends on the time frame you trade for.

24. *What kind of quotes do you have? What kind of software would you recommend? Are there any systems or software that you would definitely not recommend?*

I get daily quotes, that's all I care about. What kind of software would I recommend? TradeStation.

25. *How much data do you think is necessary to be tested as far as assessing a day-trade session on five-minute bars? A daily bar system? A 60-minute system?*

Well, a daily bar system works well for me. I did a system one time that had over a thousand trades in it using daily bars, so it covered about 15 years and it was really good. It was accurate 85 percent of the time. But from the day that I developed it, it never made a nickel. I don't think that the size of the university or sample means very much. A mathematician and statisticians will tell you that 30 samples is enough or 150 trades is enough or whatever, but real-time experience says that is not the way it is. There might be something else going on in the market that we are not able to account for, so you just have to give it your best shot; you develop your system, and you test it on a lot of data. You do have to have a good amount of data, but you have to look at what it is you are testing as well as just saying that it worked on so many days.

26. *Why do some systems consistently perform year after year, and other systems fail or need to be continually optimized?*

Well, I think the ones that performed consistently every year are: 1.) few and far between, and, 2.) they are long-term trend following.

27. *How important are drawdowns in your research? How important is average trade size?*

Drawdowns are very, very important. And I've already commented on average profit per trade. Obviously if you are drawdown versus what you make, let's say the system makes $100,000 but your drawdown is $80,000, are you willing to risk 80 to make 100? No. I think you should be willing to risk between 10 and at the most 20 percent to, say, $10,000 to $20,000 to make $100,000. Obviously, the lower the better.

28. *Do you do portfolio management—linking several commodities of different systems together? Do you do pyramiding? Why or why not?*

No, I just try to trade one or two markets the best I can. The other stuff is a little complicated, a little too highbrow for me.

29. *Let's get a little morbid. You've died. You've left a sealed letter to your heirs. It contains the secret of your fortune. It's the secret to allow them to continue the lifestyle to which they have been accustomed. What one sentence is in the letter?*

It would be, "Become a broker." And I say that because I think that's more certain. You could take the name Larry Williams and say, hey, I know Larry Williams' secrets, so trade with me and you'd be able to make a real good living as a broker, because of all the books and stuff that I've done. I don't think it would necessarily be the lifestyle one would want to lead but, I mean, brokers always make money. Now, traders, we have a problem. We have run ups and run downs, but the secret would be to pay attention to the commercials, pay attention to seasonals, pay attention to open interest, pay attention to the trend and buy at volatility expansion breakouts; sell at volatility expansion breakdowns.

PART 2

The Systems

MICHAEL CONNOR

Conner 19 JAPANESE YEN 65/99-Daily   01/05/87 - 01/02/96

Performance Summary: All Trades

Total net profit	$ 54657.50	Open position P/L	$ 1875.00
Gross profit	$ 104285.00	Gross loss	$ -49627.50
Total # of trades	81	Percent profitable	28%
Number winning trades	23	Number losing trades	58
Largest winning trade	$ 22795.00	Largest losing trade	$ -2267.50
Average winning trade	$ 4534.13	Average losing trade	$ -855.65
Ratio avg win/avg loss	5.30	Avg trade(win & loss)	$ 674.78
Max consec. winners	2	Max consec. losers	11
Avg # bars in winners	46	Avg # bars in losers	5
Max intraday drawdown	$ -21865.00		
Profit factor	2.10	Max # contracts held	1
Account size required	$ 24865.00	Return on account	220%

Performance Summary: Long Trades

Total net profit	$ 37257.50	Open position P/L	$ 0.00
Gross profit	$ 58897.50	Gross loss	$ -21640.00
Total # of trades	36	Percent profitable	36%
Number winning trades	13	Number losing trades	23
Largest winning trade	$ 13795.00	Largest losing trade	$ -1830.00
Average winning trade	$ 4530.58	Average losing trade	$ -940.87
Ratio avg win/avg loss	4.82	Avg trade(win & loss)	$ 1034.93
Max consec. winners	3	Max consec. losers	7
Avg # bars in winners	41	Avg # bars in losers	4
Max intraday drawdown	$ -7290.00		
Profit factor	2.72	Max # contracts held	1
Account size required	$ 10290.00	Return on account	362%

Performance Summary: Short Trades

Total net profit	$ 17400.00	Open position P/L	$ 1875.00
Gross profit	$ 45387.50	Gross loss	$ -27987.50
Total # of trades	45	Percent profitable	22%
Number winning trades	10	Number losing trades	35
Largest winning trade	$ 22795.00	Largest losing trade	$ -2267.50
Average winning trade	$ 4538.75	Average losing trade	$ -799.64
Ratio avg win/avg loss	5.68	Avg trade(win & loss)	$ 386.67
Max consec. winners	3	Max consec. losers	9
Avg # bars in winners	53	Avg # bars in losers	5
Max intraday drawdown	$ -22192.50		
Profit factor	1.62	Max # contracts held	1
Account size required	$ 25192.50	Return on account	69%

MICHAEL CONNOR

//\\\\\\\\\\\\\\\\\\\\\\\\\\\\\\\\\\\\\

SYSTEM

Name   : Conner 19
Notes :

Last Update : 03/21/96 05:22pm
Printed on : 03/21/96 05:23pm
Verified   : YES

/////////////////////////////////// CODE \\\\\\\\\\\\\\\\\\\\\\\\\\\\\\\\\\\\\

```
Input: LEConsec(4),SEConsec(4);
IF MRO(Close <= Close[1],LEConsec,1) = -1 Then
 Buy ("LE1")tomorrow at Lowest(H,4) stop;
IF MRO(Close >= Close[1],SEConsec,1) = -1 Then
 Sell ("SE1")tomorrow at Highest(L,4) stop;
{
If MarketPosition=1 then exitlong  ("LX1")
 from entry ("LE1") at Highest(L,4)[1] limit;

If MarketPosition=-1 then exitshort  ("SX1")
 from entry ("SE1") at Lowest(H,4)[1] limit;}

{ Anchors Stop to EntryBar low and high}
If Barssinceentry >0  then exitlong ("LX2") from entry ("LE1")
at$ Low - 2 points stop;
If Barssinceentry >0  then exitshort ("SX2") from entry ("SE1")
at$ High + 2 points stop;

{JKNote: Done in TradeStation Power Editor, $1000 MM stop used,
 LX1 and SX1 coded but not used.}
```

//\\\\\\\\\\\\\\\\\\\\\\\\\\\\\\\\\\\\\

Prepared using Omega TradeStation Version 3.50 by Omega Research, Inc.

JOSEPH DINAPOLI

Dinapoli5 S&P 500 INDEX 67/99-Daily   01/02/90 - 06/06/96

Performance Summary: All Trades

Total net profit	$ 87480.00	Open position P/L	$ -12325.00
Gross profit	$ 177140.00	Gross loss	$ -89660.00
Total # of trades	54	Percent profitable	50%
Number winning trades	27	Number losing trades	27
Largest winning trade	$ 45195.00	Largest losing trade	$ -18980.00
Average winning trade	$ 6560.74	Average losing trade	$ -3320.74
Ratio avg win/avg loss	1.98	Avg trade(win & loss)	$ 1620.00
Max consec. winners	5	Max consec. losers	4
Avg # bars in winners	43	Avg # bars in losers	15
Max intraday drawdown	$ -47285.00		
Profit factor	1.98	Max # contracts held	1
Account size required	$ 54285.00	Return on account	161%

Performance Summary: Long Trades

Total net profit	$ 105615.00	Open position P/L	$ 0.00
Gross profit	$ 137620.00	Gross loss	$ -32005.00
Total # of trades	27	Percent profitable	59%
Number winning trades	16	Number losing trades	11
Largest winning trade	$ 45195.00	Largest losing trade	$ -12055.00
Average winning trade	$ 8601.25	Average losing trade	$ -2909.55
Ratio avg win/avg loss	2.96	Avg trade(win & loss)	$ 3911.67
Max consec. winners	3	Max consec. losers	4
Avg # bars in winners	55	Avg # bars in losers	14
Max intraday drawdown	$ -19955.00		
Profit factor	4.30	Max # contracts held	1
Account size required	$ 26955.00	Return on account	392%

Performance Summary: Short Trades

Total net profit	$ -18135.00	Open position P/L	$ -12325.00
Gross profit	$ 39520.00	Gross loss	$ -57655.00
Total # of trades	27	Percent profitable	41%
Number winning trades	11	Number losing trades	16
Largest winning trade	$ 26370.00	Largest losing trade	$ -18980.00
Average winning trade	$ 3592.73	Average losing trade	$ -3603.44
Ratio avg win/avg loss	1.00	Avg trade(win & loss)	$ -671.67
Max consec. winners	3	Max consec. losers	4
Avg # bars in winners	26	Avg # bars in losers	16

Dinapoli5 S&P 500 INDEX 67/99-Daily   01/02/90 - 06/06/96

Account size required $ 69260.00 Return on account   -26%

JOSEPH DINAPOLI

```
Type          : System
Name          : Dinapoli5
Notes         :

Last Update   : 02/10/97 12:56pm
Printed on    : 02/10/97 12:57pm
Verified      : YES
```

```
Input:Length1(3),Length2(7),Length3(25);
If (Average(Close,Length1)[3]< Average(Close,Length2)[5]   OR
Average(Close,Length2)[5]< Average(Close,Length3)[5]) AND
  (Average(Close,Length1) > Average(Close,Length2) AND   (Average(Close,Length2)>
 Average(Close,Length3))) Then Buy at   (Average(Close,Length1)[3]) limit;

If (Average(Close,Length1)[3]> Average(Close,Length2)[5]   OR
Average(Close,Length2)[5]> Average(Close,Length3)[5]) AND
  (Average(Close,Length1) < Average(Close,Length2) AND   (Average(Close,Length2)<
 Average(Close,Length3))) Then Sell at   (Average(Close,Length1)[3]) limit;
```

STAN EHRLICH

Ehrlich17 Heating Oil - NYMEX-Daily   01/02/80 - 03/31/94

Performance Summary: All Trades

Total net profit	$ 36109.00	Open position P/L	$ 0.00
Gross profit	$ 86847.19	Gross loss	$ -50738.19
Total # of trades	80	Percent profitable	54%
Number winning trades	43	Number losing trades	37
Largest winning trade	$ 7925.00	Largest losing trade	$ -2575.00
Average winning trade	$ 2019.70	Average losing trade	$ -1371.30
Ratio avg win/avg los	1.47	Avg trade(win & loss)	$ 451.36
Max consec. winners	11	Max consec. losers	5
Avg # bars in winners	33	Avg # bars in losers	21
Max intraday drawdown	$ -11248.60		
Profit factor	1.71	Max # contracts held	1
Account size required	$ 11248.60	Return on account	321%

Performance Summary: Long Trades

Total net profit	$ 24404.40	Open position P/L	$ 0.00
Gross profit	$ 49224.40	Gross loss	$ -24820.00
Total # of trades	36	Percent profitable	56%
Number winning trades	20	Number losing trades	16
Largest winning trade	$ 6035.00	Largest losing trade	$ -2453.20
Average winning trade	$ 2461.22	Average losing trade	$ -1551.25
Ratio avg win/avg los	1.59	Avg trade(win & loss)	$ 677.90
Max consec. winners	5	Max consec. losers	3
Avg # bars in winners	39	Avg # bars in losers	23
Max intraday drawdown	$ -6743.40		
Profit factor	1.98	Max # contracts held	1
Account size required	$ 6743.40	Return on account	362%

Performance Summary: Short Trades

Total net profit	$ 11704.60	Open position P/L	$ 0.00
Gross profit	$ 37622.80	Gross loss	$ -25918.20
Total # of trades	44	Percent profitable	52%
Number winning trades	23	Number losing trades	21
Largest winning trade	$ 7925.00	Largest losing trade	$ -2575.00
Average winning trade	$ 1635.77	Average losing trade	$ -1234.20
Ratio avg win/avg los	1.33	Avg trade(win & loss)	$ 266.01
Max consec. winners	8	Max consec. losers	5
Avg # bars in winners	29	Avg # bars in losers	20
Max intraday drawdown	$ -7263.40		
Profit factor	1.45	Max # contracts held	1
Account size required	$ 7263.40	Return on account	161%

STAN EHRLICH

Page 1

```
Type        : System
Name        : Ehrlich17
Notes       :

Last Update : 12/10/96 03:17pm
Printed on  : 12/10/96 03:18pm
Verified    : YES
```

```
{
Use DAILY bars for the Heating Oil}


If Low of Today < Lowest(Low,13)[3]
Then buy tomorrow at @Highest(High,3)[1] Stop;

If High of Today > Highest(High,13)[3]
Then Sell tomorrow at @Lowest(Low,3)[1] Stop;

{$$2500 money management stop, $2500 trailing stop,$55 comm. deducted}
```

DAVID FOX

Fox31 JAPANESE YEN 65/99-Daily   01/05/87 - 01/02/96

Performance Summary: All Trades

Total net profit	$	37927.50	Open position P/L	$ 8450.00
Gross profit	$	37927.50	Gross loss	$ 0.00
Total # of trades		2	Percent profitable	100%
Number winning trades		2	Number losing trades	0
Largest winning trade	$	31357.50	Largest losing trade	$ 0.00
Average winning trade	$	18963.75	Average losing trade	$ 0.00
Ratio avg win/avg loss		100.00	Avg trade(win & loss)	$ 18963.75
Max consec. winners		2	Max consec. losers	0
Avg # bars in winners		802	Avg # bars in losers	0
Max intraday drawdown	$	-2312.50		
Profit factor		100.00	Max # contracts held	1
Account size required	$	5312.50	Return on account	714%

Performance Summary: Long Trades

Total net profit	$	31357.50	Open position P/L	$ 0.00
Gross profit	$	31357.50	Gross loss	$ 0.00
Total # of trades		1	Percent profitable	100%
Number winning trades		1	Number losing trades	0
Largest winning trade	$	31357.50	Largest losing trade	$ 0.00
Average winning trade	$	31357.50	Average losing trade	$ 0.00
Ratio avg win/avg loss		100.00	Avg trade(win & loss)	$ 31357.50
Max consec. winners		1	Max consec. losers	0
Avg # bars in winners		1259	Avg # bars in losers	0
Max intraday drawdown	$	-1412.50		
Profit factor		100.00	Max # contracts held	1
Account size required	$	4412.50	Return on account	711%

Performance Summary: Short Trades

Total net profit	$	6570.00	Open position P/L	$ 8450.00
Gross profit	$	6570.00	Gross loss	$ 0.00
Total # of trades		1	Percent profitable	100%
Number winning trades		1	Number losing trades	0
Largest winning trade	$	6570.00	Largest losing trade	$ 0.00
Average winning trade	$	6570.00	Average losing trade	$ 0.00
Ratio avg win/avg loss		100.00	Avg trade(win & loss)	$ 6570.00
Max consec. winners		1	Max consec. losers	0
Avg # bars in winners		344	Avg # bars in losers	0
Max intraday drawdown	$	-2312.50		
Profit factor		100.00	Max # contracts held	1
Account size required	$	5312.50	Return on account	124%

DAVID FOX

////////////////////////////////Quick System: Fox31\\\\\\\\\\\\\\\Page 1 of 1\\\\

```
Notes     :
Last Update : 03/21/96 07:42pm
Printed on  : 03/21/96 07:44pm
Verified  : Yes
```

/////////////////////////////////INPUTS\\\\\\\\\\\\\\\\\\\\\\\\\\\\\\\\\\\

```
InputName      Default Value
-------------------------------------------------------------------------------
Length         220
```

////////////////////////////////////LONG ENTRY\\\\\\\\\\\\\\\\\\\\\\\\\\\\\\\\\\\

If   : CurrentBar > 1 and Close > Highest(High,Length)[1]

Then   Buy on Close

////////////////////////////////////SHORT ENTRY\\\\\\\\\\\\\\\\\\\\\\\\\\\\\\\\

If   : CurrentBar > 1 and Close < Lowest(Low,Length)[1]

Then   Sell on Close

////////////////////////////////////STOPS\\\\\\\\\\\\\\\\\\\\\\\\\\\\\\\\\\\\

Enabled	Stop	Enabled	Stop
No	Money Management Amount : $0.00	No	Breakeven Stop Floor : $0.00
No	$ Risk Trailing Stop Amount : $0.00	No	Profit Target Amount : $0.00
No	% Risk Trailing Stop Amount : $0.00 Floor : $0.00	No	Close all trades at end of day session

NELSON FREEBURG

Nelson Freeburg JAPANESE YEN 65/99-Daily   01/02/87 - 01/02/96

Performance Summary: All Trades

Total net profit	$ 93747.50	Open position P/L	$ 0.00
Gross profit	$ 162050.00	Gross loss	$ -68302.50
Total # of trades	83	Percent profitable	42%
Number winning trades	35	Number losing trades	48
Largest winning trade	$ 24220.00	Largest losing trade	$ -2855.00
Average winning trade	$ 4630.00	Average losing trade	$ -1422.97
Ratio avg win/avg loss	3.25	Avg trade(win & loss)	$ 1129.49
Max consec. winners	7	Max consec. losers	5
Avg # bars in winners	33	Avg # bars in losers	9
Max intraday drawdown	$ -10212.50		
Profit factor	2.37	Max # contracts held	1
Account size required	$ 13212.50	Return on account	710%

Performance Summary: Long Trades

Total net profit	$ 63220.00	Open position P/L	$ 0.00
Gross profit	$ 92005.00	Gross loss	$ -28785.00
Total # of trades	41	Percent profitable	46%
Number winning trades	19	Number losing trades	22
Largest winning trade	$ 22895.00	Largest losing trade	$ -2430.00
Average winning trade	$ 4842.37	Average losing trade	$ -1308.41
Ratio avg win/avg loss	3.70	Avg trade(win & loss)	$ 1541.95
Max consec. winners	2	Max consec. losers	5
Avg # bars in winners	33	Avg # bars in losers	9
Max intraday drawdown	$ -7597.50		
Profit factor	3.20	Max # contracts held	1
Account size required	$ 10597.50	Return on account	597%

Performance Summary: Short Trades

Total net profit	$ 30527.50	Open position P/L	$ 0.00
Gross profit	$ 70045.00	Gross loss	$ -39517.50
Total # of trades	42	Percent profitable	38%
Number winning trades	16	Number losing trades	26
Largest winning trade	$ 24220.00	Largest losing trade	$ -2855.00
Average winning trade	$ 4377.81	Average losing trade	$ -1519.90
Ratio avg win/avg loss	2.88	Avg trade(win & loss)	$ 726.85
Max consec. winners	8	Max consec. losers	6
Avg # bars in winners	34	Avg # bars in losers	9
Max intraday drawdown	$ -21825.00		
Profit factor	1.77	Max # contracts held	1
Account size required	$ 24825.00	Return on account	123%

NELSON FREEBURG

Page 1 of 1

///\\

SYSTEM

Name   : Pathfinder Currency
Notes : Nelson Freeburg

Last Update : 12/11/95 01:55am
Printed on : 12/11/95 01:55am
Verified   : YES

///////////////////////////////// CODE \\\\\\\\\\\\\\\\\\\\\\\\\\\\\\\\\\\\\\\

{_____Long Entries/Exits_____}

```
If Average(Close,6)[0] > Average(Close,6)[1] and
   Average(Close,9)[0] > Average(Close,18)[0] and
      Average(Close,3)[0] of data2 > Average(Close,25)[0] of data2 then
         BUY tomorrow market;

If Average(Close,9)[0] < Average(Close,18)[0] then
   ExitLong tomorrow market;
```

{_____Short Entries/Exits_____}

```
If Average(Close,6)[0] < Average(Close,6)[1] and
   Average(Close,9)[0] < Average(Close,18)[0] and
      Average(Close,3)[0] of data2 < Average(Close,25)[0] of data2 then
         SELL tomorrow market;

If Average(Close,9)[0] > Average(Close,18)[0] then
   ExitShort tomorrow market;
```

///\\\

Prepared using Omega TradeStation Version 3.01 by Omega Research, Inc.

LEE GETTESS

Gettess30   S&P 500 INDEX 65/99-Daily   01/05/87 - 01/02/96

Performance Summary: All Trades

Total net profit	$ 65705.00	Open position P/L	$ 0.00
Gross profit	$ 168120.00	Gross loss	$-102415.00
Total # of trades	159	Percent profitable	79%
Number winning trades	126	Number losing trades	33
Largest winning trade	$ 9270.00	Largest losing trade	$ -4505.00
Average winning trade	$ 1334.29	Average losing trade	$ -3103.48
Ratio avg win/avg loss	0.43	Avg trade(win & loss)	$ 413.24
Max consec. winners	17	Max consec. losers	2
Avg # bars in winners	2	Avg # bars in losers	2
Max intraday drawdown	$ -14525.00		
Profit factor	1.64	Max # contracts held	1
Account size required	$ 17525.00	Return on account	375%

Performance Summary: Long Trades

Total net profit	$ 65705.00	Open position P/L	$ 0.00
Gross profit	$ 168120.00	Gross loss	$-102415.00
Total # of trades	159	Percent profitable	79%
Number winning trades	126	Number losing trades	33
Largest winning trade	$ 9270.00	Largest losing trade	$ -4505.00
Average winning trade	$ 1334.29	Average losing trade	$ -3103.48
Ratio avg win/avg loss	0.43	Avg trade(win & loss)	$ 413.24
Max consec. winners	17	Max consec. losers	2
Avg # bars in winners	2	Avg # bars in losers	2
Max intraday drawdown	$ -14525.00		
Profit factor	1.64	Max # contracts held	1
Account size required	$ 17525.00	Return on account	375%

Performance Summary: Short Trades

Total net profit	$ 0.00	Open position P/L	$ 0.00
Gross profit	$ 0.00	Gross loss	$ 0.00
Total # of trades	0	Percent profitable	0%
Number winning trades	0	Number losing trades	0
Largest winning trade	$ 0.00	Largest losing trade	$ 0.00
Average winning trade	$ 0.00	Average losing trade	$ 0.00
Ratio avg win/avg loss	100.00	Avg trade(win & loss)	$ 0.00
Max consec. winners	0	Max consec. losers	0
Avg # bars in winners	0	Avg # bars in losers	0
Max intraday drawdown	$ 0.00		
Profit factor	100.00	Max # contracts held	0
Account size required	$ 0.00	Return on account	0%

LEE GETTESS

```
//////////////////////////////Quick System: Gettess30\\\\\\\\\\\\\\Page 1 of 1\\\\
```

Notes   :
Last Update : 03/21/96 06:09pm
Printed on   : 03/21/96 06:12pm
Verified   : Yes

```
///////////////////////////////////////INPUTS\\\\\\\\\\\\\\\\\\\\\\\\\\\\\\\\\\\\\\\\\\
```

InputName   Default Value

LEConsec   2

```
///////////////////////////////////LONG ENTRY\\\\\\\\\\\\\\\\\\\\\\\\\\\\\\\\\\\\\\\\\\
```

If   : MRO(Close >= Close[1],LEConsec,1) = -1 and O of tomorrow < C

Then   Buy at Market

```
////////////////////////////////////LONG EXIT\\\\\\\\\\\\\\\\\\\\\\\\\\\\\\\\\\\\\\\\\\
```

If   : MarketPosition=1 and O of tomorrow > EntryPrice

Then   ExitLong at Market

```
//////////////////////////////////////STOPS\\\\\\\\\\\\\\\\\\\\\\\\\\\\\\\\\\\\\\\\\\\\
```

Enabled	Stop	Enabled	Stop
Yes	Money Management Amount : $4000.00	No	Breakeven Stop Floor : $0.00
No	$ Risk Trailing Stop Amount : $0.00	No	Profit Target Amount : $0.00
No	% Risk Trailing Stop Amount : $0.00 Floor : $0.00	No	Close all trades at end of day session

```
///////////////////////////////////////////////\\\\\\\\\\\\\\\\\\\\\\\\\\\\\\\\\\\\\\\\\\
```
Prepared using Omega TradeStation Version 3.50 by Omega Research, Inc.

CYNTHIA KASE

```
Kase30  BRITISH POUND 67/99-Daily   01/02/85 - 06/06/96
```

Performance Summary: All Trades

Total net profit	$ 91067.50	Open position P/L	$ 1850.00
Gross profit	$ 183291.25	Gross loss	$ -92223.75
Total # of trades	139	Percent profitable	35%
Number winning trades	48	Number losing trades	91
Largest winning trade	$ 16945.00	Largest losing trade	$ -1936.25
Average winning trade	$ 3818.57	Average losing trade	$ -1013.45
Ratio avg win/avg loss	3.77	Avg trade(win & loss)	$ 655.16
Max consec. winners	3	Max consec. losers	8
Avg # bars in winners	33	Avg # bars in losers	5
Max intraday drawdown	$ -12242.50		
Profit factor	1.99	Max # contracts held	1
Account size required	$ 12242.50	Return on account	744%

Performance Summary: Long Trades

Total net profit	$ 72953.75	Open position P/L	$ 1850.00
Gross profit	$ 113227.50	Gross loss	$ -40273.75
Total # of trades	68	Percent profitable	40%
Number winning trades	27	Number losing trades	41
Largest winning trade	$ 16945.00	Largest losing trade	$ -1936.25
Average winning trade	$ 4193.61	Average losing trade	$ -982.29
Ratio avg win/avg loss	4.27	Avg trade(win & loss)	$ 1072.85
Max consec. winners	3	Max consec. losers	6
Avg # bars in winners	36	Avg # bars in losers	5
Max intraday drawdown	$ -11327.50		
Profit factor	2.81	Max # contracts held	1
Account size required	$ 11327.50	Return on account	644%

Performance Summary: Short Trades

Total net profit	$ 18113.75	Open position P/L	$ 0.00
Gross profit	$ 70063.75	Gross loss	$ -51950.00
Total # of trades	71	Percent profitable	30%
Number winning trades	21	Number losing trades	50
Largest winning trade	$ 14420.00	Largest losing trade	$ -1711.25
Average winning trade	$ 3336.37	Average losing trade	$ -1039.00
Ratio avg win/avg loss	3.21	Avg trade(win & loss)	$ 255.12
Max consec. winners	3	Max consec. losers	7
Avg # bars in winners	28	Avg # bars in losers	5
Account size required	$ 8103.75	Return on account	224%

CYNTHIA KASE

Page 1
_____

Type   : System
Name   : Kase30
Notes   :

Last Update : 12/10/96 09:26pm
Printed on : 12/10/96 09:27pm
Verified   : YES

_____

{ Use on Daily Bars,British Pound,
$1000 Money management stop,$55 commission}

Input: Length(2);

IF CurrentBar > 1 and Average(C,Length*2) crosses
 over Average(C,Length*3)
Then Buy Highest(High,Length) + 1 point Stop;

IF CurrentBar > 1 and Average(C,Length*2) crosses
 below Average(C,Length*3)
 Then Sell Lowest(Low,Length) - 1 point Stop;

_____

JOE KRUTSINGER

One Night Stand JAPANESE YEN 65/99-Daily   01/05/87 - 01/02/96

Performance Summary: All Trades

Total net profit	$ 27817.50	Open position P/L	$ 0.00
Gross profit	$ 49842.50	Gross loss	$ -22025.00
Total # of trades	114	Percent profitable	61%
Number winning trades	69	Number losing trades	45
Largest winning trade	$ 3882.50	Largest losing trade	$ -1067.50
Average winning trade	$ 722.36	Average losing trade	$ -489.44
Ratio avg win/avg loss	1.48	Avg trade(win & loss)	$ 244.01
Max consec. winners	9	Max consec. losers	7
Avg # bars in winners	1	Avg # bars in losers	1
Max intraday drawdown	$ -4510.00		
Profit factor	2.26	Max # contracts held	1
Account size required	$ 7510.00	Return on account	370%

Performance Summary: Long Trades

Total net profit	$ 20417.50	Open position P/L	$ 0.00
Gross profit	$ 34390.00	Gross loss	$ -13972.50
Total # of trades	64	Percent profitable	58%
Number winning trades	37	Number losing trades	27
Largest winning trade	$ 3882.50	Largest losing trade	$ -1055.00
Average winning trade	$ 929.46	Average losing trade	$ -517.50
Ratio avg win/avg loss	1.80	Avg trade(win & loss)	$ 319.02
Max consec. winners	7	Max consec. losers	7
Avg # bars in winners	1	Avg # bars in losers	1
Max intraday drawdown	$ -4087.50		
Profit factor	2.46	Max # contracts held	1
Account size required	$ 7087.50	Return on account	288%

Performance Summary: Short Trades

Total net profit	$ 7400.00	Open position P/L	$ 0.00
Gross profit	$ 15452.50	Gross loss	$ -8052.50
Total # of trades	50	Percent profitable	64%
Number winning trades	32	Number losing trades	18
Largest winning trade	$ 2357.50	Largest losing trade	$ -1067.50
Average winning trade	$ 482.89	Average losing trade	$ -447.36
Ratio avg win/avg loss	1.08	Avg trade(win & loss)	$ 148.00
Max consec. winners	5	Max consec. losers	3
Avg # bars in winners	1	Avg # bars in losers	1
Max intraday drawdown	$ -2345.00		
Profit factor	1.92	Max # contracts held	1
Account size required	$ 5345.00	Return on account	138%

JOE KRUTSINGER

```
///////////////////////////Quick System: One Night Stand\\\\\\\\\\Page 1 of 1\\\\

Notes        :
Last Update  : 03/21/96 02:46pm
Printed on   : 03/21/96 02:47pm
Verified     : Yes


/////////////////////////////////////INPUTS\\\\\\\\\\\\\\\\\\\\\\\\\\\\\\\\\\\\\

InputName        Default Value
--------------------------------------------------------------------------------


///////////////////////////////////LONG ENTRY\\\\\\\\\\\\\\\\\\\\\\\\\\\\\\\\\\\

If   :  Average(C,10) >Average(C,40) and DayOfWeek(date)=4

Then    Buy next bar at Highest(H,4) Stop

////////////////////////////////////LONG EXIT\\\\\\\\\\\\\\\\\\\\\\\\\\\\\\\\\\\

If   :  MarketPosition=1

Then    ExitLong at Market

///////////////////////////////////SHORT ENTRY\\\\\\\\\\\\\\\\\\\\\\\\\\\\\\\\\\

If   :  Average(C,10) < Average(C,40) and DayOfWeek(date)=4

Then    Sell next bar at Lowest(L,8) Stop

///////////////////////////////////SHORT EXIT\\\\\\\\\\\\\\\\\\\\\\\\\\\\\\\\\\\

If   :  MarketPosition=-1

Then    ExitShort at Market

/////////////////////////////////////STOPS\\\\\\\\\\\\\\\\\\\\\\\\\\\\\\\\\\\\\\
```

Enabled	Stop	Enabled	Stop
Yes	Money Management Amount : $1000.00	No	Breakeven Stop Floor : $0.00
No	$ Risk Trailing Stop Amount : $0.00	No	Profit Target Amount : $0.00
No	% Risk Trailing Stop Amount : $0.00 Floor : $0.00	No	Close all trades at end of day session

```
//////////////////////////////////////////\\\\\\\\\\\\\\\\\\\\\\\\\\\\\\\\\\\\\\\
Prepared using Omega TradeStation Version 3.50 by Omega Research, Inc.
```

JOE KRUTSINGER

Buy Mon,1400 St,XMOC S&P 500 INDEX 65/99-Daily   01/05/87 - 01/02/96

                    Performance Summary: All Trades

Total net profit	$ 108765.00	Open position P/L	$ 0.00
Gross profit	$ 302085.00	Gross loss	$-193320.00
Total # of trades	452	Percent profitable	55%
Number winning trades	248	Number losing trades	204
Largest winning trade	$ 10270.00	Largest losing trade	$ -1455.00
Average winning trade	$ 1218.08	Average losing trade	$ -947.65
Ratio avg win/avg loss	1.29	Avg trade(win & loss)	$ 240.63
Max consec. winners	11	Max consec. losers	7
Avg # bars in winners	0	Avg # bars in losers	0
Max intraday drawdown	$ -12905.00		
Profit factor	1.56	Max # contracts held	1
Account size required	$ 15905.00	Return on account	684%

                    Performance Summary: Long Trades

Total net profit	$ 108765.00	Open position P/L	$ 0.00
Gross profit	$ 302085.00	Gross loss	$-193320.00
Total # of trades	452	Percent profitable	55%
Number winning trades	248	Number losing trades	204
Largest winning trade	$ 10270.00	Largest losing trade	$ -1455.00
Average winning trade	$ 1218.08	Average losing trade	$ -947.65
Ratio avg win/avg loss	1.29	Avg trade(win & loss)	$ 240.63
Max consec. winners	11	Max consec. losers	7
Avg # bars in winners	0	Avg # bars in losers	0
Max intraday drawdown	$ -12905.00		
Profit factor	1.56	Max # contracts held	1
Account size required	$ 15905.00	Return on account	684%

                    Performance Summary: Short Trades

Total net profit	$ 0.00	Open position P/L	$ 0.00
Gross profit	$ 0.00	Gross loss	$ 0.00
Total # of trades	0	Percent profitable	0%
Number winning trades	0	Number losing trades	0
Largest winning trade	$ 0.00	Largest losing trade	$ 0.00
Average winning trade	$ 0.00	Average losing trade	$ 0.00
Ratio avg win/avg loss	100.00	Avg trade(win & loss)	$ 0.00
Max consec. winners	0	Max consec. losers	0
Avg # bars in winners	0	Avg # bars in losers	0
Max intraday drawdown	$ 0.00		
Profit factor	100.00	Max # contracts held	0
Account size required	$ 0.00	Return on account	0%

JOE KRUTSINGER

```
/////////////////////////Quick System: Buy Mon,1400 St,XMOC\\\\\\\\\Page 1 of 1\
Notes        :
Last Update  : 03/21/96 02:48pm
Printed on   : 03/21/96 02:55pm
Verified     : Yes


//////////////////////////////////INPUTS\\\\\\\\\\\\\\\\\\\\\\\\\\\\\\\
InputName      Default Value
---------------------------------------------------------------------------


//////////////////////////////////LONG ENTRY\\\\\\\\\\\\\\\\\\\\\\\\\\\\\\
If    :  DayOfWeek(date)=5

Then     Buy at Market

//////////////////////////////////STOPS\\\\\\\\\\\\\\\\\\\\\\\\\\\\\\\\\\\
```

Enabled	Stop	Enabled	Stop
Yes	Money Management Amount : $1400.00	No	Breakeven Stop Floor : $0.00
No	$ Risk Trailing Stop Amount : $0.00	No	Profit Target Amount : $0.00
No	% Risk Trailing Stop Amount : $0.00 Floor : $0.00	Yes	Close all trades at end of day session

```
////////////////////////////////////////\\\\\\\\\\\\\\\\\\\\\\\\\\\\\\\\\\\\\'
```
Prepared using Omega TradeStation Version 3.50 by Omega Research, Inc.

JOE KRUTSINGER

EZ Bonder TQ 65/99-Daily   01/05/87 - 01/02/96

Performance Summary: All Trades

Total net profit	$ 41798.75	Open position P/L	$ 2000.00
Gross profit	$ 121538.75	Gross loss	$ -79740.00
Total # of trades	119	Percent profitable	43%
Number winning trades	51	Number losing trades	68
Largest winning trade	$ 9851.25	Largest losing trade	$ -4305.00
Average winning trade	$ 2383.11	Average losing trade	$ -1172.65
Ratio avg win/avg loss	2.03	Avg trade(win & loss)	$ 351.25
Max consec. winners	6	Max consec. losers	8
Avg # bars in winners	21	Avg # bars in losers	9
Max intraday drawdown	$ -13966.25		
Profit factor	1.52	Max # contracts held	1
Account size required	$ 16966.25	Return on account	246%

Performance Summary: Long Trades

Total net profit	$ 41798.75	Open position P/L	$ 2000.00
Gross profit	$ 121538.75	Gross loss	$ -79740.00
Total # of trades	119	Percent profitable	43%
Number winning trades	51	Number losing trades	68
Largest winning trade	$ 9851.25	Largest losing trade	$ -4305.00
Average winning trade	$ 2383.11	Average losing trade	$ -1172.65
Ratio avg win/avg loss	2.03	Avg trade(win & loss)	$ 351.25
Max consec. winners	6	Max consec. losers	8
Avg # bars in winners	21	Avg # bars in losers	9
Max intraday drawdown	$ -13966.25		
Profit factor	1.52	Max # contracts held	1
Account size required	$ 16966.25	Return on account	246%

Performance Summary: Short Trades

Total net profit	$ 0.00	Open position P/L	$ 0.00
Gross profit	$ 0.00	Gross loss	$ 0.00
Total # of trades	0	Percent profitable	0%
Number winning trades	0	Number losing trades	0
Largest winning trade	$ 0.00	Largest losing trade	$ 0.00
Average winning trade	$ 0.00	Average losing trade	$ 0.00
Ratio avg win/avg loss	100.00	Avg trade(win & loss)	$ 0.00
Max consec. winners	0	Max consec. losers	0
Avg # bars in winners	0	Avg # bars in losers	0
Max intraday drawdown	$ 0.00		
Profit factor	100.00	Max # contracts held	0
Account size required	$ 0.00	Return on account	0%

JOE KRUTSINGER

```
////////////////////////////Quick System: EZ  Bonder\\\\\\\\\\\\\Page 1 of 1\\\\
Notes        :
Last Update  : 03/21/96 04:28pm
Printed on   : 03/21/96 04:29pm
Verified     : Yes


/////////////////////////////////INPUTS\\\\\\\\\\\\\\\\\\\\\\\\\\\\\\\\\\\\

InputName       Default Value
-------------------------------------------------------------------------------
Length1         1
Length2         1.8


////////////////////////////////LONG ENTRY\\\\\\\\\\\\\\\\\\\\\\\\\\\\\\\\\\\

Buy next bar at C + Range * Length1 Stop

////////////////////////////////LONG EXIT\\\\\\\\\\\\\\\\\\\\\\\\\\\\\\\\\\\\

If   : MarketPosition=1

Then    ExitLong next bar at (c-Range*Length2 ) Stop

////////////////////////////////STOPS\\\\\\\\\\\\\\\\\\\\\\\\\\\\\\\\\\\\\\\\\
```

Enabled	Stop	Enabled	Stop
Yes	Money Management Amount : $1000.00	No	Breakeven Stop Floor : $0.00
No	$ Risk Trailing Stop Amount : $500.00	No	Profit Target Amount : $0.00
No	% Risk Trailing Stop Amount : $0.00 Floor : $0.00	No	Close all trades at end of day session

```
/////////////////////////////////////////\\\\\\\\\\\\\\\\\\\\\\\\\\\\\\\\\\\\\\\\\
```
Prepared using Omega TradeStation Version 3.50 by Omega Research, Inc.

GLENN NEELY

```
Neeley31  JAPANESE YEN 65/99-Weekly    01/09/87 - 01/05/96
```

Performance Summary: All Trades

Total net profit	$ 60442.50	Open position P/L	$ 30762.50
Gross profit	$ 86575.00	Gross loss	$ -26132.50
Total # of trades	24	Percent profitable	42%
Number winning trades	10	Number losing trades	14
Largest winning trade	$ 18457.50	Largest losing trade	$ -3055.00
Average winning trade	$ 8657.50	Average losing trade	$ -1866.61
Ratio avg win/avg loss	4.64	Avg trade(win & loss)	$ 2518.44
Max consec. winners	2	Max consec. losers	3
Avg # bars in winners	27	Avg # bars in losers	8
Max intraday drawdown	$ -9100.00		
Profit factor	3.31	Max # contracts held	1
Account size required	$ 12100.00	Return on account	500%

Performance Summary: Long Trades

Total net profit	$ 48772.50	Open position P/L	$ 0.00
Gross profit	$ 64207.50	Gross loss	$ -15435.00
Total # of trades	13	Percent profitable	46%
Number winning trades	6	Number losing trades	7
Largest winning trade	$ 18457.50	Largest losing trade	$ -3055.00
Average winning trade	$ 10701.25	Average losing trade	$ -2205.00
Ratio avg win/avg loss	4.85	Avg trade(win & loss)	$ 3751.73
Max consec. winners	3	Max consec. losers	4
Avg # bars in winners	28	Avg # bars in losers	5
Max intraday drawdown	$ -8707.50		
Profit factor	4.16	Max # contracts held	1
Account size required	$ 11707.50	Return on account	417%

Performance Summary: Short Trades

Total net profit	$ 11670.00	Open position P/L	$ 30762.50
Gross profit	$ 22367.50	Gross loss	$ -10697.50
Total # of trades	11	Percent profitable	36%
Number winning trades	4	Number losing trades	7
Largest winning trade	$ 14932.50	Largest losing trade	$ -3055.00
Average winning trade	$ 5591.88	Average losing trade	$ -1528.21
Ratio avg win/avg loss	3.66	Avg trade(win & loss)	$ 1060.91
Max consec. winners	3	Max consec. losers	6
Avg # bars in winners	26	Avg # bars in losers	10
Max intraday drawdown	$ -8797.50		
Profit factor	2.09	Max # contracts held	1
Account size required	$ 11797.50	Return on account	99%

GLENN NEELY

//////////////////////////////////Quick System: Neeley31\\\\\\\\\\\\\\\\Page 1 of 1\\\\

```
Notes       :
Last Update : 03/21/96 08:14pm
Printed on  : 03/21/96 08:14pm
Verified    : Yes
```

/////////////////////////////////////INPUTS\\\\\\\\\\\\\\\\\\\\\\\\\\\\\\\\\\\

```
InputName      Default Value
-------------------------------------------------------------------------
Length         50
```

/////////////////////////////////////LONG ENTRY\\\\\\\\\\\\\\\\\\\\\\\\\\\\\\\\

If   : CurrentBar > 1 and RateOfChange(c,10) > 0

Then   Buy next bar at H Stop

/////////////////////////////////////SHORT ENTRY\\\\\\\\\\\\\\\\\\\\\\\\\\\\\\\\

If   : CurrentBar > 1 and RateOfChange(c,10) <0

Then   Sell next bar at L Stop

/////////////////////////////////////STOPS\\\\\\\\\\\\\\\\\\\\\\\\\\\\\\\\\\\\\\

Enabled	Stop	Enabled	Stop
Yes	Money Management Amount : $3000.00	No	Breakeven Stop Floor : $0.00
No	$ Risk Trailing Stop Amount : $0.00	No	Profit Target Amount : $0.00
No	% Risk Trailing Stop Amount : $0.00 Floor : $0.00	No	Close all trades at end of day session

//\\\\\\\\\\\\\\\\\\\\\\\\\\\\\\\\\\\\\\\
Prepared using Omega TradeStation Version 3.50 by Omega Research, Inc.

GLENN NEELY

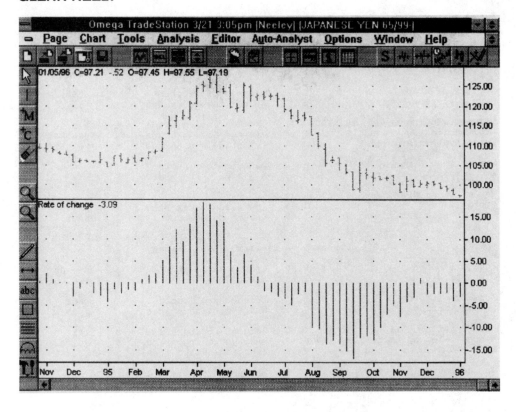

JEFFREY ROY

DeTrend SWISS FRANC 65/99-Daily   01/02/90 - 01/02/96

Performance Summary: All Trades

Total net profit	$	56430.00	Open position P/L	$	0.00
Gross profit	$	75957.50	Gross loss	$	-19527.50
Total # of trades		44	Percent profitable		59%
Number winning trades		26	Number losing trades		18
Largest winning trade	$	13545.00	Largest losing trade	$	-1442.50
Average winning trade	$	2921.44	Average losing trade	$	-1084.86
Ratio avg win/avg loss		2.69	Avg trade(win & loss)	$	1282.50
Max consec. winners		5	Max consec. losers		4
Avg # bars in winners		39	Avg # bars in losers		3
Max intraday drawdown	$	-3845.00			
Profit factor		3.89	Max # contracts held		1
Account size required	$	6845.00	Return on account		824%

Performance Summary: Long Trades

Total net profit	$	36787.50	Open position P/L	$	0.00
Gross profit	$	47202.50	Gross loss	$	-10415.00
Total # of trades		25	Percent profitable		68%
Number winning trades		17	Number losing trades		8
Largest winning trade	$	13532.50	Largest losing trade	$	-1442.50
Average winning trade	$	2776.62	Average losing trade	$	-1301.88
Ratio avg win/avg loss		2.13	Avg trade(win & loss)	$	1471.50
Max consec. winners		5	Max consec. losers		2
Avg # bars in winners		36	Avg # bars in losers		3
Max intraday drawdown	$	-3375.00			
Profit factor		4.53	Max # contracts held		1
Account size required	$	6375.00	Return on account		577%

Performance Summary: Short Trades

Total net profit	$	19642.50	Open position P/L	$	0.00
Gross profit	$	28755.00	Gross loss	$	-9112.50
Total # of trades		19	Percent profitable		47%
Number winning trades		9	Number losing trades		10
Largest winning trade	$	13545.00	Largest losing trade	$	-1255.00
Average winning trade	$	3195.00	Average losing trade	$	-911.25
Ratio avg win/avg loss		3.51	Avg trade(win & loss)	$	1033.82
Max consec. winners		5	Max consec. losers		4
Avg # bars in winners		45	Avg # bars in losers		3
Max intraday drawdown	$	-2885.00			
Profit factor		3.16	Max # contracts held		1
Account size required	$	5885.00	Return on account		334%

JEFFREY ROY

///\\\

SYSTEM

```
Name      : DeTrend
Notes : Jeff Roy DeTrend Oscillator System

Last Update : 04/15/96 01:39pm
Printed on  : 04/15/96 01:39pm
Verified    : YES
```

/////////////////////////////////// CODE \\\

```
INPUTS:   Period(37), Thresh(1.00);
VARS:   DeTrend(0), LastTrade(1), LongPositionHigh(0), ShortPositionLow(999999);

{      Calculate DeTrend Oscillator      }

DeTrend = Close[0] - Average(Close, Period)[0];


{      Entries      }

If DeTrend[0] > Thresh and LastTrade = -1 then
   Buy market;

If DeTrend[0] < -Thresh and LastTrade = 1 then
   Sell market;


{      Re-Enter With Trend      }

If MarketPosition = 0 and LastTrade = 1 then
   Buy at LongPositionHigh stop;

If MarketPosition = 0 and LastTrade = -1 then
   Sell at ShortPositionLow stop;


{      Track Last Position High / Low      }

If MarketPosition > 0 then LastTrade = 1;
If MarketPosition < 0 then LastTrade = -1;

If MarketPosition > 0 then begin
   If High[0] > LongPositionHigh then LongPositionHigh = High[0];
   ShortPositionLow = 999999;
End;

If MarketPosition < 0 then begin
   If Low[0] < ShortPositionLow then ShortPositionLow = Low[0];
   LongPositionHigh = 0;
End;
```

///\\\

Prepared using Omega TradeStation Version 3.01 by Omega Research, Inc.

RICHARD SAIDENBERG

```
Saidenberg30  S&P 500 INDEX 67/99-Daily    01/02/85 - 06/06/96

                    Performance Summary:  All Trades

Total net profit      $ 111865.00   Open position P/L      $      0.00
Gross profit          $ 408825.00   Gross loss             $-296960.00

Total # of trades           965     Percent profitable            49%
Number winning trades       477     Number losing trades          488

Largest winning trade $   5550.00   Largest losing trade   $  -1050.00
Average winning trade $    857.08   Average losing trade   $   -608.52
Ratio avg win/avg loss       1.41   Avg trade(win & loss)  $    115.92

Max consec. winners           7     Max consec. losers              8
Avg # bars in winners         0     Avg # bars in losers            0

Max intraday drawdown $  -9425.00
Profit factor                1.38   Max # contracts held            1
Account size required $   9425.00   Return on account           1187%
```

```
                    Performance Summary:  Long Trades

Total net profit      $  85515.00   Open position P/L      $      0.00
Gross profit          $ 216575.00   Gross loss             $-131060.00

Total # of trades           510     Percent profitable            55%
Number winning trades       278     Number losing trades          232

Largest winning trade $   3650.00   Largest losing trade   $  -1050.00
Average winning trade $    779.05   Average losing trade   $   -564.91
Ratio avg win/avg loss       1.38   Avg trade(win & loss)  $    167.68

Max consec. winners           7     Max consec. losers              8
Avg # bars in winners         0     Avg # bars in losers            0

Max intraday drawdown $  -5250.00
Profit factor                1.65   Max # contracts held            1
Account size required $   5250.00   Return on account           1629%
```

```
                    Performance Summary:  Short Trades

Total net profit      $  26350.00   Open position P/L      $      0.00
Gross profit          $ 192250.00   Gross loss             $-165900.00

Total # of trades           455     Percent profitable            44%
Number winning trades       199     Number losing trades          256

Largest winning trade $   5550.00   Largest losing trade   $  -1050.00
Average winning trade $    966.08   Average losing trade   $   -648.05
Ratio avg win/avg loss       1.49   Avg trade(win & loss)  $     57.91

Max consec. winners           5     Max consec. losers             10
Avg # bars in winners         0     Avg # bars in losers            0


Saidenberg30  S&P 500 INDEX 67/99-Daily    01/02/85 - 06/06/96

Account size required $  15325.00   Return on account            172%
```

RICHARD SAIDENBERG

Page 1
_____

```
Type        : System
Name        : Saidenberg30
Notes       :

Last Update : 12/09/96 11:13pm
Printed on  : 12/09/96 11:13pm
Verified    : YES
```
_____

```
If TradesToday(Date) < 2 then begin;
    Buy at H + (Range*0.66) stop;
    Sell at L - (Range*0.66) stop;
End;

{ Use Daily S&P 500 Bars, exit market on close,
$50 commission, no slippage,use a $1000 Money management stop}

{ Use Daily US Bonds Bars,
$50 commission, no slippage,use a $500 Money management stop}
```

RANDY STUCKEY

Stuckey19 JAPANESE YEN 65/99-Daily   01/05/87 - 01/02/96

Performance Summary: All Trades

Total net profit	$ 42247.50	Open position P/L	$ 26175.00
Gross profit	$ 76430.00	Gross loss	$ -34182.50
Total # of trades	23	Percent profitable	61%
Number winning trades	14	Number losing trades	9
Largest winning trade	$ 13132.50	Largest losing trade	$ -6330.00
Average winning trade	$ 5459.29	Average losing trade	$ -3798.06
Ratio avg win/avg loss	1.44	Avg trade(win & loss)	$ 1836.85
Max consec. winners	4	Max consec. losers	3
Avg # bars in winners	117	Avg # bars in losers	51
Max intraday drawdown	$ -13777.50		
Profit factor	2.24	Max # contracts held	1
Account size required	$ 16777.50	Return on account	252%

Performance Summary: Long Trades

Total net profit	$ 43565.00	Open position P/L	$ 0.00
Gross profit	$ 57230.00	Gross loss	$ -13665.00
Total # of trades	12	Percent profitable	75%
Number winning trades	9	Number losing trades	3
Largest winning trade	$ 13132.50	Largest losing trade	$ -6255.00
Average winning trade	$ 6358.89	Average losing trade	$ -4555.00
Ratio avg win/avg loss	1.40	Avg trade(win & loss)	$ 3630.42
Max consec. winners	4	Max consec. losers	1
Avg # bars in winners	121	Avg # bars in losers	53
Max intraday drawdown	$ -8092.50		
Profit factor	4.19	Max # contracts held	1
Account size required	$ 11092.50	Return on account	393%

Performance Summary: Short Trades

Total net profit	$ -1317.50	Open position P/L	$ 26175.00
Gross profit	$ 19200.00	Gross loss	$ -20517.50
Total # of trades	11	Percent profitable	45%
Number winning trades	5	Number losing trades	6
Largest winning trade	$ 10870.00	Largest losing trade	$ -6330.00
Average winning trade	$ 3840.00	Average losing trade	$ -3419.58
Ratio avg win/avg loss	1.12	Avg trade(win & loss)	$ -119.77
Max consec. winners	3	Max consec. losers	2
Avg # bars in winners	112	Avg # bars in losers	50
Max intraday drawdown	$ -18922.50		
Profit factor	0.94	Max # contracts held	1
Account size required	$ 21922.50	Return on account	-6%

RANDY STUCKEY

////////////////////////////Quick System: Stuckey19\\\\\\\\\\\\\Page 1 of 1\\\\

```
Notes        :
Last Update  : 03/21/96 07:27pm
Printed on   : 03/21/96 07:28pm
Verified     : Yes
```

/////////////////////////////////////INPUTS\\\\\\\\\\\\\\\\\\\\\\\\\\\\\\\\\\\\\

InputName	Default Value
Length	40

////////////////////////////////////LONG ENTRY\\\\\\\\\\\\\\\\\\\\\\\\\\\\\\\\\\\

If : CurrentBar > 1 and Close > Highest(High,Length)[1]

Then   Buy on Close

///////////////////////////////////SHORT ENTRY\\\\\\\\\\\\\\\\\\\\\\\\\\\\\\\\\\\

If : CurrentBar > 1 and Close < Lowest(Low,Length)[1]

Then   Sell on Close

/////////////////////////////////////STOPS\\\\\\\\\\\\\\\\\\\\\\\\\\\\\\\\\\\\\\

Enabled	Stop	Enabled	Stop
No	Money Management Amount : $0.00	No	Breakeven Stop Floor : $0.00
No	$ Risk Trailing Stop Amount : $0.00	No	Profit Target Amount : $0.00
No	% Risk Trailing Stop Amount : $0.00 Floor : $0.00	No	Close all trades at end of day session

GARY WAGNER

Wagner31 COMEX GOLD 67/99-Weekly   04/01/88 - 01/05/96

Performance Summary: All Trades

Total net profit	$ 22615.00	Open position P/L	$ 1130.00
Gross profit	$ 27660.00	Gross loss	$ -5045.00
Total # of trades	17	Percent profitable	71%
Number winning trades	12	Number losing trades	5
Largest winning trade	$ 3185.00	Largest losing trade	$ -2335.00
Average winning trade	$ 2305.00	Average losing trade	$ -1009.00
Ratio avg win/avg loss	2.28	Avg trade(win & loss)	$ 1330.29
Max consec. winners	4	Max consec. losers	3
Avg # bars in winners	13	Avg # bars in losers	27
Max intraday drawdown	$ -10090.00		
Profit factor	5.48	Max # contracts held	1
Account size required	$ 17090.00	Return on account	132%

Performance Summary: Long Trades

Total net profit	$ 1955.00	Open position P/L	$ 1130.00
Gross profit	$ 6505.00	Gross loss	$ -4550.00
Total # of trades	7	Percent profitable	43%
Number winning trades	3	Number losing trades	4
Largest winning trade	$ 2945.00	Largest losing trade	$ -2335.00
Average winning trade	$ 2168.33	Average losing trade	$ -1137.50
Ratio avg win/avg loss	1.91	Avg trade(win & loss)	$ 279.29
Max consec. winners	1	Max consec. losers	2
Avg # bars in winners	14	Avg # bars in losers	33
Max intraday drawdown	$ -9595.00		
Profit factor	1.43	Max # contracts held	1
Account size required	$ 16595.00	Return on account	12%

Performance Summary: Short Trades

Total net profit	$ 20660.00	Open position P/L	$ 0.00
Gross profit	$ 21155.00	Gross loss	$ -495.00
Total # of trades	10	Percent profitable	90%
Number winning trades	9	Number losing trades	1
Largest winning trade	$ 3185.00	Largest losing trade	$ -495.00
Average winning trade	$ 2350.56	Average losing trade	$ -495.00
Ratio avg win/avg loss	4.75	Avg trade(win & loss)	$ 2066.00
Max consec. winners	7	Max consec. losers	1
Avg # bars in winners	13	Avg # bars in losers	6

Wagner31 COMEX GOLD 67/99-Weekly   04/01/88 - 01/05/96

Account size required	$ 10940.00	Return on account	189%

Gary Wagner   **237**

///////////////////////////Quick System: Wagner31\\\\\\\\\\\\\Page 1 of 1\\\\

Notes   :
Last Update : 02/10/97 12:10pm
Printed on   : 02/10/97 12:27pm
Verified   : Yes

///////////////////////////////////INPUTS\\\\\\\\\\\\\\\\\\\\\\\\\\\\\\\\\\\

InputName   Default Value

Vara   2

/////////////////////////////////LONG ENTRY\\\\\\\\\\\\\\\\\\\\\\\\\\\\\\\\\

If   : C < C[1] and C[1] < C[2] and C[3] < C[4] and o Of tomorrow < C

Then   Buy next bar at c + 1 point Stop

/////////////////////////////////SHORT ENTRY\\\\\\\\\\\\\\\\\\\\\\\\\\\\\\\\

If   : C > C[1] and C[1] > C[2] and c[3] > c[4] and O of tomorrow > C

Then   Sell next bar at c- 1 point Stop

/////////////////////////////////STOPS\\\\\\\\\\\\\\\\\\\\\\\\\\\\\\\\\\\\\\

Enabled   Stop   Enabled   Stop
--------------------------------   ------------------------------
No   Money Management   No   Breakeven Stop
            Amount : $0.00   Floor : $0.00

No $ Risk Trailing Stop   Yes   Profit Target
            Amount : $0.00   Amount : $3000.00

No   % Risk Trailing Stop   No   Close all trades at
            Amount : $0.00   end of day session
            Floor : $0.00

///\\\\\\\\\\\\\\\\\\\\\\\\\\\\\\\\\\\
Prepared using Omega TradeStation Version 4.01 by Omega Research, Inc.

BILL WILLIAMS

B Williams19 JAPANESE YEN 65/99-Daily   01/05/87 - 01/02/96

Performance Summary: All Trades

Total net profit	$ 52077.50	Open position P/L	$ 1450.00
Gross profit	$ 242825.00	Gross loss	$-190747.50
Total # of trades	367	Percent profitable	44%
Number winning trades	160	Number losing trades	207
Largest winning trade	$ 11882.50	Largest losing trade	$ -10155.00
Average winning trade	$ 1517.66	Average losing trade	$ -921.49
Ratio avg win/avg loss	1.65	Avg trade(win & loss)	$ 141.90
Max consec. winners	9	Max consec. losers	7
Avg # bars in winners	8	Avg # bars in losers	4
Max intraday drawdown	$ -16150.00		
Profit factor	1.27	Max # contracts held	1
Account size required	$ 19150.00	Return on account	272%

Performance Summary: Long Trades

Total net profit	$ 36767.50	Open position P/L	$ 0.00
Gross profit	$ 113922.50	Gross loss	$ -77155.00
Total # of trades	184	Percent profitable	45%
Number winning trades	83	Number losing trades	101
Largest winning trade	$ 11882.50	Largest losing trade	$ -3617.50
Average winning trade	$ 1372.56	Average losing trade	$ -763.91
Ratio avg win/avg loss	1.80	Avg trade(win & loss)	$ 199.82
Max consec. winners	4	Max consec. losers	9
Avg # bars in winners	5	Avg # bars in losers	3
Max intraday drawdown	$ -16030.00		
Profit factor	1.48	Max # contracts held	1
Account size required	$ 19030.00	Return on account	193%

Performance Summary: Short Trades

Total net profit	$ 15310.00	Open position P/L	$ 1450.00
Gross profit	$ 128902.50	Gross loss	$-113592.50
Total # of trades	183	Percent profitable	42%
Number winning trades	77	Number losing trades	106
Largest winning trade	$ 9432.50	Largest losing trade	$ -10155.00
Average winning trade	$ 1674.06	Average losing trade	$ -1071.63
Ratio avg win/avg loss	1.56	Avg trade(win & loss)	$ 83.66
Max consec. winners	6	Max consec. losers	8
Avg # bars in winners	11	Avg # bars in losers	6
Max intraday drawdown	$ -27982.50		
Profit factor	1.13	Max # contracts held	1
Account size required	$ 30982.50	Return on account	49%

BILL WILLIAMS

```
Notes       :
Last Update : 03/21/96 07:08pm
Printed on  : 03/21/96 07:16pm
Verified    : Yes
```

////////////////////////////////////INPUTS\\\\\\\\\\\\\\\\\\\\\\\\\\\\\\\\\\\

```
InputName     Default Value
--------------------------------------------------------------------------
Length        20
```

////////////////////////////////////LONG ENTRY\\\\\\\\\\\\\\\\\\\\\\\\\\\\\\\

If   : Range/MaxList(1,V)>Average(Range/MaxList(1,V),Length)

Then   Buy next bar at H Stop

///////////////////////////////////SHORT ENTRY\\\\\\\\\\\\\\\\\\\\\\\\\\\\\\\

If   : Range/MaxList(1,V)< Average(Range/MaxList(1,V),Length)

Then   Sell next bar at L Stop

////////////////////////////////////STOPS\\\\\\\\\\\\\\\\\\\\\\\\\\\\\\\\\\\\

Enabled	Stop	Enabled	Stop
No	Money Management Amount : $4000.00	No	Breakeven Stop Floor : $0.00
No	$ Risk Trailing Stop Amount : $0.00	No	Profit Target Amount : $0.00
No	% Risk Trailing Stop Amount : $0.00 Floor : $0.00	No	Close all trades at end of day session

LARRY WILLIAMS

```
Williams 19  BRITISH POUND 65/99-Daily   01/05/87 - 01/02/96
```

Performance Summary: All Trades

Total net profit	$ 85887.50	Open position P/L	$ 456.25
Gross profit	$ 150560.00	Gross loss	$ -64672.50
Total # of trades	70	Percent profitable	47%
Number winning trades	33	Number losing trades	37
Largest winning trade	$ 19970.00	Largest losing trade	$ -3655.00
Average winning trade	$ 4562.42	Average losing trade	$ -1747.91
Ratio avg win/avg loss	2.61	Avg trade(win & loss)	$ 1226.96
Max consec. winners	4	Max consec. losers	7
Avg # bars in winners	44	Avg # bars in losers	21
Max intraday drawdown	$ -10027.50		
Profit factor	2.33	Max # contracts held	1
Account size required	$ 13027.50	Return on account	659%

Performance Summary: Long Trades

Total net profit	$ 59125.00	Open position P/L	$ 456.25
Gross profit	$ 91528.75	Gross loss	$ -32403.75
Total # of trades	35	Percent profitable	51%
Number winning trades	18	Number losing trades	17
Largest winning trade	$ 17145.00	Largest losing trade	$ -3555.00
Average winning trade	$ 5084.93	Average losing trade	$ -1906.10
Ratio avg win/avg loss	2.67	Avg trade(win & loss)	$ 1689.29
Max consec. winners	3	Max consec. losers	3
Avg # bars in winners	49	Avg # bars in losers	19
Max intraday drawdown	$ -6565.00		
Profit factor	2.82	Max # contracts held	1
Account size required	$ 9565.00	Return on account	618%

Performance Summary: Short Trades

Total net profit	$ 26762.50	Open position P/L	$ 0.00
Gross profit	$ 59031.25	Gross loss	$ -32268.75
Total # of trades	35	Percent profitable	43%
Number winning trades	15	Number losing trades	20
Largest winning trade	$ 19970.00	Largest losing trade	$ -3655.00
Average winning trade	$ 3935.42	Average losing trade	$ -1613.44
Ratio avg win/avg loss	2.44	Avg trade(win & loss)	$ 764.64
Max consec. winners	3	Max consec. losers	6
Avg # bars in winners	38	Avg # bars in losers	23
Max intraday drawdown	$ -8768.75		
Profit factor	1.83	Max # contracts held	1
Account size required	$ 11768.75	Return on account	227%

LARRY WILLIAMS

`/////////////////////////`/Quick System: Williams 19`\\\\\\\\\\\`Page 1 of 1`\\\\`

```
Notes       :
Last Update : 03/21/96 05:49pm
Printed on  : 03/21/96 05:50pm
Verified    : Yes
```

`////////////////////////////////////`/INPUTS`\\\\\\\\\\\\\\\\\\\\\\\\\\\\\\\\\\\`

```
InputName       Default Value
-------------------------------------------------------------------------
Length          16
PH              ((H+L+C)/3*2)-L
PL              ((H+L+C)/3*2)-H
```

`////////////////////////////////////`/LONG ENTRY`\\\\\\\\\\\\\\\\\\\\\\\\\\\\\\\`

Buy next bar at Highest(PH,Length) + 1 point Stop

`////////////////////////////////////`/SHORT ENTRY`\\\\\\\\\\\\\\\\\\\\\\\\\\\\\\`

Sell next bar at Lowest(PL,Length) - 1 point Stop

`////////////////////////////////////`/STOPS`\\\\\\\\\\\\\\\\\\\\\\\\\\\\\\\\\\\\`

Enabled	Stop	Enabled	Stop
No	Money Management Amount : $0.00	No	Breakeven Stop Floor : $0.00
No	$ Risk Trailing Stop Amount : $0.00	No	Profit Target Amount : $0.00
No	% Risk Trailing Stop Amount : $0.00 Floor : $0.00	No	Close all trades at end of day session

Index

ADX, 82, 186

agricultural markets (*see* consumables/agricultural products)

All In One, 104

All Star Traders Hotline, 163, 173

All-Season Investor, 57

American Stock Exchange, 134, 135

Angell, George, 92, 200

Appel, Gerald, 49, 55, 135, 140, 200

Aspen Graphics, 25, 30, 73, 85, 92

Auer, Ivan, 34

average modified moving average (AMMA), 48

averages, moving averages, 22-24, 26, 29, 48, 52, 53, 54, 83, 99, 111, 142, 164

Babcock, Bruce, 55, 200

bars, 12-13, 14-15, 17-18, 19, 27, 42-43, 49, 55, 58, 68, 73, 80, 83, 89, 90-91, 93, 100, 103, 118, 122, 127, 137-138, 141, 142, 156, 160, 174-175, 180-181, 189, 191, 200, 203

Beatrice Foods Corp., 37

Bernstein, Jake, 12, 21, 33, 35, 38, 174, 200

Berry, Tom, 96

Black-Scholes Model, 13

BMI data feeds/quotes, 73, 144

Board of Trade, 28, 34-35

bonds (*see* T-bond trading)

Bonneville quotes, 103

breakout systems, 6, 47-50, 63, 70, 99, 106, 137, 154, 157, 194, 196

Bressert Investment Group, 120

broker selection, 16-17, 26-27, 49-50

Business One/Irwin Guide to Commodity Trading, 55

buy (*see* entry points)

calls (*see* options)

Candlestick Forecaster, 162-184

candlestick patterns, 86, 87, 162-169, 177

Cashman, Gene, 34

Catscan/Catscan II, 147-159

cattle (*see* consumable/agricultural products)

change, rate of change theory, 106

channel breakout method, 6, 47-50, 63, 70, 99, 154, 157, 194

chaos theory (*see* fractal research)

chart analysis (*see also* Japanese Candlestick Charting), 16, 121-122

Chart XL software, 153

Chemical Bank, 79, 80

Chevron International, 79

Chicago Mercantile Exchange, 3-4, 13, 15, 16, 144

choppy markets, 149-150, 154, 155

CIS Trading Package, 30

Clean Products, 79

CNBC quotes/ticker, 144

Coast Investment Software, 20-32

cocoa (*see* consumable/agricultural products)

code/customizing commands, 54

coffee (*see* consumable/agricultural products)

commands, customizing, 54

Commodities Futures Game, 116

Commodity Futures Game, The, 30

Commodity Perspective Chart Service, 35, 36

Commodity Quotes Graphics, 103

Commodity Timing, 198

Complete Guide to the Futures Market, A, 59

CompStock (S&P), 92

Computer Analysis of the Technical Markets, 179

Computer Analysis...Futures Market, 16

computer-generated trading, 13

Computrac, 36-37, 39, 171

Connor, Michael, 3-19

consumables/agricultural products, 13, 43-44, 98, 101, 114, 121, 127, 154, 175, 181, 190, 201

Conti Commodities Services, 33, 34, 37

contingency orders, 17

Contrary Opinion, 116

cotton (*see* consumable/agricultural products)

CQG, 17, 188

Crash of 1987, 28

CRB, 175

CSI, 159

currency trading, 13, 49, 51-60, 89, 98, 106, 121, 123-124, 128, 141, 142, 154, 160, 177, 189, 194, 201-202

cycle activity charting, 33, 36, 38-40, 41, 44, 72

dampened stochastic methods, 81-82

Data Broadcast Co., 180

data feeds (*see* quotation systems)

Davis, Ned, 55, 200

day-of-the-week study, 196

delta neutral, 135

DeMark, Thomas R., 51-52, 55, 170, 174, 200

Dennis, Richard, 175, 176

Design Testing and Optimization, 158

DeTrend oscillator, 123-124, 128

Dev-Stop, 81, 87

developing trading systems, 19, 31-32, 46, 50, 59-60, 76-77, 86-95, 97-103, 105, 107-110, 112, 113-114, 119, 121-128, 132-133, 135-142, 146-157, 163-171, 173-174, 182-184, 186-187, 189, 190, 192-193, 195-197, 200-202

Dial Data, 17

DiNapoli, Joseph, 20-32

Disciplined Trader, The, 117

Displaced Moving Averages system, 23-24

divergence of markets, 85, 87

diversification, 75

DMI, 82, 186

Doji (*see also* Japanese Candlestick Charting), 165, 170

Dollar Trader system, 47-50

Donchian, 6

Donchian price-channel breakout, 154, 157

Douglas, Mark, 117

Dow Jones 20 Bond Average, 56-57

drawdowns, 18, 31, 46, 50, 53, 59, 64-65, 74, 93, 98, 104, 118, 123, 131, 138, 145, 146, 152, 160, 181-182, 192, 204

DTN, 188

dual systems, 101-102

DuPont, 148

Easy Language, 135

Economist magazine, 88

Ehrlich Cycle Finder, 33-42

Ehrlich cycle forecaster software, 42

Ehrlich, Stan, 33-46

Elder, Alexander, 72

Electronic Data Systems (EDS), 62

Elliott wave, 37, 106-108, 110, 116, 189

Elliott Wave Institute, 106-107

empirical approach to trading, 43

energy markets, 35, 69, 79-80, 82, 154

entry points/rules, 18, 26, 28-29, 56, 66-67, 70, 87-88, 99, 105, 115, 124, 126, 137-138, 140, 142, 146, 154, 157, 166, 173-174, 177, 199, 201-202

evaluating trading systems, 8-9, 11-12, 14, 24, 26-28, 31, 41-44, 46, 48-49, 53-54, 58-59, 62-65, 67-68, 73-74, 83-86, 97-98, 103-104, 107-112, 115, 118, 124-125, 131, 136-141, 143-145, 149-150, 152, 160, 169-172, 174, 181, 187-188, 198, 203

Excalibur software, 153, 158

Excel, 17, 153, 177

exit points/rules, 26, 28-29, 56, 66-67, 70, 81-83, 87-88, 99, 102, 105, 115, 124, 126, 137-138, 140, 142, 146, 157, 166, 173-174, 177, 199

facilitation index, in fractal research, 190

Faciss, Leo, 163

Fibnode software, 25, 30, 31

Fibonacci analysis, 22-29

Fibonacci Money Management/Trend Analysis, 20

filtering systems, 79

Financial Trader magazine, 163

Formula Research newsletter, 54-55

Fox 31 system, 47

Fox, David, 47-50

fractal research, 185-193

Franklin Street Mercantile Exchange, 34

Freeberg, Nelson, 51-60

fundamental analysis, 35, 41, 52, 195-196

Future Source, 92, 171, 180

FutureLink, 50

Futures International Conferences, 163

Futures magazine, 16, 97, 163, 168, 173, 181

Futures Symposium International, 21

Futures Truth Co., 149-160

Futures Truth magazine, 47

Gallep Trading Applications of Japanese Candlestick Charting, 163

Gan, W.D., 174

Gehm, Frank, 75

General Motors, 62

Genesis, 159

Gettess, 30, 61

Gettess, Lee, 61-77

Glasgow & Gorman Futures Corp., 4

gold/silver (*see* precious metals)
Goldsmidt, Walter, 37-38
grain (*see* consumable/agricultural products)

Hadady, R. Earl, 116
Haller, Gil, 197, 200
handheld systems, 103
Harlow, 30
Harvard Chart XL software, 153
head-and-shoulders formations, 167
hedging, 35, 37, 86, 92, 175
Heiser, Ralph, 196
Hi Ho Silver, 97-98
Hikita, Takahiro, 174
Hill, John, 155, 200
hogs (*see* consumables/agricultural products)
Hoil, Herbert, 176
Honma, Sokyu, 163-165
How I Made a Million Dollars, 195
Hulbert, 161
Hunt Brothers, 37, 46

IDA, 171
indicators (*see also* signals), 9-11, 22-24, 26, 29, 40,
    48, 78-81, 82-83, 86, 101, 106, 141-143, 155,
    157, 162, 164, 167-168, 171, 187, 191, 197
Information Services, 180
interest rates, 52, 108
Intermarket Technical Analysis, 57
International Pacific Trading Co., 162
Intraday Analysis, 171
Investors Business Daily Publication magazine, 163

Japanese Candlestick Charting, 162-169
Japanese Chart of Charts, 168
Jones, Paul T., 51-52, 175, 176
Joseph, Tom, 189

Kase Analytica, 85
Kase and Company, Inc., 78, 79
Kase, Cynthia, 78-95
KaseCD, 80, 81, 86-87
Kaufman, Perry, 16, 50, 55
Kondratiev wave, 41
Krutsinger & Krutsinger Inc., 96
Krutsinger, Joseph, 53, 96-105, 121, 126-127,
    129, 155-156, 158, 189, 191, 200, 202

Lane, George, 6
Lavally, Art, 35-36, 35

LeBeau, Charles, 16, 55, 143, 179
limited slope method, 67
linear regression oscillators, 67
Livermore, Jessie, 100, 116
livestock (*see* consumables/agricultural products)
London Times, The, 16
loss (*see* risk management)
Lotus 1-2-3, 153
Lucas, David, 16, 55, 143, 179
lumber (*see* consumables/agricultural products)

M.O.A.T. Index, 112, 115
MACD, 81, 86, 171
MACD/Stochastic combination, 22, 29
Major Market Index, 135
margin trading, 20
Market Watch fax service, 3-19
Market Wizards, 16, 88
MarketSolve, 120, 121
MasterChartist, 135
Mastering Elliott Wave, 113
Matheny, Brad, 162, 172
mechanical trading systems (*see* developing
    trading systems)
Meehan, Bill, 200
Merc, 28, 34
MetaStock, 54, 177, 180
MidAmerica Commodity Exchange, 6, 7
Miller-Lane, 6
Mirza, David, 120-121
modeling, 55, 130-131
momentum (*see* trend analysis)
money management, 8, 59, 74, 79, 84, 92, 107,
    140, 154, 166, 181-182, 194
moving averages, 22-24, 26, 29, 48, 52, 53, 54,
    99, 111, 142, 164
Murphy, John J., 57, 179

Neely, Glenn, 31, 106-119
NEo Wave, 107-114
neural networks, 186
New Commodity Trading Systems & Methods, 50
New Ways Book, 202-203
New York Stock Exchange, 69
New York Times, The, 16

oats (*see* consumable/agricultural products)
OCOs (One Cancels Other), 17
often-inverted method, 67
oil market (*see* energy markets)
Omega Research Inc. software, 15, 16, 99, 103,
    134, 135

Omega Solutions, 96
One Night Stand, 51, 97, 104, 105
OOPS! system, 101
OPEC oil embargo (c.1970), 35
Optimal F money management, 59, 74
optimal left method, 65
options trading, 13, 20, 108, 134, 135
orange juice (*see* consumable/agricultural products)
Oscillator Predictor, 24, 26, 29, 30
oscillators/oscillator-based systems, 24-30, 67,
    80-81, 86-87, 123-124, 128, 164, 171, 177

Pardo Group Limited, 120, 121
Pardo, Robert, 121, 158
Path Finder, 51-60, **53**
pattern analysis, 69-70, 196-199
Paul Revere trading system, 98
PeakOscillator, 80-81, 86, 87
PeakOut, 86-87
Permission Screen, 81
Perot, Ross, 62
Petronal (BVI), 79
Piper Jeffrey and Hopwood, 97
Pit Boss, 121-126
pivot formulas/points, 5-6, 48
Polaroid, 79
pork bellies (*see* consumable/agricultural
    products)
Portana, 96, 97, 132
Portfolio Analyzer Software, 96
portfolio management, 10, 18-19, 31, 46, 50, 55,
    59, 74-75, 94, 104, 118, 132, 145-146, 161,
    182, 192
Prechter, Robert, 33, 37
precious metals, 37, 56, 58, 89, 97-98, 107, 108,
    110-111, 175
price patterning, 69-70
Pring, Martin, 57
probability analysis, 80-81
Profit data feed, 180
profits/profit targets, 12, 17-19, 28-29, 31, 40, 44-
    45, 50, 53, 57, 64-67, 70, 74, 77, 87-88, 93,
    102, 104, 118, 122-123, 126, 129, 131, 138,
    139, 145, 146, 152, 154, 158, 160, 166, 177,
    181-182, 198, 199, 204
Prudential Bache, 88
puts (*see* options)
pyramiding, 18-19, 31, 46, 50, 59, 74-75, 94,
    104, 118-119, 132, 146, 161, 182, 192

Quadram, 59
quantitative analysis, 79
Quick Editor system, 47, 106, 194

quotation systems, 16, 30, 45, 50, 58, 72-73, 92-
    93, 103, 117, 124, 129-130, 135, 144, 159-160,
    179-180, 191, 203

R-Breaker, 134-140
R-Levels, 134-140
rate of change theory, 106
real-time quotes, 16-17, 30, 45, 50, 58, 72, 92,
    103, 117, 124, 129-130, 135, 144, 159, 179-
    180, 191
Relative Strength Index (RSI), 86, 137-138, 186,
    187
Reminiscences of a Stock Market Operator, 100,
    117
Republic Securities, 4
resistance/support levels, 122-133
retracements, 8, 42, 50, 59
risk management, 9, 18, 28, 31, 32, 44-45, 53, 58,
    59, 65, 68, 71-72, 75, 77, 84, 86, 91-92, 94,
    102, 107, 119, 124-125, 129, 132, 138, 143,
    158, 175-177, 179, 191, 198, 202, 204
Robbins Trading Co., 96, 126, 128, 129
Rodman & Renshaw, 4
Ross, Joseph, 12, 16, 72
Roy, Jeff, 120-133
Russian Grain Deal (c.1970), 35

Saidenberg, Richard, 134-146
Sakata Five technique, 163-169
Sakata's Constitution, 165
Samarec, 79
Sanku pattern (*see also* Japanese Candlestick
    Charting), 166
Sanminoden, 165
Sanpei pattern (*see also* Japanese Candlestick
    Charting), 166
Sansen pattern (*see also* Japanese Candlestick
    Charting), 166-167
Sanzan pattern (*see also* Japanese Candlestick
    Charting), 166-167
Saperstein, Robert, 33
Savage, Terry L., 35
scaling (*see also* pyramiding), 182
Schwager, Jack, 57, 59
Scientific Investment System Research Group
    (SISRG), 135, 140
sell (*see* exit points)
Sharpe ratio, 59
Shimizu, Seiki, 168
Signal Data Feed, 17, 30, 103, 117, 180
signals (*see also* indicators), 52, 86, 171, 172
size of trade (*see* trade size evaluation)
Slater, Tim, 37

Smarter Trading, 55

Smith, Gary, 159

SoundView Advisors, 136

Speculator King, 116

Standard & Poor's, 27-28, 56-59, 61, 63, 66, 89,
    92, 104, 108, 114, 121, 122, 123, 126, 127,
    134, 135, 136, 141, 143, 151, 156, 171, 188,
    191, 197, 201

standard deviation, 59, 83

Standard Oil Co., 79

statistical analysis, 80-81

Stauffer Chemical Co., 79

stochastic methods (*see also* MACD/Stochastic),
    6, 29, 81-82, 86, 171, 186, 187

stock market, 43, 56, 100, 134, 197

Stone, 30

stop-loss routines, 4-5, 8, 9, 12, 15-17, 18, 40, 81-
    83, 87, 98, 99, 105, 123-124, 126, 133, 136-
    137, 140, 142, 146, 154, 172-174, 199, 202

Stowell, Joseph, 200

Stuckey, Randy, 147-161

sugar (*see* consumables/agricultural products)

Super Charts, 16, 45-47, 85, 97, 106, 130, 134,
    153, 158, 194

support/resistance levels, 122-133

Swager, Jack, 88

Synergistic Technical Analysis (STA), 164-165

System Assist program, 102, 128

System Writer, 9, 25, 42, 49, 54, 65-66, 81, 85,
    97, 99, 100, 112, 125, 139, 153, 158, 172-173,
    177, 199, 203

Systems and Forecasts newsletter, 135, 140

T-bond trading, 37, 52, 58, 63-64, 68-69, 99, 100,
    101, 104, 108, 121, 154, 197

Taguchi robustness theory, 148-149, 151-152, 157

TC 2000, 180

technical analysis, 33, 35, 41, 53, 79-81, 106,
    110, 115, 121, 134, 162-168, 170, 195-196

Technical Analysis of Futures Markets, 179

Technical Analysis of Stocks and Commodities
    magazine, 189

*Technical Traders Guide...Computerized
    Analysis ...*, 55

Technical Traders Guide...Futures Market, 143

Telerate, 92

Teletrac, 188

testing trading systems, 17-18, 30-31, 50, 52, 70,
    73, 83-84, 93, 103, 118, 130-131, 141, 144-
    145, 150, 160, 177, 180-181, 191, 203

Teweles, 30

tick-by-tick quotes, 16-17, 30, 45, 50, 58, 72, 92,
    103, 117, 129-130, 144, 159, 179-180, 191

Time Trend II/III, 135

timing trades (*see also* bars; indicators; signals),
    86, 198-199

trade size, 18, 31, 46, 50, 53, 59, 64-65, 74, 104,
    118, 122-123, 131, 145, 161, 181-182

Traders World magazine, 163

TradeStation, 3-19, 25, 26, 42, 45-46, 47, 49, 54,
    65-66, 73, 85, 91, 92, 97, 100, 103, 106, 112,
    122, 125, 130, 134, 135, 136, 138, 139, 143, 153,
    158, 172-173, 177, 180, 188, 194, 199, 203

Trading Chaos, 188

Trading for a Living, 72

Trading System Development video, 96

Trading System Toolkit, 53, 96, 129, 156, 158,
    202

Trading with the Odds, 78, 95

trend analysis, 22-23, 26, 28, 29, 40, 42, 58, 63, 67,
    69-70, 72, 73, 82, 84, 86, 108, 101-102, 109-112,
    119, 121-122, 141, 149-150, 154, 155, 170

Turtle Trading Method, 6

USDX, 49

Value Line Investment Survey, 135

variance, 83

Vince, Ralph, 59, 65, 74, 75

volatility, 12-13, 20, 57, 63, 70, 82-83, 90-91,
    100, 126, 196, 199

volatility breakout systems (*see also* breakout;
    channel breakout; volatility), 70, 99

Volker, T., 182

volume trading, 190

Wagner, Gary, 162-184

wave theory, 37, 41, 106-107, 110, 112, 114, 116,
    189

Westerland, Gary, 172

wheat (*see* consumable/agricultural products)

Wilder, Welles, 82, 96, 200, 202-203

Williams 19, 194

Williams Reports, 197

Williams, Bill, 185-193

Williams, Larry, 55, 67, 72, 100, 101, 102, 129,
    158, 174, 194-204

windows (*see also* Japanese Candlestick
    Charting), 166

Winning in the Futures, 92

Winning On Wall Street, 57

Winthrop Securities Inc., 4

Worth magazine, 163

XMI (*see* Major Market Index)

zero balance theory, 196

Zweig, Martin, 55, 57, 200